SAN FRANCISCO
SOLANO DE SONOMA

SAN RAFAEL ARCANGEL
SAN FRANCISCO DE ASIS
(DOLORES)

SAN JOSE
DE GUADALUPE

SAN
FRANCISCO

SANTA CLARA
DE ASIS

SANTA CRUZ

SAN JUAN BAUTISTA

SAN CARLOS
BORROMEO
DEL RIO CARMELO

NUESTRA SENORA DE LA SOLEDAD

SAN ANTONIO DE PADUA

SAN MIGUEL ARCANGEL

SAN LUIS OBISPO DE TOLOSA

LA PURISIMA CONCEPCION

SANTA INES

SANTA BARBARA

SAN
BUENAVENTURA

EL CAMINO REAL

Showing a number of Franciscan missions,
from a map of 1821.
(The road at the time
was merely a horse and mule trail.)
The map also shows U.S. 101,
which today covers
substantially the same route.

N

W E

S

CALIFORNIA

SAN FERNANDO
REY DE ESPANA

SAN GABRIEL
ARCANGEL

OS
NGELES

SAN JUAN CAPISTRANO

SAN LUIS
REY
DE FRANCIA

SAN DIEGO DE ALCALA

SAN DIEGO

THE
GOLDEN
ROAD

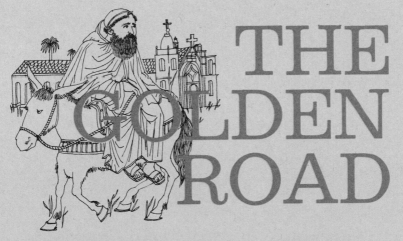

THE GOLDEN ROAD

The Story of California's Spanish Mission Trail

FELIX RIESENBERG, JR.

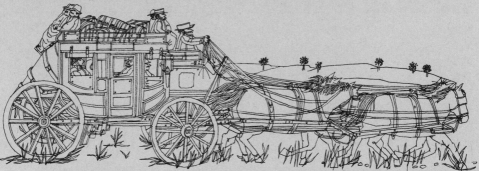

McGRAW-HILL BOOK COMPANY, INC.

New York   Toronto   London

to
Grandson Billy
WILLIAM SCOFIELD BARRETT

Contents

One   Seaside Route

THE PREHISTORIC CORRIDOR

One million years ago a series of great quakes ruptured the Pacific Coast of North America, crushing vegetation and stampeding prehistoric beasts into chasms or deep water. Amid thundering detonations, under a haze of volcanic ash, ponderous cascades of lava surged downward to hiss and steam and harden in the cold blue sea. From the violent upheavals there lifted a variform escarpment destined to everlasting change because it lay above a permanent split in the earth's crust.

The coastal range that arched five hundred miles between the future cities of San Francisco and San Diego was wrenched and buckled by continuous, slowly lessening shocks as the plane of the fracture slipped. Mountains rose and tilted to envelop gold-bearing quartz and petroleum in rocky folds; quakes kneaded the rich land into magnificent ridges, canyons, rolling hills and valleys. With the heritage of change and varied beauty the earth fault gave this section of California one constant—a seaside corridor along which life has moved through the millenniums.

Survivors of the recurring cataclysms grazed and hunted on land that turned fertile as torrential rains washed the mountain sides and strong westerly gales cleared the air. The mulch of dawn redwoods, oak, cypress and chaparral settled over the remains of ground sloths, three-toed giant horses, vultures and the mesasaurus, a huge sea lizard whose ancestors had spawned in fetid shallows of the vanished Great Basin Sea.

The trail of prehistory led from hills around San Francisco Bay through forests and valleys down to a great bight at Monterey. Out of the sea to the south mountains, which Spanish sailors would name for Santa Lucia, became the hunting ground of saber-tooth cats and condors. The path skirted the sea to pass Santa Barbara, cut inland through a pass that opened the San Fernando Valley and more grazing land for the imperial mastodon. Farther south lay the La Brea tar pits, covered with a deceptive sheet of water, where giant bison, the dire wolf and other beasts met death in the sucking asphalt. The trace swerved east near San Diego, out into deserts and to Mexico.

The trickle of southward-moving carnivore became steady along that trail on the Pacific slope about 50,000 years ago. And there was less leisure to the grazing of the herds. More frequent roars of pain and terror echoed out of canyons, and smoke that curled up from protected ledges carried the smell of burnt flesh. Nervous animals crashed off the trail to seek safety in forests and underbrush.

At the flanks of the mammoths, beating them to death with bone clubs and slashing their hides with stone knives, came strong-jawed, short-legged creatures who carried fire. Early man had reached California.

THE NOMADS

Back of that arrival lay a tremendous migration of more than 150,-000 years' duration. Thousands of generations had trekked from

Africa to Asia Minor, then through India to China and around the perimeter of the Pacific over a land bridge at Bering Strait. From Alaska some followed the Central Plain eastward of the Rocky Mountains and fanned out to the Atlantic; others headed south through the Great Basin corridor, left their petrified footprints in Nicaragua, and did not cease wandering until they viewed the mountainous Cape Horn seas from the ragged shores of Tierra del Fuego. The earliest nomads from Siberia may have kept the sea in sight as a bearing, walking on the shelf of the ten-fathom curve in one of the ages when the Pacific was lower by several hundreds of feet. Along countless lost trails they left spear points, arrowheads and crude knives. Down until some time five thousand years ago, the wanderers spread, backtracked and explored new wilderness all over the Western Hemisphere. One of the earliest tribes to find a permanent hunting ground in North America stopped on the Pacific coastal trail more than 30,000 years ago.

SANTA ROSA MAN

In 1960 Southern California scientists were unearthing evidence that a contemporary of Europe's Neanderthal man inhabited California, which may point to either a very early migration from Asia or the independent rise of man in America.

The scene of discovery was Santa Rosa Island, possibly once a part of the mainland, but today one of the channel group some thirty miles seaward of Santa Barbara. From prehistoric charcoal pits came bones of "dwarf mammoths" together with cutting tools used to dismember the beasts, and finally a human skeleton. The remains were subjected to a process known as the Carbon-14 test, a post–World War II use of radioactivity to determine the age of fossils. Technicians claimed the Santa Rosa barbecues were held *at least* 30,000 years ago: Carbon-14 was then limited to that span.

Louis A. Brennan, a writer and amateur archeologist, has interestingly traced recent developments in the search for Santa Rosa

Man and his contemporaries, to show the "Amerind" as the true predecessor of the native who would be called Indian after the first voyage of Columbus.[1]

More than one mystery surrounds that early California hunter: did his race die out with other Neanderthals or did he mate with later nomads and pass along a Western Hemisphere seed? It is not even certain that Santa Rosa Man came down a trail from the north. At the time of his migration solid land may have filled the South China Sea, extending out beyond the Philippines and isles of Micronesia, on along the equator to the Galápagos, then northward above the Easter Island Rise to the shores of Mexico.

A possible southern route, and the Bering land bridge, had been long sunk four thousand years ago when Oriental sailors first ventured offshore. Tribes on the coast of California, hemmed in from three sides by deserts or snow-capped mountains, knew the ocean only as a treacherous, formidable water. From far away it brought gales, fogs and long rollers that crashed on their shore. Great tides, undertows and sudden storms made that sea too perilous to venture upon for very far. To those who followed Santa Rosa Man, the Pacific loomed as a wet wilderness that each day swallowed the sun, often sending blood-colored emissions across the sky. The dead, with knees under chins, were buried facing the ocean which was their infinity.

THE SEA LEGENDS

Other men attached myths and legends to the Pacific, almost as though to shrink a frightful vastness. Ancient sagas told of Lemuria and the Southern Continent, huge land areas that broke the open sea. By 500 B.C. man had embarked on long voyages from the Asian coast, and through the centuries mariners yarned of fabulous countries.

Scholars seeking contacts to explain characteristics of India and the Levant in America believe ships must have navigated the Pacific at an early date. Harold Sterling Gladwin, an authority on

4

Mayan, Aztec and Inca history, has suggested that vessels from the fleet of Alexander the Great crossed the Pacific midway in the third century B.C. to give natives a legend of blond sea gods.

The archeologist Gordon Ekholm, considering such oddities as toys with wheels—in a land whose people did not use the wheel —stated his belief that "ships and navigation were sufficiently advanced by the eighth century to allow trans-Pacific voyages." [2]

Any eastward passage out of an Asian port in those days would have brought ships in sight of the California coast: the only possible sailing route is above the Calms of Cancer, a run before the prevailing westerlies to a landfall near the fortieth parallel of latitude, thence south along the shore. There are two—questionable —records of such Great Circle voyages.

The monk Hwui Shan, with other Buddhist priests of the fifth century as witnesses, described California as "an Island 4,000 miles in circumference on which grows a tree 20,000 feet high whose fruit makes men immortal."

An even less believable visitor was the navigator Hee Li who, as a result of a 180-degree compass error caused by a cockroach wedged beneath the needle, sailed a reverse homeward course to enter San Francisco Bay which he named Hong-Tsi (Great Harbor). The "evidence" offered for Hee Li's landing is the dawn redwood trees that grow outside of California only in Central China's "Valley of the Tiger."

No logs or narratives of Pacific voyages have come down from medieval times. The skillful seamen of Polynesia could have taken their big outriggers eastward; Japanese fishermen and pirates had even a shorter distance to sail. That great Chinese ships were at sea in the twelfth century we know from the authority Chau Ju-Kua who wrote of vessels "as big as houses and when their sails are spread they are like great clouds in the sky." [3]

If mariners landed or were wrecked on California's shores in ancient times they left no mark yet found. Siftings of shell mounds around San Francisco—thirty-foot layers of refuse from daily living deposited in kitchen middens—show no trace of a foreign sailor. Shell, ash and earth point only to a culture virtually unchanged through more than forty centuries, a primitive existence untouched by seafarers.

INDIAN ARCADIA

The shell mound record of Pacific Coast Indians begins at the time when chained slaves of Egypt were being whipped to death dragging blocks to build the monstrous pyramid at Gizeh. In California's land of plenty hide tents were pitched at random; from almost any campfire it was but a few dozen paces to herds of half-tame deer, easily caught small game, or streams chocked with trout and salmon. The only potential predator, the grizzly bear, was too well fed to be a menace.

So mild was the climate that natives lounged in nakedness through most of the year. Rabbit and sea otter skins gave them what protection they required against fog at Monterey and San Francisco, and there was no heat to compare with that described by nomads from the southwestern desert. Rude shelters were thrown together with no thought of permanence: when a dwelling became overly infested with fleas and vermin, it was burned.

That race whose generations had trekked the longest migratory arc of all time responded to the promised land by starting a pattern of stationary living that would be likewise notable. In an ever slowing perambulation along their coastal aisle, loosely formed tribes blended the past with the creatures and things of the new country. Chiefs were chosen by the people; medicine men and women—called Shamans—arose to minister to the ill and explain the unknown.

A healthy population practiced open polygamy and discovered herbs that would still be in use during the twentieth century—for poison oak, constipation and the common cold. Doctors prescribed diets of raw lion heart to bolster courage; roasted deer leg to increase fleetness; and milkweed for nursing mothers.

In the religion that developed, God was some animal—Hawk,

Eagle or Coyote. Devils were the giants of the inner earth whose wrath caused terrorizing quakes. Without warning the ground would shake, then hills and mountains split; gaping crevices opened; rocks and trees fell on a few unfortunates. Not even the Shamans could predict when and where the giants might strike. The terrestrial revolutions caused no exodus; neither did they discourage a great dual migration which began five hundred years before the birth of Christ.

Tribes moving down the Great Basin found summer passes through the Sierra Nevada. Hunting with bows and arrows, ferocious dogs at their heels, the Athabascans, Algonkins and Penutians followed the crooked Sacramento River to the Coast. In the sparsely populated hills around the huge bay of San Francisco they founded villages that would last one hundred generations.

The second migration into California, which did not end until 500 A.D., was a series of tortuous marches from the southern part of the Great Basin through passes and along desert trails destined to a much later fame. Tribes of Shoshoneans, with women carrying babies and bundles on their backs, reached the coastal corridor at points from San Diego and Los Angeles up beyond Santa Barbara.

The immigrants of ancient history made the first division of Northern and Southern California. Being prolific, healthy and peaceable they gave the Pacific Coast both above and below Point Concepción the densest population of any Indian territory in what would be the United States of America. But even with a population of 150,000, ample room remained for hunters.

The new tribes and the native settlers—strangers all—set up separate villages about fifty miles apart and in a few centuries had attained almost complete isolation. More than one hundred dialects of twenty different languages developed; when rare meetings occurred to settle boundary disputes tribesmen were forced to use signs.

With game becoming scarce and wary, the Indians learned to use the acorn for food. Mashed, washed free of tannic acid and

7

crushed into a yellow meal, it was cooked in baskets over hot stones and eaten either as a thick soup or stored in unleavened loaves. The great stands of oak insured an indefinite supply and made the drudgery of agriculture unnecessary. The acorn represented some absolute minimum of effort to secure nourishment. For variety cooks prepared a porridge made from chia seeds and a black lump of paste the size of an orange flavored with something that tasted like almond. Grasshoppers were a delicacy and whenever a whale stranded, tribes would gather on the beach for a blubber feast.

In the numerous secluded villages women prepared feather skirts and body paint for ceremonial dances or wove intricate baskets that were watertight. Men hid for hours watching traps or cages into which small game and birds were lured by bait. The coast trail dimmed under a blanket of chaparral and weeds; rocks and shale were left to pile up in canyons after slides; wind, rain and growth obliterated rude signs. Grievance raids and the kidnapping of women were carried out through wilderness terrain. Travel lessened every decade.

By the eleventh century—the age of Europe's fanatical Crusades—the California Indian had reached a physical and mental plateau on which he would bask in comparative peace until the standard bearers of white civilization darkened his horizon.

An early observer, José Espinosa y Tello, wrote that the *Costañoans*—one of the Spaniard's names for all tribes north of Monterey—preserved customs too old to trace and described one that puzzled him:

> ...in their leisure moments they will lie on the ground face downwards for whole hours with the greatest content.[4]

Father Miguel Venegas confirmed and found abhorrent a similar dedication to relaxed living in southern California where the Indians "take no heed for the morrow and regard any work and exertion with horror." [5]

Acquisitive sea venturers bred in a world of strife were amazed to find warfare treated as a game in which combatants often lost interest and repaired as friends to a *temescal*, or steam bath. Gambling was likewise a vagary: debts were paid in dentalium shells, clam-disk beads or deerskins. No one owned property; no merchants sold food, clothing or any service. The word poverty did not exist in any of the numerous dialects.

The first descriptions of the natives were given by sixteenth century monks and sailors who observed great differences among tribes. Heights ranged from below five feet to five feet, eight inches. There was a Mongolian cast to all features, but some approached fineness; in others, thick lips and flat noses made them appear ugly. Skin coloring varied between a deep brown and tan; builds ran a wide gamut: the *Costañoan* of San Francisco was squat; the *Canaleño* of Santa Barbara Channel tall, heavily muscled and symmetrical; the *Diegueño* small, slim and wiry. In villages of the south the women were adjudged beautiful—by celibates and mariners long at sea.

Some untraceable change must have affected these simple and superstitious California villagers near the start of the sixteenth century to build up a foreboding expectancy. Among the *Diegueños* and their neighbors the *Luiseños*, it had become the custom for adventurous young braves to embark on long treks and travelers may have returned with news of the *conquistadores*.

By 1540 Cortés had landed on the peninsula of lower California, Cabeza de Vaca had pushed into Arizona, and the captains of Coronado were on the Colorado, just one week's march from the Pacific Coast. That summer the lost navigator Francisco de Ulloa may have reached the latitude of the *Diegueño* or *Luiseño* domains. Along the shores of California the word spread and Shamans attempted to explain such oddities as golden hair, skin the color of the moon, beasts who laughed and fire-sticks that killed. The legends told of no such gods, or devils; the jimson weed produced no visions so wondrously strange.

More than two hundred years passed before white horsemen

9

thundered over the Indian trail, but during that time coastal villages would meet the Spaniard whose ships used the sea as a highway.

THE COASTAL MARINERS

On the afternoon of September 29, 1542 the caravels *San Salvador* and *Victoria* ghosted into San Diego harbor, dropped anchors off a sandy beach and sent bearded men in armor to the shore. At their head was Captain Juan Rodríguez Cabrillo, a native of Portugal then past his fiftieth year, who had served with distinction under Cortés. He was considered by Viceroy Antonio de Mendoza to be "a person very expert in all matters of the sea" and a commander to be entrusted with the most important mission of the time.

Cabrillo christened the bay San Miguel, after the Saint's Day, and enticed some Indian boys to the beach by waving bright-colored beads. In gentle fashion he sent the children back to waiting tribesmen loaded with baubles. The diarist of the expedition narrated the result:

> ... The following day in the morning three large Indians came to the ships and explained by signs that some people like us were going about inland ... and were killing many of the natives, and for this reason they were afraid.[6]

The captain questioned the three men at length about the object of his mission—an estuary somewhere to the north whose mouth was thought to be marked by giant redwood trees. This was the fabled Northwest Passage which was believed then, and for the next one hundred years, to connect the Pacific and Atlantic oceans. The Spanish hoped to locate and fortify the strait, establishing if possible an overland route through California, and thus block off the South Sea from any Protestant maritime nation. The Indians knew of no strait so Cabrillo gave orders to make sail.

At San Pedro harbor, which he named *Bahía de los Fumos* be-

cause of smog from many fires, Cabrillo again had word of northward marching explorers who were paralleling his course. The little
armada ran up to the Santa Barbara Channel, heard of their soldier
countrymen for the third time, but could learn nothing of any transcontinental river or strait.

On one of the islands near ancient Santa Rosa the commander
broke an arm at the shoulder. He remained on deck while the ships
labored northward, sometime scudding under forecourses alone,
often hove-to in boisterous weather. Threatening the *San Salvador*
and *Victoria* always was the ragged, unknown coast to leeward
which must be kept in sight lest they miss the opening to the Atlantic. One log entry read:

> There are mountains which seem to reach the heavens, and the sea
> beats on them . . . it appears as though they would fall on the ships.

A sea-facing highway along such mountains is all that would remain to honor the name of Cabrillo whose ships reached the Cali-
fornia-Oregon border without discovering a coastal break. The commander died from complications of his untended arm, was buried
on one of the Santa Barbara Channel islands, and Spanish exploration ships did not come north again for sixty years.

Mystery shadows the voyage of Cabrillo. His rough log disappeared after being transcribed by landsmen. Rumors of a mo-
mentous discovery reached Lisbon, then filtered to England where
it was believed that Spain had discovered the continental passage
and was keeping it under wraps to prevent foreign invasion of a
land she could not yet traverse and settle.

In London the sea historian Richard Hakluyt wrote of "A
Very Late and Great Probability of a Passage by the Northwest
Part of America in 58 Degrees of Northerly Latitude." Hakluyt had
his information from "An excellent learned man of Portingale, of
singular gravety [*sic*], authority, and experience." [7]

Faith in what the English called the Strait of Anian, or Stock-
fish Strait, sent Master Francis Drake coursing northward from
Cape Horn to ravage the Pacific shores of New Spain in 1579, con-

fident that he could make his homebound easting somewhere in the high latitudes. Failing, he turned back and put into a cove north of San Francisco Bay where the little *Golden Hind*, loaded with gold and ballasted with silver bars, was careened in safety.

Drake named the land *Nova Albion*—New England—because its white cliffs reminded him of the Dover Coast. On June 17, he ordered a plate of brass erected to claim the country for Queen Elizabeth. Chaplain Francis Fletcher of the *Golden Hind* recorded that the natives in the vicinity "supposed us to be gods and would not be persuaded to the contrary." The Chaplain described the Indians as peaceable and friendly, yet:

> ...commonly so strong of body, that that which two or three of our men could hardly beare, one of them could take upon his backe and carrie it easily away, up hill and downe hill an English mile together.[8]

As Indians came to the beach "weeping and tearing their flesh," Drake put to sea and voyaged round the world. His plate of brass must have been honored for many years because it was found on a Marin County road above the anchorage in 1936 by a chauffeur who kept it in his car for a time, thinking the metal might be useful. When he discarded the plate another motorist retrieved and held it for possible car repairs. After four hundred years the marker, now at the Bancroft Library, seemed to have an affinity to the automobile.

Drake's failure to discover the Northwest Passage was scarcely noticed in England amid excitement caused by the unbelievable manifest of the *Golden Hind*—thirteen chests of royals of plate, four score pound weight of gold, six-and-twenty tons of silver, priceless jewels and precious stones. To gentlemen-adventurers who would "seek golde while sluggardes lye at home," the circumnavigator related that each year Spain dispatched from the Philippines toward Acapulco a slow, ill-armed treasure galleon that merited the attention of all "valiaunt mindes." The response brought Cavendish, Woodes Rogers, Clipperton, Shelvocke and Anson into the Pacific.

The ponderous Manila galleons had been seen by Indians for fifteen years before the voyage of Drake. The annual ships, trailing long streamers of weed from their barnacled bilges, sick men stretched out on cluttered decks, most often came in sight of the high trail along the Sierra de Santa Lucia, then bore away for Mexico. At one of the harbors south of the range a galleon finally anchored, in 1587, and natives from Morro Bay and San Luis Obispo gathered in the hills to watch sailors and marines land.

Pedro de Unamuno debarked passengers and crew who were ill with scurvy to camp in a beach cave for two days. He led a party of soldiers on a two days' march along an *arroyo* lined with heavy underbrush and pursued bands of frightened Indians. Some women were likely raped, for the villagers attacked in force to drive the Spaniards back aboard ship.[9]

When two boatloads of castaways struggled ashore near Morro Bay eight years after the call of Unamuno, the grievance apparently had been forgotten, or runners from up the coast told that the sailors were helpless. The men in open boats had survived the foundering of the galleon *San Augustin* at Drake's Bay after Captain Sebastían Rodríguez Cermeñon anchored to commence a survey of California ports. Those shipwrecked victims received food and water every hundred miles from Point Sur down to Acapulco where Cermeñon reported the loss of a precious cargo of porcelain, beeswax and Oriental silk.[10]

THE MAPMAKER

As the seventeenth century opened, irate merchants of New Spain and the Philippines pressured the Crown for relief from great losses being suffered in the galleon trade which should "normally" bring 1,000 per cent profit on investment. From the gloomy Escorial near Madrid the pious philanderer, Philip III, decreed that action be taken to eradicate foreign piracy, scurvy and the perils of shipwreck on the California coast.

To carry out the royal command Gaspar de Zuñiga y Azevedo,

Count of Monte Rey, then Viceroy of New Spain, decided to send an expedition of two hundred men in three ships to find a suitable harbor on the coast of California where the Manila galleons might overhaul and people recover after the transPacific voyage before running the gantlet of corsairs. From the list of available commanders the Viceroy chose a man of "medium yet adequate ability" whose past disappointments and great ambition would make him eager to succeed. Named Captain General was Sebastián Vizcaíno, a robust, energetic man of about fifty years.

Reared to the sea in the Basque Provinces, Vizcaíno had branched out as a trader, invested in Manila cargoes and was on the verge of affluence when the Englishman Thomas Cavendish took the galleon *Santa Ana* off Cape San Lucas in 1587. The personal loss to the sailor-merchant was 60,000 ducats but he gained favor in the viceroyalty through his energy in salvaging the hulk of the treasure ship. In ten years Vizcaíno returned to the shores of Baja (Lower) California at the head of a pearl-hunting party, charged with blazing a northerly trail; his failure caused the Count of Monte Rey to order a sea approach.

With many dead or ill of scurvy, Vizcaíno brought his little fleet to anchor on November 10, 1602, at a port discovered by Cabrillo but renamed by him San Diego. The Captain General, accompanied by his son, soldiers and a priest, followed a seaside trail north for ten leagues. They found signs of amber and gold; Indians who stalked the party were afraid to approach, excepting

> a very old woman who appeared to be more than 150 years old and
> . . . had wrinkles on her belly which looked like a blacksmith's bellows, and her navel protruded bigger than a gourd.[11]

Vizcaíno's *diario* told of sailing north by way of an isle he christened Catalina where inhabitants had "dogs like those in Castile." An old woman displayed rags of figured Chinese silk she "had got from people like ourselves, who had Negroes," and were shipwrecked at some undetermined time. Pointing north, the Indians directed the mariners vaguely toward marching men in armor, again mentioning Negroes for whom they seemed to have great respect.

On the shores of Santa Barbara Channel head winds and fog delayed the ships. The Carmelite monk Antonio de la Ascención, a sailor who had taken holy vows and was cosmographer of the expedition, noted in his *derrotero* that a *Canaleño* chief offered ten wives to each Spaniard if the Captain General would remain; instead some "quite old" women were entertained aboard the flagship.

Vizcaíno discovered nothing that had not been seen by Cabrillo but he affixed many lasting names: capes, Concepción, Pinos, Año Nuevo and Reyes; and the bays, San Diego, Carmel and—for his sponsor—Monterey.

It was at the open roadstead of Monterey that Vizcaíno attempted to insure the success of his expedition which by late December of 1602 was in desperate circumstances, with many dead of scurvy and few on their feet to work the ships. Of that desolate bay he wrote:

> ... it is all that can be desired as a harbor for ships making the voyage from the Philippines ... surrounded by settlements of friendly Indians ... with plenty of wood and water.[12]

Upon his return to Mexico Vizcaíno embellished his description, averring that Monterey was a *puerto famoso*, and to Spain went charts, sketches and directions. Father Ascención declared that California was an island but he made a prophetic recommendation:

> ... go by land to settle, some at the port of San Diego and others at the port of Monterey for to endeavor to go by sea will be a very great and difficult task.[13]

As was so often the way with Spanish colonial policy, plans changed and the idea of a northern settlement lost favor. The log and charts of Sebastián Vizcaíno were preserved to be made good use of in the next century by another opportunist. Meanwhile the Manila galleon used the newly named capes and islands as passing points, but felt no relief from the scourge of privation, scurvy and piracy. The Indians strangled children born of unions with the white explorers, and impoverished Spain left California in peace for another 165 years.

Two   Pathfinders of New Spain

THE DEVIL'S ROAD

For one hundred years after Vizcaíno's expedition, the best globes and charts fixed California as a club-shaped coastal island that widened northward from Cape San Lucas to be headed by the mythical Northwest Passage; between island and continent, mapmakers placed a wide arm of the sea. The imaginative geography matched the source which suggested California as a name to early Spaniards —an island described in the medieval romance *Las Sergas de Esplandián* "on the right hand of the Indies, very near the Terrestial Paradise . . . rich in pearls and gold and peopled with black Amazons whose queen was Calafia." [1]

First to suspect that California belonged to the mainland was the remarkable Jesuit missionary, explorer and scholar, Eusebio Francisco Kino who blazed the earliest southwestern trails, proved Baja California a peninsula, and started a chain of missions that would enable Spain to occupy her last stronghold in the New World. The versatile priest also envisioned a road from Mexico to Monterey.

17

Father Kino was thirty-six years of age when he landed at La Paz on the eastern shore of Baja California in 1683. Already well known in Europe as a mathematician and astronomer he had been appointed Royal Cosmographer of the one hundred–man expedition that hoped to secure a foothold along the bleak littoral where others had failed since the time of Hernán Cortés. In addition to scientific knowledge Kino brought with him a zeal for missionary work born of the conviction that divine providence had spared him ten years earlier when he lay gravely ill. The black robe of the scholarly priest covered a rugged body, the heritage of his boyhood in the alpine Tyrol; for thirty years after he stepped ashore at La Paz his long marches and horseback journeys awed even the natives.

The colony at La Paz fought starvation, extreme heat and disease for two years. The few Indians in the area were hostile and hungry; supply ships arrived late or not at all from across the stormy gulf; cattle died for want of food and water in that semi-arid country whose native plant was the cactus. Only Kino and his Jesuit companion, Juan María Salvatierra of Milan, explored the territory north of the cowering settlement.

The *Sierra de la Giganta* reminded the two priests of Italy's savage-peaked Apennines; the Gulf of California showed the same deep blue as the Adriatic. Two hundred miles above La Paz the explorers found a coastal site that again suggested Italy—here a dozen years later they dedicated an American shrine to Our Lady of Loreto. Many features of the terrain, and some instinct reserved for great explorers, caused Father Kino to doubt the insularity of the land he trod.

When La Paz was abandoned, the two priests went to the frontier of Pimería Alta, later to be the border of Arizona and Mexico. Kino then commenced a series of fifty marches westward, often accompanied only by Indians. Founding one tiny mission after another, harassed by heat and lack of water, the strong priest reached the Colorado. The trail he broke became known as *El Camino del Diablo*, and many who followed would agree that it was, indeed, The Devil's Road. After he crossed the great red river and saw the gulf coast fall away to the south, Kino was able to write with certainty: *"California no es isla."* [2]

THE PIOUS FUND

Chanting prayers as they led a small company up the beach in 1697, Fathers Kino and Salvatierra embraced in joy while a single brass cannon was dragged to the side of a rude cross. Again they were at Loreto, this time to attack Baja California with an invincible weapon—adequate cash under complete control. The Society of Jesus planned a mission trail that would extend from Cape San Lucas up to San Diego, be joined by *El Camino del Diablo*, and continue northward to the *puerto famoso* at Monterey. It was not impossible that the holy highway would one day reach the shores of the Northwest Passage, thanks to their Pious Fund.

Wealthy patrons in Spain made large contributions to this Pious Fund, bequeaths that eventually amounted to almost $200,-000. For the first few years the barren peninsula remained unconquerable, but by 1700 two missions and a guard of thirty soldiers were established. A nucleus of converted Indians—*neophytes*—were taught husbandry and catechism by priests who knew how to get the most out of unpromising soil; a roadway out of Loreto began to take permanent shape. Eusebio Kino departed for the northern trail where he labored until his death in 1711, leaving Salvatierra in charge.

By the time that pioneer Jesuit died six years later, the short mission trail of Baja California approached La Paz. At the port of past defeats, Father Jaime Bravo founded another mission in 1720. Father Juan de Ugarte, a Mexican of great strength, built a small vessel; he and his *neophyte* crew battled tremendous tides and foul weather to explore the Gulf of California coastline all the way north, charting the waters and marking pearl beds.

A mission near the southern tip of the peninsula, honoring Saint Joseph of the Cape, was thriving in 1734 when the Manila galleon of that year made port in great distress. On to the deck of the ship went one hundred and forty head of sheep, hogs and cattle together with fruits, vegetables and game birds. But the following year, when the galleon *Encarnación* called, the mission had been wiped out by an Indian attack.

Like the mighty Pacific tides, the fortunes of the Jesuit frontier appeared to rise and fall to extremes. Indian attacks, famine, epidemics and shipwrecks were met with a persevering courage that grew stronger through seventy years. Father Fernando Consag explored both ocean and gulf coasts; Father Wenceslao Link laid out a trail from Loreto up to the thirtieth parallel where the Mission of Santa Maria was founded. *Neophytes* showed reluctance to go farther and told garbled stories of white soldiers, black priests, Amazons and the savage *Diegueño* natives.

In Mexico traders complained that they were not welcome at Baja California—that the Jesuits were hoarding fortunes gained from pearl fishing and a smuggling trade carried on with pirates and the Manila galleons. When inspectors visited Loreto they were led away from such comforts as the town offered, onto the desolate trail. Saddle-weary and parched, the officials returned to Mexico City with tales of a primitive country: mountain lions boldly snatched animals and men; snakes and scorpions lurked in cactus jungles; the mosquitoes were unbearable.

For all its apparent wildness the mission trail of Baja California represented an outpost as solid as any on the North American frontier of the mid–eighteenth century. At the time Russian fur traders were only commencing to advance along the chain of the Aleutians; south and west out of Canada came a mere dribble of *voyageurs*; Daniel Boone, with his "good gun, good horse, and good wife" had just begun to eye the Tennessee end of the Wilderness Road; *El Camino del Diablo* was fading before the onslaught of Apache raiders. But the black-robed padres who carried on after Kino and Salvatierra controlled almost four thousand natives, had land under cultivation, and the Pious Fund by 1767 was reckoned at half a million dollars. Then an unexpected, fatal blow was dealt the Society of Jesus.

THE KING'S INSPECTOR

With no more explanation than warning Charles III, the Bourbon King of Spain, expelled the Jesuits and ordered the confiscation of their holdings at home and abroad. This display of "enlightened despotism" was one of numerous reforms in a reign destined to extend its influence over California for more than half a century. And the personality, policies and representatives of the monarch would shadow the founding of missions up to Monterey.

Charles III, a peculiar-looking man with a comical, triangular face, led a spartan life and divided each day between carefully scheduled morning business sessions and afternoon hunting. Bans were placed on institutions he disliked and these included dancing, theatricals, music, and even the much-loved sport of bullfighting. The Spanish people were expected to show enthusiasm for such reforms as sanitation, highway building, freedom for Moslems, Jews and Gypsies, and military academies. Robbed of fun, taxed on every hand, the only group to show gratitude was the growing family of bureaucrats. One of the shrewdest and most ambitious of these devoted civil servants stormed into the viceroyalty of New Spain to oversee the banishment of the Jesuits and expedite the flow of revenue to Madrid; chance would place him in charge of founding settlements in northern California.

José de Gálvez, hard, thin lips scarcely visible above a square chin, held the title *Visitador General* and was responsible only to the King whose written orders admonished that "it being necessary, on account of the large sums needed in attending to the obligations of my royal crown, to exhaust all means. . . ." [3] The former shepherd boy who studied law and took as second wife a Frenchwoman of influence, immediately showed Mexico that he intended to carry out the orders of King Charles. (*¡Que Diós guarde!*)

Word from the provinces told of grumbling among Indian and mestizo subjects over such "voluntary" levees as the *medio réal de ministeros*—a tax to pay the salaries of those who protected the natives—and of demonstrations which had the effrontery to protest the Jesuit expulsion. The forty-six-year-old Gálvez moved swiftly at the head of cavalry troops into Potosí and other towns.

Mass trials were held and Gálvez quickly passed sentences: 85 hangings; 75 public floggings; 670 life imprisonments; 117 banishments. In a fervent speech to the bereaved, the *Visitador General* declared:

> ... before God, and with all sincerity, I have not upon my conscience the slightest scruple of having exceeded the limits of justice ...

Exiles, with the families of their executed friends, carried the story of horror to the seacoasts and borders: men had been hung, quartered and beheaded; a secretary who drew up an oath had his hand cut off; the heads of ringleaders, fixed to pikes, were left to rot atop houses; daughters and young widows were given to the soldiers. Fear of this justice guaranteed an obedience which gave Gálvez a reputation for efficiency as he departed for Baja California to inspect the wealth taken from the Jesuits.

On the Guadalajara Road between Mexico City and San Blas a courier overtook the *Visitador General* with startling news and urgent orders. Secret dispatches advised Charles III that the Russians were moving southward through Alaska. They were said to have suffered losses of three hundred men in a single battle with Indians, yet they were pushing on toward California in what appeared to be considerable numbers. Gálvez was directed to fit out suitable expeditions to fortify and defend the ports of San Diego and Monterey, especially the latter which—according to the authoritative account of Sebastián Vizcaíno—would make an ideal northern bulwark against the Muscovite.

"FOR GOD AND THE KING OF SPAIN!"

The ruthlessness of Gálvez belonged in a measure to the times; but his tremendous energy and administrative ability were unique and in lethargic New Spain tended to be magnified. The qualities which would later make him Minister of the Indies were in disturbing evidence from the moment of his arrival at the Pacific Coast naval port of San Blas in April of 1768. Two vessels were commandeered and a third was ordered built; all available arms and supplies must be earmarked for the invasion; couriers to Mexico City, Sonora and Baja California rode night and day carrying directives to assemble troops. In the wake of the executive action there piled up voluminous correspondence, always pleasing to His Majesty.

In planning the defense against the Russians Gálvez did not at first favor a march through territory known only by reports 165 years old. Apache and Yuma tribes were then hostile; in California there might no longer be the docile natives described by Vizcaíno. But a stormy six-weeks voyage from San Blas to Baja California—with average headway less than half a mile an hour—decided the *Visitador General* that the success of his enterprise depended on a highway.

In September Captain Fernando Javier Rivera y Moncada, field-hardened commander of Peninsula troops, was sent from Cape San Lucas northward with orders to "borrow" livestock, supplies, implements and church property at the Jesuits' abandoned missions. Rivera was to await further orders north of Santa María, the end of the trail opened by Father Link.

The Jesuit empire had been inherited by the Franciscan Order whose seventeen gray-frocked padres were under Junípero Serra, destined to future fame and possibly sainthood. Gálvez invited the fifty-five-year-old, lame missionary to headquarters at Santa Ana and skillfully enlisted the Church's aid. Beforehand he knew something of Serra—as a penance the priest had *walked* from Vera Cruz to Mexico City suffering a spider bite on the way which caused his limp; in fashionable churches he practiced flagellation; only with difficulty could anyone silence his almost incessant chatter on the glory of placing "the gentle yoke of Christ" on the heathen Indian. The adroit Gálvez stressed the importance of obtaining and never relinquishing a hold on Northern California, regardless of obstacles.

23

Persons standing in the way—Spaniard or enemy, soldier or priest—must be swept aside: "for God and Charles III."

Serra toured the Baja missions, spreading the word that Gálvez understood the primary reason for the settlement of Northern California—the spread of Christianity. The priest wrote numerous letters, helped with the work of packing for the expedition, and finally blessed the caravels *San Carlos* and *San Antonio* before their sailings toward San Diego with supplies and troops under Captain Pedro Fages, veteran of the Sonora frontier. Serra limped up to Loreto to join the tough, likable Gaspar de Portolá who would lead Spanish pathfinders to Monterey and the shores of San Francisco Bay.

Captain Portolá, a middle-aged officer of the renowned Catalan Dragoons, and newly appointed Governor of California, received orders to head out of Loreto in March. The veteran of campaigns in Portugal and Italy—a bluff, professional soldier—he had welcomed the American assignment that took him away from new military academy soldiers who gossiped in the officers' mess about such *paja* as the King making hangmen wear Hapsburgian hats.

Portolá led his few men and forty-odd Indian converts up a dusty trail that had been well-trampled and lapped dry by four hundred head of livestock, horses and mules in Rivera's cattle drive one month earlier. At Velicatá, a village north of the thirtieth parallel, Serra joined the party. The priest kept a diary which noted naked Indians, the theft of his spectacles, and the temporary relief given his leg ulcer by ointment used to treat the saddle sores of mules. The entries also told of great hunger among the Indian converts who "joyfully ate" a newborn mule as well as a "she ass killed when it stumbled and raised the ire of the Genoese cook, who was fined four times the value of the beast and made to walk the rest of the way, by order of the commander." [4] One week out of San Diego many of the converts deserted.

Nine months after his arrival in Baja California Gálvez had sent three ships to sea and two land parties up the Peninsula. Surrounded by reams of parchment, dictating until he fell asleep exhausted, the King's Inspector composed elaborate reports of the work that included names, manifests, itemized lists of church material and—to indicate that even price regulations on playing cards, cigarettes and liquor set by the Council of the Indies were being observed—outlined the setting up of California's first roadhouse north of Loreto under the retired soldier Felipe Romero. Near the end of this preliminary report Gálvez indulged himself to express regret that he could not share the adventure, at sea or on the march, but must remain behind where his satisfaction lay in the hope "that I have not been a servant entirely useless to my master and to my nation." [5] The enemies of Gálvez claimed that he did spend some time in the field—secretly hunting for a treasure said to have been buried by the Jesuits.

DEAD MEN'S POINT

The experience of the sea expedition confirmed Gálvez's opinion that Spain's new domain must be opened and held by road. Scurvy contracted aboard the *San Carlos* and *San Antonio*—the latter taking 110 days to reach San Diego—caused the deaths of more than fifty men; the third ship was never heard from after leaving Cape San Lucas. The two land parties reached their destination without loss of a single Spaniard.

Of the hundred seaborne soldiers, priests and muleteers who set up a makeshift combination of fort and hospital, almost half were unable to stand—let alone march through wilderness country. Indians lost all fear of the Spaniards whom they at first believed to be approaching in some kind of huge fish; apparently they preserved no tales of Vizcaíno from great grandparents, and knew only of white men said to be far inland.

The *Diegueños* hung around camp, playfully stealing any loose article in sight. One night several hundred staged a raid in which they removed canvas, belaying pins, deck cargo and line from the ships and even dragged sheets from under the dying. After daybreak the goods were returned with smiles, then restolen. When a group was shown a life-size painting of Mary holding the infant Jesus several young mothers stepped forward, bared their breasts and offered milk for the child of the Virgin.

But on several occasions these childlike people showed signs of ugliness. Only the urgency of his orders decided Portolá to march with his most able men and leave behind forty persons in care of Serra and the surgeon, Don Pedro Prat. Half of that company would join other scurvy victims below the sandpoint named by the Spaniards, *Punta de los Muertos*.

THE TRAILBLAZERS

After Mass on the morning of July 14, 1769 Gaspar de Portolá rode to the head of a sixty-four-man column, waved his gauntleted right hand, and led the cavalcade to the northwest several miles where the first camp was pitched for a final check and to permit Sergeant José Francisco Ortega to scout ahead.

Around the fire that night the explorers talked of what might be encountered on the four-hundred-mile trek. Portolá, with a proud tradition of the Spanish soldier's valor since the days of the famous Captains of Compliments, would know how to combat any Russian, but Indians were outside his experience. Captain Rivera regarded the natives as pests who might without warning attack their converted brothers. Captain Pedro Fages had fought the fierce Apaches in the Sonora country and pointed out that many of his Catalan soldiers who had started with him by sea were either dead or ill. Ensign Miguel Costansó, of the regular Army and a topographical engineer, advised that according to every account some rough terrain lay before the party.

Portolá had loaded one hundred mules for the expedition and counted on being met either by the *San José*—which sank—or the returned *San Antonio*, sent south for additional men and supplies. The seven muleteers warned the Governor that the pack animals, and horses, would be easily stampeded if the Indians were not kept away. The natives in California took great delight in teasing the beasts at night to make them "speak."

On the morning of the 15th Portolá again gave the order to march. Ortega and eight *soldados de cuera* (so called from their leather jackets) led the way with spades, crowbars and mattocks to clear any heavy underbrush that could not be circled. Portolá rode at the head of an armed column with Father Juan Crespí at his side. Crespí, the alert, good-humored boyhood friend of Serra, was then forty-eight years of age but had become inured to hardship after sixteen years in the Sierra Gordo missions.

Fages, ill of scurvy from the start, had charge of the men escorting four divisions of loaded mules while Rivera guarded the flank of spare horses and pack animals. Portolá, Crespí, Fages and Costansó all kept *diarios* of the historic and near-disastrous march along a route that would forever after be the main north-south artery of California.

For the first week the pace was slow, considering the easy terrain, and the average of six miles per day was explained in Costansó's diary:

> Camp was pitched early each afternoon so that the explorers could scout ahead to plan the next day's march. More protracted halts were called after unusually fatiguing marches, or if a stampede necessitated recovery of the animals.[6]

Those first stampedes occurred one week after departure as the expedition approached a river they christened for *Jesus de los Temblores* when violent shocks gave them their first taste of California's quakes. Where the Spanish animals pounded the ground in fright they also gave the name *Santa Ana* for the feast day; a week later Portolá bestowed another name which would survive in abbreviated form: *Nuestra Señora de Los Angeles de Porciuncúla.*

Moving slowly northward through beautiful valleys shaded by oak, then turning west between slopes of a natural trail, Portolá came in sight of the sea at Santa Barbara Channel and for the first time recognized descriptions in the account of Cabrillo's landing 227 years earlier. Here were large numbers of strong, even-featured natives who lived in rush houses cemented with clay and built seaworthy craft—*Pueblo de Canoas.*

27

The *Canaleños* excitedly drew pictures in the sand and explained this art in pantomime: ships and men with beards and hats. Costansó and Fages were dragged into the water as the natives tried to convey the idea that they had seen these very two men on the deck of the *San Antonio* two moons ago when that ship overran San Diego coming north. And to show that they knew of other ships, the Indians brought out the rusted blades of old swords and knives.

A more disturbing exhibit was viewed farther up the coast near the end of August when Indians showed new European-made beads and indicated that they came from the north. Some of Portolá's men "recognized" the Russian design; others disagreed—"*Compañeros*, I met this girl in San Lucar. . . ."

All the way up the arching shore the natives showed a friendliness that was not abused, a tribute to the strong leadership of commander and officers. Fages wrote:

> . . . the Indians came voluntarily to nearly every place where our men camped that they might present themselves to us and show us honors demonstrating the most complete confidence. . . . Our men made themselves understood by signs and they in like manner indicated to us the road, the watering places and other matters concerning which we required information for our guidance on the march. It was never necessary for us to use our weapons for any purpose save to obtain some game which was generally bears whose flesh had a pleasant flavor.[7]

It was near San Luis Obispo in the first week of September that the pathfinders came upon fierce grizzly bears who hunted in bands of a dozen to terrorize the tribes. One huge beast almost killed a soldier after receiving nine shots. The miraculous guns of the Spaniards, and the bear meat, made friends of Indians whose leader had a large tumor growing from his neck. For this deformity the area was named *El Buchón*.

Along the trail they blazed the explorers gave either the names of saints—insisted upon by the priests—or as often a simple, descriptive label such as *Gaviota* (seagull); *Olla* (kettle); *Pájaro* (bird); *Oso Flaco* (thin bear); *Pulgas* (fleas); and at first they called the murky Salinas the Chocolate River.

On September 16th Portolá, who had followed a sea path instead of going inland at San Luis Obispo, found himself stopped by the sheer drop of the Sierra de Santa Lucía near San Simeon. They were still one hundred miles from Monterey but according to the mistaken latitude reckoned by astrolabe the Commander believed himself much closer. He must break a path inland yet it would not be wise to by-pass the port and be cut off by a Russian force. Provisions were beginning to run low; after two months a number of the men were showing signs of scurvy, including the scout Ortega. The decision reached by Portolá sent the expedition up into the mountains, laboring one mile a day to gain a ridge along which they could proceed northward. On every side mountains reached away out of sight. According to Crespí the magnificent view presented

> a sad outlook for poor travelers, tired and worn by the fatigues of the journey, by the task of clearing rough passages and breaking roads through hills, woods, dunes and swamps . . .[8]

The intense ascent, men dragging reluctant mules, and another struggle down steep hills, brought the Spaniards to the Salinas none too soon. From the strain came crippling scurvy for more than a dozen of the soldiers. Limbs useless, it was necessary to lash them to *tijeras*—wooden frames—borne by the mules. The only relief for the sufferers was a nightly rubdown with oil until the cavalcade approached the coast, and rainfall eased the pains in swollen arms and legs.

On the last day of September the distant sound of breakers told Portolá he was again near the sea. Scouts went ahead and returned with the assurance that no enemy forces occupied the area. At dawn the following morning the Commander took Crespí, Costansó and five soldiers with him to a hill that overlooked the coast. They unrolled the chart of Vizcaíno and another by the Manila admiral, José Cabrera Buena, weighed down the edges with swords, and compared the pictured shoreline with what they could see in the distance. Far north loomed what must be *Punta de Año Nuevo*; on their left rose the headland of *Punta de Pinos*. But the great bight between the capes showed no break. Where was the famous, sheltered harbor of Monterey? When Rivera returned from a careful examination of the shore he reported a solid front of sand dunes, sparsely populated by stupid, inferior natives. Father Crespí wrote:

> At Punta Pinos there is no port, nor have we seen in all our journey a country more desolate than this, or people more rude, Sebastián Vizcaíno to the contrary notwithstanding.

For three days the weakening company probed the coast for signs of Vizcaíno's "port sheltered from all winds ... thickly settled with people ... a harbor that is all that can be desired for the Manila ships." [9] Finally, to leave no doubt, Portolá gave the order to break camp and head north.

In the rugged mountains beyond Santa Cruz, three men believed to be dying were given extreme unction. Portolá dropped on the trail, too ill to walk, but had himself propped in a litter and urged on the tired expedition. The 22nd of October Rivera joined the sick list and two days later a halt was called on the beach thirty miles below the then undiscovered Golden Gate. Every man reported ill while heavy rain soaked and chilled them to bring on an epidemic of diarrhea. *Valle de los Soldados de los Cursos*, they called the camp site on San Gregorio Creek—Valley of the Soldier's Curses. Meat and vegetables had given out; the men were too weak to hunt. Rations were reduced to five small tortillas per man per day.

The epidemic relieved the swelling of scurvy and some of the natives came to offer their black lumps of almond-tasting pastry. Although Portolá was thought near death he gave the order to march. It was necessary to construct rude bridges over three *arroyos* on this later abandoned coastal trail, but finally they made the shores of Half Moon Bay. Carried to a height above Point San Pedro, the Commander saw the bleak Farallon Islands and beyond the white cliffs that led to Point Reyes. Crespí recognized the great bight outside the hidden Golden Gate and wrote, "It is of our Father San Francisco and we have left Monterey behind."

Perplexed, wearied to the point of almost complete exhaustion, the men huddled around a great campfire on the first day of November, and delayed the slaughter of a mule while Ortega led volunteers toward a herd of deer seen silhouetted on Sweeney Ridge. The hunters returned with venison but also brought startling and discouraging news: they had sighted San Francisco Bay, a huge estuary which blocked off any chance of advancing northward. There was no sign of the *San José*, of Russians, or of a *puerto famoso*. Sadly Portolá pointed south. Candles were lit, prayers were said, and penances were promised as the defeated Spaniards began the trek back to San Diego.

THE RETREAT

Only Indian converts and a few of the more hardy Catalonians could eat the mule meat whose rank smell and taste added nausea to the miseries of the company as it staggered down to Monterey Bay. On the shore there, and at Point of Pines, Portolá left bottle messages beneath wooden crosses—pleas for help which told the route they would attempt to follow.

By an extraordinary effort Portolá left his litter and assured the men that the march south would be easier. When demoralized, starving soldiers stole flour he called a halt, and measured the remaining supply into shares.

As the year 1768 ended the explorers were bogged down in mud at San Luis Obispo, but the next day they shot a mother bear and cub; the nourishment helped them on to Point Concepción. Around the headland the sun broke out, and with good weather luck changed. Plied with food by the friendly natives, warmed by the mild seacoast climate, the ill recovered. Portolá reached San Diego without losing a man during four hard months of trail breaking. Crespí summed up the arrival:

> ... with the merit of having been compelled to eat the flesh of male and female mules and without having found the Port of Monterey, which we judge to have been filled up by great sand dunes ... [10]

AN OFFICIAL REVISION

The failure to find Monterey was matched by Serra's lack of success in attracting converts to his mission at San Diego. The united pioneers watched the road and the sea to the south for the coming of provisions that would enable them to retire from California.

In Sonora José de Gálvez stood speechless as he read the report of Portolá:

> What should be the Carmel River is only a brook; what should be a seaport is only a little cove; what have been described as great lakes are puddles ... [11]

With astonishment the King's Inspector hastily scanned the other reports; Crespí, Fages, Rivera—and even the engineer Costansó—confirmed the Governor. ¡Nombre de Dios! Had these tontos lost all reason? His Majesty had been explicit in the order that Monterey should be fortified. Were months of time, thousands of pesos, and the future of Gálvez to be thrown away because of unasked-for opinions?

No word of the failure to fortify Monterey went beyond Gálvez. The San Antonio was hastily loaded; her captain given orders for delivery to Portolá and Serra along with the admonition to crack on sail for a record passage to San Diego. The ship arrived just in time to prevent the desertion of northern settlement.

Portolá, the good soldier, shrugged when he read his blistering message from the Visitador General. With Crespí, Fages and another expedition he set off to retrace his steps to Monterey while the elated Serra embarked for the northern roadstead aboard ship. Arriving at Monterey where his wooden cross above the untouched bottle stood decorated with flowers of the natives, Portolá, the priest and the soldier walked to the beach accompanied by a scribe and other witnesses. On the afternoon of May 24, 1770, the three exchanged nods, then for the record spoke in unison:

> We were mistaken for this *is* the port of Monterey which we seek, just as it was described by the navigators Sebastián Vizcaíno and José Cabrera Buena.[12]

The *San Antonio* arrived the last day of May after a forty-eight-day passage and Junípero Serra led the cheering people ashore. Because there was a scarcity of wood and water around Monterey, dedication ceremonies were held at Carmel on June 3 near the spot at which a Carmelite monk had blessed a cross in 1603. *San Carlos de Borromeo de Monterey* became the northern terminal of the road from Loreto.

The first couriers to use the route were a young sailor and soldier who volunteered to carry the great news of rediscovery. With spare horses they departed June 14 and reached the southern tip of Baja California in just under fifty days. Word was relayed to Mexico City by fast lugger and professional messengers; soon after August 10 Gálvez had published, and sent to Madrid, a joyous brochure that heralded the founding of New Spain's northernmost stronghold in the New World.

Gálvez disposed of Portolá by having him "promoted" to be Governor of Pueblo where the honest soldier remained until his retirement, under the eyes of the Viceroy. Fages and Rivera were pitted against each other; Serra was used as a check against the rivals. José de Gálvez weathered an attack of *accidente* (insanity) and returned to Spain in glory to nurse California through infancy from his high post as Minister of the Indies.

THE TROUBLED TRAIL

First to hold the reins in command of the California coast frontier was the blunt, honest Captain Pedros Fages who took over at Monterey when Portolá departed. During his four years as *comman-*

dante, until Serra's efforts had him removed, Fages reconnoitered the trail between San Diego and San Francisco, personally supervised road work, pursued runaways, disciplined soldiers and scttlers at distant points, and became an authority on the route he had helped to open.

A glimpse of the troubles that came as Indians reacted to the early conversion efforts of the Franciscans and the abuses of crude solders is seen in a report made to the Viceroy by Fages:

> In order to travel and transport goods from San Diego to Monterey it is necessary to pass twenty or more Indian towns either directly through them, along their borders, or at least within sight of them at about gunshot distance and there are numerous cliffs, bluffs, and difficult passages where the natives might, to advantage, dispute the way and even prevent travelers from passing. Instances of this are not lacking. For example, in the year '72 they threw stones and darts at me when I was going down to San Diego at a place which we call El Rincon; the Indians took advantage of an opportunity to surprise me and my escort when we were occupied in effecting a difficult passage, and we found ourselves in such straits that it was necessary, assuming the defensive, to punish the boldness of the insolent fellows, killing one or more of them but losing none of our men. Since then they have shown some caution but whenever they see a small number of travelers not well armed the Indians do not hesitate to try their fortune. It is plain to see that there is no means of forfending these injuries than to establish presidios and missions in suitable places. . . .[13]

At the time of Fages' defensive action only three sites had been blessed between San Diego and Monterey, mere outposts where the Franciscans planted mustard seed and radishes while they enticed the first *neophytes.* In Apache country the few guards and priests would have been quickly wiped out.

In his report to Viceroy Antonio María Bucareli y Ursúa, one of New Spain's greatest rulers, Fages urged that a strong presidio be established on the shores of San Francisco Bay. He and Crespí made two *entradas* along the coastal range, up to the Sacramento River, but the commander objected to founding any mission until he was given soldiers in sufficient numbers. For this insistence Serra was able to persuade the Viceroy to replace Fages. However, Bucareli did heed the soldier's advice to settle San Francisco, which led to a new "feeder" route from Mexico into the coast trail—an ancient westward course used by aborigines and then by Eusebio Kino: *El Camino del Diablo*.

THE HARD-RIDING CAPTAIN

Fifty miles in a day was a common ride for Captain Juan Bautista Anza, son and grandson of Sonora frontier soldiers, who was chosen by Bucareli to break trail and lead the first large party of settlers from New Spain to San Francisco. Just past forty years of age, in his prime, Anza was as hard on foot as on horseback and had killed a famous Apache chief in a hand to hand fight. Feared by the natives, trusted by his soldiers, he was a man who would insure as much as possible the safety of women and children on a 1,600-mile journey through a near wilderness of deserts, mountains and ambush terrain held by hostile Indians.

To survey the land over which he would lead colonists, Anza left Tubac near Tucson, Arizona, in January of 1774 with a party of thirty-four that included Sebastián Tarabel, a Baja California *neophyte* who had "run away" from San Gabriel near Los Angeles and made the eastward trek to Sonora on foot. Another guide was Juan Valdés, one of Portolá's soldiers. Anza made San Gabriel in ten weeks, spotting waterholes found one hundred years before by Kino, leaving markers for the later migration. He rode up to Monterey and back with a few men, then returned to Mexico.

On January 4, 1775, Anza again came onto the coast road at San Gabriel, this time at the head of what seemed like a huge cavalcade. There were 243 persons, including infants born on the desert, and more than one thousand animals. Mission bells rang and volleys were fired by the presidial soldiers; fires had been lit and as many sheep as could be spared were slaughtered for a barbecue to welcome the travelers.

In the long train that had braved the desert with the loss of only one life—a woman—were families with as many as nine children. California soldiers eyed the young señoritas; *neophytes* thronged around the golden horse of Juan Palamino, first of the famous breed of "Isabellas" to reach the country that would give them the name of the rider.

After a number of delays, and when supplies had run low, Anza took his charges onto what had become a recognizable road in six years of even sparse travel. Hurrying the expedition along toward Monterey, anxious to deliver the people safely, Anza sighted the Santa Barbara Channel three days after leaving San Gabriel. Father Pedro Font, diarist, recorded that the road

> ...runs along the sea beach almost touching the waves; for this reason it is a very diverting way and it would have been more so if the day had been clear and not so murky from fog. The people of the expedition, who had never seen the sea, found many things to marvel at.... In places there is no other way except along the beach and in other stretches there is a road which they call "along the heights" which runs on the edge of the sliced off part of the hills with great precipices from which the sea is visible far below.[14]

Font's diary reflected the changes come about since Portolá first traveled up the Santa Barbara shore. He found the *Canaleños* who had welcomed and helped the early explorers to be "very thievish" and at times openly insulting to the soldiers. The priest wrote of the women:

> ...they were very cautious and hardly a one left their huts because the soldiers, since they were not married, had offended them with various excesses which the unbridling of their passions caused them to commit with them. This shyness I observed in all the villages of the channel.[15]

At San Luis Obispo the Anza party turned inland to avoid the Santa Lucia Mountains, and followed a route opened by Fages that took them along the Salinas with a short cut to the little mission on the San Antonio River where they ate shoats and fat. Soaked by rain and weary, but in better shape than many a later wagon train, Anza's people arrived at Monterey after 130 days on the road.

The late Herbert Eugene Bolton, one of the West's most distinguished historians, made a twentieth century crossing of the historic route from which he concluded:

> Among the men who helped to plant European civilization on the shores of the Pacific Ocean Anza occupies an honorable place. First to open a route across the Sierras and first to lead a colony overland to the North Pacific shores, he was the forerunnner of Mackenzie, Thompson, Lewis and Clark, Smith, Frémont, the Forty-niners, and all the eager-eyed throng who since have yielded to the urge of Westward Ho.[16]

Anza rode to the tip of the San Francisco peninsula, then around the Contra Costa to the Sacramento River. The trail he found to what is now Salinas, on through the Santa Clara Valley and northward past Palo Alto, became the main highway. On his return Anza bid the colonists good-bye and started back to Mexico with nineteen loaded mules and a small escort.

Thinking ahead to the stretches of desert they must cross Font wrote of California's first fields under cultivation and rolling hills with many pretty larkspurs and little red marigolds in bloom. Even after half a dozen years there were signs of a rich pastoral country, and one of the priest's diary notes implies the start of granaries at the missions:

> And in a cage we carried from the Mission of Carmelo four cats; two for San Gabriel and two for San Diego at the requests of the Fathers, who urgently asked us for them since they are very welcome on account of the great abundance of mice.[17]

Pathfinding along the Pacific Coast from Cape San Lucas to San Francisco Bay—from Eusebio Kino to Juan Anza—had been completed by the summer of 1776. That was the year José Gálvez became Minister of the Indies; through the next decade he favored the interests of the territory he had maneuvered into occupancy.

These trails leading northward and northwestward from San Diego toward the upper shores of that great bay of San Francisco would be criss-crossed by foot and by horseback as the explorers—Portolá, Anza and others—pathfound the ancient littoral that would one day be the King's Highway, and later, the route of a great freeway.

Three   The Mission Trail

THE LONG GOWNS

The Spanish missionary record of tenacity in the New World—from the *reducciónes* of Paraguay to the chapels of Baja California—was expected to continue along the Pacific coastal trail opened by the pathfinders. Expensive military establishments could be maintained for a time, justified by the threat of Russian or English invasion; but statesmen such as Floridablanca, Arrillaga and Gálvez counted on the religious zeal of the Franciscans to make the outpost tenable through conversion of the natives and cultivation of the virgin soil.

Those Franciscan padres of the late eighteenth century were among the best educated men of their day and had been schooled to teach not only religion but also the crafts of husbandry, weaving, carpentry and masonry. Many brought from the college of San Fernando specially developed skills; all were imbued with an apostolic devotion that was put to the most severe test by their difficult assignment.

The unpromising start to found missions one day's ride apart between Monterey and San Diego came on July 14, 1771, in the beautiful undulating country of the Santa Lucia's southeastern valley where oak trees lined the San Antonio River. Junípero Serra walked seventy-five miles from Monterey to hang a wooden, metal-lined bell from a limb and cry out shrilly as he pealed: "Hear O Gentiles! Come! Come to the Holy Church of God! Come and receive the faith of Christ!" [1] A single curious native approached and at a distance watched the priest celebrate Mass on an altar of branches. The eighteen head of cattle allowed each of the newly found missions were turned loose to graze; olive and pomegranate seeds were planted.

Two months later other Franciscans walked one hundred miles up the road from San Diego and performed a fourth dedication on the banks of the San Gabriel River, planted orange trees and grape vines, then put the cattle to pasture and waited for converts.

A small guard was stationed at each of the missions, relieved at intervals from the presidios of Monterey and San Diego. Pack mules came with tools, farm implements, food and loads of vestments, chalices, silver caskets, baptismal fonts, statuary and copies of Betancourt's Manual. Serra limped between the four little churches, undismayed by the reluctance of the Indians to embrace Christianity.

Curiosity brought native children to watch the work of the "long gowns," as they called the priests from their full length robes of gray sackcloth, secured at the waist by a heavy white cord. Boys and girls would wait for the fathers to throw back their cowls or re-move broad, round-brimmed hats to reveal tonsured crowns. Those who stayed to hear Mass, or the chanting of the *Alabado*, were re-warded by gifts of beads and bits of colored cloth. At Carmel a few were taught to say "*Amar a Diós*" (To love God).

The Franciscans knew from the start they were dealing with a race that must be attracted like children; once their confidence was gained the way to saving souls might be opened. The fathers attempted to learn the dialects, offered food, protection and an opportunity to help. They persuaded little girls to wear dresses of

39

blue maguey cloth and passed out baize and striped sackcloth. Under ideal conditions it would have been difficult to convince those free and idle people that labor, routine, regulations and memory tasks represented an ideal life. But when soldiers moved in to abuse the Indians the missionary effort seemed doomed.

At San Gabriel Archangel, soon after its founding, soldiers returned from a hunting trip with the head of an Indian which was set on a pole before their stockade. The native, they said, had attempted to kill one of the soldiers who warded off the arrow with his bullhide shield, then shot the attacker. The next day a band of Indians appeared to ask for the head of their chief whom they claimed had been grievously provoked: the soldier had raped his wife.

The fathers thought their prayers were answered when the first child brought in to be baptized was the son of the murdered chief. The soldiers, a rough lot, sulked at the remonstrances and to show that they were not *frailéros* (those fond of priests) engaged in a game around San Gabriel; riding into the villages they lassoed women, raped them, then shot any Indian who attempted to interfere. In this heavily populated area only two Indians a month were baptized during the first year.

When a fifth mission was founded at San Luis Obispo the Indians gathered to help with building shelters and offered roots to the Spaniards who came with only fifty pounds of flour and a few *almudes* of wheat; they also brought children to be baptized and a woman named Lilila insisted on doing heavy work although she was very old. These tribes were attempting to show appreciation for the white man's slaughter of fearsome bears. Here lay a great opportunity for the priests but again there was trouble, as Serra recorded:

> . . . let us leave time to tell the story of the progress which I hope Christianity will make among them in spite of the Enemy who already began to lash his tail by means of a bad soldier, who soon after arrival was caught in actual sin with an Indian woman.[2]

40

Where soldiers were stationed in force converts refused to remain overnight; young women avoided the road between the missions and hid when horsemen approached their *rancheria*, as the villages were called. At isolated San Antonio *neophytes* built their huts near the church and invited friends to stay overnight so they could hear the long gowns at daybreak sing the *Canticle of Dawn*:

> *Now comes the dawn*
> *Brightness of morn*
> *Oh, let all of us say*
> *Hail-Mary-Hail . . .*

The protests of the fathers against soldier conduct, along with pleas for more missions, were presented to Captain Fages, and Serra wrote detailed letters of complaint to the Viceroy. The *commandante*, who rivaled the Franciscan president as a correspondent, foolishly urged the curtailment of religious effort: the quarrelsome California native was amiable to discipline only in the form of vigorous chastisement; he was incapable of ever understanding the mysteries of the holy Catholic faith—let him therefore be used to build much needed roads, forts and dwellings and to till the soil.

The presumption of Pedro Fages in offering unsolicited criticism on a policy already approved was made good use of by Serra, who never hesitated to employ his political acumen in maneuvers against the military. He departed for Mexico, laid his case before Viceroy Bucareli, made strong reference to the Pious Fund, and engaged in heavy correspondence with Madrid. As a result Fages was removed, but in his place came that rival veteran of the first expedition, Capitán Rivera, with whom Serra soon found himself at odds.

The Father President brought home news of plans to insure success for the Franciscans. Colonists—including prospective brides for soldiers—were to come north with Captain Anza; other settlers would be sent from Loreto. The mission chain was to be immediately increased so the road from San Diego, extended to San Francisco, might show an establishment every thirty-five to sixty miles.

Finally, Baja California had been turned over to the Dominicans and fifteen relieved padres now were available for the north, including Serra's former student at Mallorca, Francisco Palou.

THE GRAY OX

From the writings of the devoted Palou there emerges a picture of Serra which beneath the eulogizing shows the indefatigable spirit of man with a dream. Palou subjugated himself to the dynamic teacher and accompanied him across the Atlantic, to the San Gordo missions of Mexico, then followed his wanderings in California. Despite remarkable energy and dedication, Serra owes much of his lasting fame to the dark-eyed, silent biographer, for like all crusaders he was known in his day as a nuisance to those in power and a tyrant of sorts among inferiors.

In Mexico Serra dubbed himself "the gray ox" and he made that nickname apt during the decade preceding his death. Few have ever covered so many purposeful miles in such great and continuous pain as the fair-looking priest. The ulcer on his leg remained open to make walking or even riding a torture; a skin cancer spread over his body; attacks of asthma grew worse. Great zeal and the enthusiasm that comes with planning kept Serra alive.

At Carmel, his headquarters, the Father President worked on maps with Palou and his other staunch friend, Crespí. They marked areas where the new missions were to rise and indicated slight direction changes to be made in the road. Couriers dashed between the first struggling missions and brought back reports of slow but certain progress: a few more *neophytes* every day at San Antonio; increases of stock at San Diego and San Luis Obispo; and the soil at San Gabriel rivaled in richness the land around Carmel. The Franciscans were ready in 1775 to fill in gaps along the trail when disaster struck.

On the night of November 4th a force of eight hundred *Diegueños*, jealous of the God who had attracted sixty tribe members to the baptismal font, descended on the San Diego mission. Father

Luis Jaume was disrobed and beaten to death; a carpenter was slain and six men wounded; all the mission buildings were fired. Captain Rivera laughed at talk of "martyrdom" and "the chance for an example of Christ's forgiveness" [3] as he sought revenge; the soldier even risked excommunication by dragging a *neophyte* from the church where the native sought sanctity.

The San Diego uprising had been caused by no soldier indiscretion so the military pursued its advantage right down to the territory's first public execution of four Indian chiefs, rubbing salt into the wound as the commanding officer instructed the priests:

> You will cooperate for the good of their souls and it is the understanding that if they do not accept the salutary waters of Holy Baptism they die on Saturday morning; and if they do—they die all the same! [4]

Before that sentence was passed on April 11, 1778—during more than two years of unrest—the Franciscans had been able to bless crosses at only three additional sites: the northern end of the mission trail was marked on the shores of San Francisco Bay; another establishment dedicated in the Santa Clara Valley midway to Monterey; and the San Diego-to-San Gabriel trail was bisected on the long slope to the sea at San Juan Capistrano.

Wearing out many pairs of heavy leather sandals, sometimes forced by illness to mount a mule, Serra patrolled the eight missions where in ten years each counted converts by the hundreds and livestock by the thousands. Log buildings were ready to give way to adobe structures; in many areas *neophytes* had graded the road; full storage bins and acres under cultivation relieved the hungry eyes that once watched the road and the sea for supplies.

Through those years of survival the guiding influence of José de Gálvez underlay the pompous directives of Charles III and the endless stream of petty regulations that reiterated the precept of his benevolent despotism—"everything *for* the people; nothing *by* the people." Alta California became a separate territory, more important than the parent peninsula, with Felipe de Neve replacing Rivera at Monterey under the title of governor; provisions were made for pueblos at San Jose and Los Angeles; in 1780 His Majesty decreed that a "voluntary tax" of two dollars per head for Spaniards and one dollar for Indians should be paid to help defray the fifty thousand dollars being spent each year to maintain the outpost; repeated dispatches warned of invasion threats by European enemies.

Along that largely defenseless coast trail there lived five hundred people of Spanish or mixed blood, including women and children, with a *neophyte* population of several thousand. Three presidios—with about fifty soldiers each—were adequate only to keep the gentile Indians at bay; one surgeon ministered to the ill between San Diego and San Francisco and could do little to combat syphilis and measles, the principal ailments visited on the Indian. The weakest stretch of the trail lay along the two hundred miles that separated the missions of San Gabriel and San Luis Obispo where Governor Neve, like his military predecessors, refused to expose soldiers. Serra might rant as he pleased about the rich field for conversion but the *Canaleños* had turned into warriors more hostile even than their cousins at San Diego.

Serra gained his way to some extent when an armed procession from San Gabriel moved to the southern shores of Santa Barbara Channel where he dedicated San Buenaventura on Easter of 1782. The soldiers then built a presidio up the coast. Serra felt full of hope on his way back to Monterey, having heard that Neve was to be replaced, but to his shocked surprise the new governor turned out to be the man he had helped remove as commandant—Fages, now wearing the epaulettes of a lieutenant colonel.

REQUIESCAT IN PACE

Fages again rode the entire mission strip, handing out pardons to runaway *neophytes*, encouraging soldiers and settlers and disciplining any who endangered the missionary effort. In spite of this show of good will Serra was suspicious; in his seventieth and last year of life he painfully walked and rode the circuit himself. On his return to Carmel he smiled wearily at the group of priests and Indians who awaited him and said: "I have come home to die." [5]

Letters of final farewell were sent to all missions; nearby priests were summoned for a personal parting. After confessing and receiving the last sacrament the old man told the carpenter to make his coffin. He died in the arms of Palou on August 28, 1784. *Neophytes* wept; Governor Fages and José de Ortega, now a captain, stood with presidial troops as Serra's body was lowered to lie alongside another veteran of the early trail, Juan Crespí, in the little cemetery at the 180-year-old *puerto famoso.*

The year Serra died Gaspar de Portolá sailed homeward, honorably retired from the Army as colonel. On the night of June 17, 1787, at the royal residence of Aranjuez near Madrid, José de Gálvez went to his reward, aged fifty-eight years, after an argument with the King. The Mexican historian Bustamente later wrote: "the death of the Minister was supposed to have been due to apoplexy, but in those days that might have been either poison or the garrote." [6] Fast-riding couriers brought another announcement of requiem two years later along with orders for the *salva funebre* at all presidios and missions: Charles III had died.

THE SEAFARERS

The successor to Junípero Serra was the courtly but vigorous Fermin Francisco de Lasuén, a native of Vitoria, Spain, whose parents had been of French extraction. In the eighteen years he would serve as president, the sturdy, prematurely gray Lasuén founded nine more missions and brought the chain to its height. About him Hubert Howe Bancroft, dean of California historians, wrote:

> Let us remember the good qualities of Junípero Serra and others like him; let us make every allowance for their weaknesses; but first among the California prelates let us ever rank Fermin de Lasuén as a friar who rose above his environment and lived many years in advance of his times. [7]

45

Badly pock-marked in early life, Lasuén cultivated a manner that made him immediately agreeable to strangers and projected into the personalities of his people. This was remarked by the first foreign navigator to land on the shores of California when the aristocratic Jean François Galaup, Comte de La Pérouse, rode the five miles from Monterey to Carmel in September of 1786:

> After crossing a little plain... we ascended the hills and heard the sound of bells announcing our coming. We were received like lords of a parish visiting their estates for the first time. The president of the missions, clad in cope, his holy-water sprinkler in hand, received us at the door of the church illuminated as on the grandest festivals; led us to the foot of the altar; and chanted a *te deum* of thanksgiving for the happy issue of our voyage.[8]

Pérouse, commanding two ships of a scientific expedition, had been instructed by the King of France to "learn the condition, force and aim"[9] of the Spanish establishments. Convinced that it would be at least a century before California became of interest to the maritime powers, the Frenchman proceeded to enjoy himself for ten days. He gave Lasuén a hand mill for grinding corn and some seed potatoes from Chile; in return he insisted on having the recipe for *pozole*—that stew of meat, maize, peas and beans—with the warning that he proposed to have his chef improve the dish with seasonings.

The tall, slender *comte*, wearing his gray hair in a long queue, found favor with the high-born wife of Pedro Fages who missed the urban life of Mexico City. From that lady the Frenchman heard of the dismal country through which she had been forced to travel between Loreto and Monterey; his sympathy was touched by her account of crude accommodations, half, or entirely, naked savages, wild animals and long, dusty marches.

The wilderness condition of California was confirmed six years later by the English navigator, Captain George Vancouver, who wore out his welcome after three visits. When he and some of the officers from HMS *Discovery* were taken on a wet ride to the Santa Clara Valley from San Francisco they saw "no single house or other man-made shelter" and at Belmont when they paused at noon one of the party broached "some grog we had brought from the ship, spirits and wine being scarce articles in this country." [10]

Vancouver presented the San Carlos mission with a music box to help dispel the loneliness and in the south found abundant supplies. He was not encouraged to linger for orders had been received from New Spain to beware of all foreigners—Englishmen, citizens of "The United States of Boston" and, especially, Russians.

Troops were alerted at presidios from San Francisco southward. Fires lay banked in the great bake ovens, ready to be fed so that cannon balls could be made red hot—*balsas rosas*—to ignite any enemy ship. Indians were repeatedly warned of the horror sure to follow a Russian invasion. Bancroft tells of conditions as they existed along the Alaskan coast as Kamchatkans and Siberians pushed southward late in the eighteenth century:

> The history of this period is a chronicle of crime, oppression, and bloodshed such as the pen recoils from recording . . . of women ravished by hundreds from their homes, casting themselves into the sea to escape their ferocious captors; of wholesale massacres; of slavery, tyranny and outrage; of fearful retribution by desperate natives; of drunken brawls, plots and counterplots, and hideous punishments . . .[11]

Colonists from Mexico and Spain were taught how to use arms and made to drill; the infirm stood sentinel duty on roads above every cove; messengers supplemented the weekly couriers riding between Loreto and Monterey. The master plan to repel an invasion was built around a cavalry force that could be assembled from all presidios at any point of attack.

The enemy threat continued through the 1790s when Spain went to war with England and during that time minimized local troubles to the extent that Lasuén was able to establish the long-sought mission at Santa Barbara in 1786, and the following year go up the road past Point Concepción to dedicate another named La Purísima.

By 1791, when sites were blessed at Santa Cruz, on the north shore of Monterey Bay, and at Soledad in the Salinas Valley thirty miles south, the mission buildings were taking their distinctive form. The old log structures, smeared with mud, gave way to stone and adobe churches. A labor force of more than seven thousand *neophytes* worked from dawn till vespers molding clay bricks, mixing lime whitewash and hewing timbers. The Franciscans at San Luis Obispo made a cast for the first roof tile, using the well-rounded thigh of an Indian as a form. Artisan settlers from Mexico—many of them convicts—supervised construction of the white-sided, red-roofed missions with their square towers, domed belfries, arches, columns and recessed windows; these were built in a quadrangle around a patio, the church flanked by low buildings that housed priests, Indians, soldiers and servants and left space for the kitchens, storage bins and granaries.

Lasuén traveled the mission trail to authorize changes, inspect the baptismal books, and make note of requests for candelabra, statues, draperies and paraphernalia needed to conduct Mass. He checked supplies with the *mavera*, the man in charge of the granary; sampled the *apolo* which was the staple food of the *neophytes*; asked questions in the *pozolera* where unmarried natives lived; gave directions for the building of stables and guest rooms for travelers. At each of those missions in the late eighties and early nineties the aging Father President watched a growing individuality, the heritage of the Indian past.

At San Juan Capistrano swallows came and departed in great migratory flights every year, roosting in crevices of sandstone which had been hauled four miles to start a great cross-shaped church. San Gabriel Archangel already had more cattle and horses than any other mission; the brand there was "T," for the *temblores* that still shook the valley. San Buenaventura featured a system of canals that made the land so rich it had been possible to supply Captain

Vancouver with twenty mule-loads of fresh vegetables. There were more canals and a great aqueduct just north at Santa Barbara, beneath the lofty "Sailor's Sycamore" that travelers sighted from a distance. The *neophytes*, and even the padre, of San Luis Obispo urged wayfarers to try the nearby mineral springs of San Miguel: grizzly bears came there at night to soak lame legs. A thing to see up the road at Mission San Antonio was the herd of golden horses, descended from the mare of Anza's soldier Juan Palamino.

The individuality of missions continued as Lasuén filled gaps in the trail, adding four more missions in 1797. Reluctant Indians were attracted to the site of San Juan Bautista, twenty-five miles northwest of Carmel, by the eighteenth century tunes played on the music box of Vancouver. New converts set heavy beams in place and secured them with rawhide thongs as the old barrel organ was ground to play "Go to the Devil," "Lady Campbell's Reel" and "The College Hornpipe." At the valley mission of San Fernando Rey, above Los Angeles, delighted *neophyte* carpenters were allowed to cut holes in heavy doors so cats could chase the rats.

Before the century ended Lasuén founded his last mission— San Luís Rey—one day's ride out of San Diego. Those eighteen establishments had eighty thousand acres of wheat, corn and barley under cultivation; each had increased herds of lean, long-horned range cattle, sheep and horses to ten thousand head; smooth *alamedas* marked the approach to the red-white quadrangles with their orchards, irrigation canals, vegetable gardens and grape vines.

The backbone of the pastoral chain was its *neophyte* population, grown to almost fifteen thousand despite a terrible mortality rate. And the finger of blame for these deaths pointed then, and through the years, at the Franciscans.

THE NEOPHYTES

In return for immediate food and future salvation the *neophyte* abandoned almost every habit of his ancestor. He wore clothing, was locked in cramped quarters from nine at night until dawn, performed labor in the fields, roads or on buildings all day, and learned the Christianity he was expected to practice. For every infraction of rules he was punished by priests who, having been reared under the harsh code of the Inquisition, did not hesitate to mortify the flesh for the soul's ultimate deliverance from evil.

For vigorous use of the lash, stocks and shackles the fathers were criticized by the military, foreign visitors, their own priests and Indians who showed their protest by running away. Into the records of San Francisco's mission went the piteous defense statements of recaptured escapees:

> Tiburcio was flogged five times by Father Antonio Dantí for crying at the death of his wife and child. . . . Otolon was flogged for not caring for his wife after she had sinned with a *vaquero*. . . . Milan had to work with no food for his family and was flogged because he went after clams. . . .[12]

Father Antonio de la Concepción Horra joined the lists against his fellow Franciscans with the charge:

> The treatment shown to the Indians is the most cruel I have ever read in history. For the slightest things they receive heavy floggings, are shackled, and put in stocks, and treated with so much cruelty that they are kept whole days without a drink of water.[13]

In the cold cell that was his office at the Mission of San Carlos de Carmelo, Lasuén read the mounting criticism: miscarriage among Indian women was being treated as purposeful abortion and after being flogged for two weeks, they were made to attend church carrying a wooden dummy of a baby; for mere suspicion of scandalous conduct females had their heads shaved; some priests were said to be wearing shoes, seducing Indian maidens, smuggling and owning silver timepieces. Finally, there was the military opinion that the principal cause for the death of half the natives each year could be found in the Franciscan policy of confining the natives at night in cramped quarters, and overworking them by day on short rations.

The Father President laboriously investigated and tried to answer each charge. Priests found guilty of excessive cruelty faced dismissal as did those who broke their vows of poverty and chastity. But Lasuén was vehement in his denial that the Indians were underfed slaves or that their quarters could be blamed for deaths from syphilis and smallpox.

With the arrival of convict artisans and poorly disciplined troops from Loreto, the fathers had no choice but to confine *neophytes* lest there be a wholesale repetition of such incidents as the Indian woman at Santa Barbara, horribly mutilated for refusing a drunken soldier; or two boys receiving light punishment because of their tender years after they drowned an Indian child—to amuse themselves. The usually calm President showed wrath to the new governor, Diego de Borcía, a jovial *bon vivant*, when he warned that unless the soldiers be curbed California could expect outbreaks similar to the massacre on the Colorado.

Charges and countercharges went into the mail pouches of weekly couriers; back from the Viceroy came warnings, orders and new regulations: soldiers visiting *rancherías*, unless on duty as escort to a priest, should receive fifteen consecutive days' guard duty, wearing four *cueras*.

Regulations were weakly enforced; the warnings of Lasuén, right up to his death in 1803, were largely ignored and never recalled a few years later when sporadic outbreaks took the lives of priests and soldiers. Along with primary and hereditary syphilis came epidemics of measles and influenza that cut a devastating swath through the mission compounds. Still the number of *neophytes* grew, reaching 21,000 in 1805.

Many of these remained docile through fear of death from starvation in the hills or at the hands of soldiers who pursued them with ruthlessness. Lieutenant José María Amador, a self-declared "Indian Fighter," reminisced in his old age about the treatment accorded captured natives in the early 1800s:

> We invited the gentile and Christian Indians to come and eat pinole and dried meat ... then we surrounded them, separated a hundred Christians from the prisoners, and at each half mile these

51

were forced on their knees in prayer and were made to understand that they were going to die.... Each one of them received four arrows, two in the front and two in each shoulder. We baptized the remaining gentile Indians and shot them. Seventy of them fell at one shot. I doubled the charge for the thirty that remained and they all fell....[14]

Punishment by the priests and drudgery on roads and in fields were mild discomforts compared to the cruelty of the soldiers. And at the missions there was music, food, shelter and the reward of praise. When the military accused the priests of overworking children the reply was made:

Of the little children over nine years of age some comb the wool in the looms and hand the shuttle and quill the lever. Others look after the tile and brick during the day so that the animals do not step in it; still others frighten away the birds; and the rest amuse themselves with their childish games.[15]

INDIANS ON HORSEBACK

While children, women and the aged were employed at routine tasks, the strong, young *neophytes* learned to master the horse. The California Indian never became the mustang-breaking, buffalo-hunting rider of the Great Plains, or a breeder like his *Cayuse* cousin in Washington and Oregon; in fact, for all his natural talent, that first mission *vaquero* was more domesticated than his mount.

Franciscan horsemen, like the broad Pablo Vincente de Sola, tucked gray robes in girdles and taught the art of breaking wild horses, tossing the *reata*, branding of cattle, and how to change a bull into a steer. Tireless on horseback, and for the first time useful with dignity, the *neophyte* made his closest approach to white equality while holding reins.

Proud *vaqueros* wearing chaps were sent to the *tierra incognita* to let themselves be seen and envied by inland gentiles. At Santa Barbara they guided mules loaded with 200-pound packs of hemp on five-day journeys along the road to the seaport. At the stock ranges of every mission the best of those cowboys were indispensable for the round-ups; those who spoke fair Spanish acted as guides when settlers or new Spanish priests came up from Loreto, bound for different missions and pueblos. Even the soldiers deigned to use Indians as trackers, mostly to search out the lair of some cattle-thieving grizzly.

Wolves and bears were making bold daylight attacks on horses and cattle at the opening of the nineteenth century; one bear killed and ate five mules and seven cows before he was tracked down; another killed an Indian guide on the road between Carmel and Monterey. A regular military campaign was ordered against the beasts—with authorization for one thousand cartridges, and poison to saturate carcasses—yet in 1805 the grizzlies killed four hundred head of livestock at Monterey.

The bears were seen often around the roadhouse of Tio Armenta, a retired soldier whose mysterious source of income was revealed to the governor at Monterey through a grizzly scare. Late one night the surgeon was called to treat two Spanish traders who were badly injured when they fell into a ravine near the roadhouse. Eight bears had chased them, the men swore; further questioning brought the admission that their nocturnal business with Armenta was gambling.

In the morning Indian trackers went to the scene, then reported to the governor: the "eight bears" had left the footprints of one human which led to the house of Victor Arroyo, a young man with a reputation for practical jokes who was also the owner of a large bearskin.

While he developed skill as *vaquero*, guide and tracker, the Indian for a long time proved almost useless as a sailor; priests and soldiers watched with yearning as thousands of sea otter came south to seek safety in California bays but they could not teach the *neophyte* to harpoon from a canoe.

Other Indians—the *Aleuts*—skimmed past *Castillo de San Joaquin* at the entrance to San Francisco harbor in their *bidarkas*, killed and skinned the sea otter, and brought the peltries back to

53

ships waiting offshore. The nutria would fetch sixty dollars each in the Canton market for the Russian-American Company: the long-dreaded Muscovite had at last reached California.

THE RUSSIAN INVASION

Nikolai Petrovich Rezánov, an official of the fur company and a chamberlain of the Czar, sailed into San Francisco in April of 1806 to plea for a cargo of wheat that would save his starving settlement at Sitka, Alaska. While he awaited a decision the Russian, then a middle-aged widower but an exceptionally handsome man, saw love in the eyes of Concepción Argüello, the beautiful young daughter of the commandant. The dashing Russian won the girl's heart and they became betrothed. "From this time," Rezánov wrote, "I managed this port of his Catholic Majesty as my interests required." [16]

The understanding was that Rezánov would return to St. Petersburg—by way of Sitka with a full cargo—gain the consent of the Czar to his marriage and return for nuptials with Concepción on whose behalf the Franciscans would seek special dispensation from Rome. The chamberlain died crossing Siberia, his sweetheart remained faithful to her death, and writers embellished the romance through the years until it became a favorite love story of California.

Historians more interested in what they believed to be facts, than in the warmth of love, unearthed a letter dated at Archangel two months before the chamberlain's meeting with Concepción in which he opined that:

> ... in the course of ten years we should become strong enough to make use of any favorable turn in European politics to include the coast of California in the Russian possessions ... and to appropriate this territory forever since the geographic position of Mexico would prevent her from sending any assistance overland.[17]

Rezánov wrote of an opportunity he believed had been lost, but four years after his departure traffic on both sea and overland routes from Mexico abruptly discontinued with the start of the revolution against Spain. Isolated, without clear orders, the Californians were helpless when Russians landed fifty miles north of the Golden Gate, purchased the land from local Indians for three blankets and some tools, and built Fort Stawianski. The Californians called it *Fuerto de los Russos;* Americans knew it as Fort Ross.

Governor José Joaquin de Arrillaga sent a detachment of troops across San Francisco Bay and up the Marin coast in the fall of 1812 to advise the Russians that they were trespassing. Lieutenant Gabriel Moraga presented only a mild protest after he viewed the fortress built of redwood logs, set on a precipice seventy feet above the sea, pierced to show twenty guns. Inside he saw the twin-steepled Greek Orthodox Church and the imposing house of Governor Ivan Alexandrovich Kuskov, the hot-tempered former merchant who wore a gold medal awarded him for the loss of a leg. *Pie de Palo,* Wooden Leg, as the soldiers called him, refused to move but his eighty Russians and one hundred Alaskan natives needed wheat and beef so he offered to trade.

Considering the report of Moraga, a son of his old comrade-in-arms under Anza, "Papá" Arrillaga decided on a course of friendship—at least until he could muster a sufficient force to oust the invader. The missions were directed to supply the Russians with cattle and grain, taking payment in ironware and whatever else the foreign mechanics could produce. At San Rafael, fifteen miles north of San Francisco, the twentieth mission was founded in 1817 as a bulwark against Kuskov.

A few months after the Russian "invasion" a series of earthquakes shook the coast from San Diego to Point Concepción. Forty *neophytes* were buried alive during early Mass at San Juan Capistrano; heavy damage was suffered at San Gabriel and San Buenaventura; the eight-year-old chapel of Santa Ynez completely crumbled. *El Año de los Temblores,* they called that year of quakes.

THE DEAD-END ROAD

The Russians and the earthquakes came as harbingers of a troubled decade. By 1810 the colonial revolutionary movement reached Mexico. Priests and officers attempted to suppress the news: foreign ships were driven away from harbor entrances by gun fire; any courier who lost, or misplaced, a dispatch received twenty-five blows and one month extra duty wearing shackles. But when transports and mule trains stopped coming north, and deserters from English and Yankee whalers slipped ashore, the word spread.

Cigarettes, mescal, newspapers and luxury foods became scarce; the pay of soldiers ceased. There was widespread discontent by 1815 when the new governor, Pablo Vincente de Sola, arrived to be greeted by demands and pleas that an abundance of hides and tallow be sold to the foreign ships. *Carretas* loaded with flowers and food bumped along the trail from as far away as San Diego, converging on Monterey to show the governor olives, oranges, wines and pastries made from mission flour. Ships from Boston, Chile and the Hawaiian Islands landed agents who tempted the people to trade their produce and hides; samples of ribbon, shoes and jewelry passed from hand to hand. The governor announced that he intended to maintain the Spanish law regardless of suffering. Being a man of notable physical strength he cowed even the roughest of his soldiers.

Governor Sola was forced to look the other way in 1818 when the rumor became persistent that insurgent vessels were fitting out in Chile and the Argentine for attacks on the California coast. Hides folded under innocent loads of produce came along the new road from Santa Clara to Monterey or to cliffs above southern anchorages; *arrobas* of tallow were smuggled out of Santa Ynez; peltries of sea otter caught in traps went to the San Francisco anchorage. Back came warnings of another invasion, this to be one of violence. Deserters from foreign ships—the Portuguese Antonio Rocha, José Bolkov of Kamchatka and the Yankee sailor Thomas

Doak, confirmed the rumors. Then, in October, a definite report reached Santa Barbara, brought from Hawaii by the American brig *Clarion*.

THE PIRATES

Commandant José de la Guerra listened to the Yankee skipper who described the thirty-eight-gun frigate *Argentina* and her consort of twenty-six guns, the *Libertad*, outfitting in Hawaii for an invasion. Commander of the insurgent forces of four hundred men was the French sailor of fortune, Capitán Hippolyte Bouchard. Guerra dispatched a *correo violento* to Monterey and sent circulars to the southern missions warning the fathers that without doubt an attack was imminent. To the 3,000 whites and 25,000 *neophytes* of California, the commandant declared:

> Under the protection of the God of battles I believe I can destroy all such villains as may have the rashness to set foot upon this soil.[18]

Until mid-October excitement mounted. Governor Sola's couriers spurred along the road out of Monterey, dashing north and south with directives for evacuation of women and children, the removal of sacred church property, and the hiding of livestock. A lookout of one soldier and two Indians was posted at each of twenty-five coast points; fifty special couriers awaited orders that would send them galloping if the enemy came in sight; at outlying defense bases soldiers received issues of five hundred cartridges each; invalids again relieved the guard at the missions.

By November 20, 1818, the scare had about worn itself thin when the two insurgent ships were sighted from the Santa Cruz mountains, carrying all sail, clawing against a strong offshore wind on tacks that would let them make Point of Pines. Bouchard entered Monterey, exchanged fire with the fort, then demanded a surrender. Sola responded with scorn:

> I will make you know the honor and firmness with which I will repel you and while there is a man alive in the province you cannot

succeed . . . since all inhabitants are faithful servants of the King and will shed the last drop of their blood in his service. . . .[19]

The governor's next roar came from headquarters twelve miles inland one week after Bouchard ignored him and landed:

> Having concentrated my forces here to hinder the pirates, foes of the human race, from going inland, up to the present time they remain about the presidio and beach of Monterey, and have not dared to cross over to San Carlos. Yesterday they showed their rage by burning down the fort and presidio, whereby they give signs of speedy departure; and it being quite likely that their depraved intention is to sack at other points . . . I keep sufficient men on lookout to advise me of the course they may follow so as to send you news with the utmost speed.

On November 27th couriers from headquarters galloped south past wagons loaded with frightened women and children to spread the word that Bouchard had sailed. The pirate landed without resistance at several places, held truce talks with Guerra, and after a raid on San Juan Capistrano December 14th, sailed out of the history of California.

One of the few to show exceptional bravery during the siege was the portly Father Luis Antonio Martinez who rose from a sick bed at San Luis Obispo and led thirty-five *neophytes* in war paint along the road to Refugio, the point at which the Spaniards were able to take three prisoners. Father Martinez, later to be removed for worldly conduct, wrote a letter to Guerra in which he criticized the commandant for failure to use that device of the Galicians against the French which would have assured a notable victory for the Californians: instead of evacuating the young women Guerra should have left them to entertain the invader, their charms supplemented with liberal amounts of *aguardiente* and mescal; then presidial troops could have slain or captured the entire pirate crew.

In the wake of the pirates came calls for action. Sola, highly critical of his subordinates, demanded that one thousand more men be sent to California. He ordered the missions to manufacture two hundred *machetes* and one hundred and fifty cartridge boxes, and each was directed to train forty archers. The missions were then required to have available at all times one hundred mounts, ready for use in the next invasion.

Into force came more stringent regulations governing travelers. Some wayfarers might not be what they claimed as in the case of a company of *maromeros*—strolling actors, or ropewalkers—who performed along the road but who were in reality revolutionary agents. All critics of His Majesty, directly and by inference in complaining about hard times, faced punishment.

The Father President issued a circular with regard to appearances of worldliness during the emergency of revolution: priests should remember the example of their predecessors and walk; only the aged should travel by muleback. It was said that some priests had been using carts with two wheels and even *coaches* of four wheels. These must be burned unless they could be converted to some other use.

The owner—and inventor-builder—of California's most luxurious vehicle in the mission era was Father José Viader of Santa Clara. His contrivance had a narrow body and hung low, hitched to a black mule. The single seat was stuffed with lamb's wool, the entire carriage covered with brown cotton cloth. A small Indian boy sat astride the mule which was guided along the wide Alameda from Santa Clara by a mounted *vaquero*. Two other *neophyte* horsemen flanked the coach, ready to place *reatas* around the axletree going up steep hills. The entourage was accompanied by several pages. Coach and horses were decorated with ribbons on such occasions as a festival at San Jose.

Soldiers and settlers thought it as well not to bring charges against Father Viader who, although a kind and pious man, was renowned for his prowess as a fighter. Once three Indians who waylaid him had been soundly beaten. Then instead of being flogged they were made to stand bleeding and listen to a long homily on the terrible sin of attacking a priest.

59

THE PARADE OF FOREIGNERS

In 1822 Mexico broke away from Spain to commence a long period of internal strife that saw outlying California butted by the policies of whatever party gained ascendency. As wise an opinion as any was that of the *neophyte*, not too Christianized to consult his ancestor's legends for profound answers: the change was good because the new flag showed a mighty eagle instead of the lion.

With the change in rule the first "Boston" ships came on the coast and New Bedford whalers boldly used San Francisco Bay and Monterey as havens. The Russians could not be ousted but their establishment offered little threat; the last of the twenty-one missions was founded thirty miles away in the Valley of the Moon at Sonoma, July 4, 1823.

That youngest Franciscan mission was thriving a year later when the Russian, Otto von Kotzebue, entered San Francisco harbor to observe and criticize the Mexican establishments. The Californians at that time had almost 200,000 acres of land yielding various crops and their combined herds numbered half a million; the only notable statistic from the Fort Ross territory was the record of 50,000 sea gulls killed in a year to serve as meat.

Captain Frederick William Beechey, commanding HMS *Blossom*, rode along the mission trail in 1826 and wrote with some disparagement about a stop made while traveling on horseback from San Francisco to Monterey. At the present site of San Mateo he observed:

> Instead of a noble mansion, in keeping with so fine a country, the party arrived at a miserable mud dwelling before the door of which a number of half-naked Indians were basking in the sun. Several dead geese, deprived of their entrails, were fixed upon pegs around a large pole, for the purpose of decoying the living game into snares. Heaps of bones also ... sadly disgraced the parklike scenery.[20]

Near the end of his ride Captain Beechey was amused by a marker near the entrance to the Carmel Valley which he described as "three large crosses erected upon Mount Calvary" and also noted "a number of smaller ones at the roadside, appraising travelers of their approach to the Mission."

Even at the time of Beechey's call England regarded the northern part of the California coast as Nova Albion, the discovery of Sir Francis Drake. Since a commercial treaty had been signed with Mexico, and there was some expectancy of annexing the land, practical patriotism indicated a course of belittling the Spanish accomplishment.

Still, Beechey was made welcome at the missions which by that time were the hostelries of the trail with food, quarters and horses free to every wayfarer. About the only person who could complain of an ungracious reception was the first American to come overland—Jedediah Strong Smith, the mountain man, trapper and trail breaker who entered California the same year as Beechey.

The tall, blue-eyed Smith followed the then abandoned route of Anza and was eager for information about fur. He had about him that irritating propensity of many inland people to ignore the customs of others. Smith, a Methodist, read aloud from the Bible, a book which had been outlawed by the Franciscans who found the work as immoral as that *escandalosísimo* dance called the "waltz." Smith marched north to spread the word of California's great potential.

As the missions approached their peak settlers, soldiers, couriers and visitors found at them an individuality grown strong through more than half a century. This might be through the personality of the priests—men like Geronimo Boscaña who wrote the Indian history *Chinigchinich*; José María Zalvidea who preached to the *neophytes* in their native tongue; Maguín de Catala, "the holy man of Santa Clara," who prophesied the Gold Rush of 1849 and the San Francisco Earthquake of 1906. Or a mission might be known for its size, wealth and beauty.

Such a superlative mission was the one toward which the Frenchman August Duhaut-Cilly rode in 1827, intent on seeing the establishment that honored the Franciscan St. Louis, King of France. Viewing the magnificent composite of Spanish, Moorish and Mexican architecture he wrote:

> ...we found before us, on a piece of rising ground, the superb buildings of Mission San Luis Rey, whose glittering whiteness was flashed back to us by the first rays of the day. In the still uncertain light of dawn, the edifices of a very beautiful model, supported upon its numerous pillars, had the aspect of a palace...[21]

San Luis Rey, started thirty years earlier as two rooms fashioned from poles and branches, had grown to be the "King of the Missions" with three thousand healthy and contented *neophytes* plus tremendous wealth. The man who had made friends, then converts, of the first *Luiseños* was Father Antonio Peyri, perhaps the best-loved of all Franciscans.

Peyri came down from San Luis Obispo with Lasuén in 1798 and was left with his initial eighteen cattle and a few supplies. The strong and handsome priest labored alongside a few Indians, showing them at the start how to float logs down the river from the Palomar mountains twenty miles away. At the time of Duhaut-Cilly's visit the vast mission stood as testimony to the loyalty inspired by the priest who had by then aged to the extent that strangers thought him very old. Many friends stopped to visit; evenings Peyri would play *Malilla*—Spanish whist—and argue vigorously.

When it came time for him to leave, Peyri slipped away at night, unable to face a farewell. But Indians rode after him to San Diego, hoping they could persuade him to remain; two Indian boys swam to the departing ship and accompanied him to Europe. For years fresh flowers and lighted candles surrounded a portrait of Peyri at San Luis Rey.

THE MISSION STRIP

After 1820, on until the Gold Rush, all California life lay along the mission trail. Northward from Sonoma only a few trappers and cattle drovers crossed the wilderness; inland the starving gentiles became horse thieves; to the south of San Diego the trail given to the Dominicans faded.

Hard-riding couriers traveled the mission circuit in 3½ days when their messages were urgent: an invasion warning or news that a Father President had died. But most of the traffic along *El Camino Real*—The Highway of the King—moved at a leisurely pace.

Mules weighted with casks of mescal and *aguardiente* plodded up from Baja California; parties of soldiers escorted priests or prisoners; *neophytes* dragged log boats to smooth the way leading into missions. Only on feast days was the highway crowded when horsemen and carts loaded with women and children converged on a mission or pueblo to witness the spectacle of a wild, starving grizzly bear pitted against a maddened bull.

Life along that pastoral highway suddenly underwent a drastic change when the first foreign traders turned El Camino Real into an artery of commerce.

Four *El Camino Real*

"FOUR EYES"

As the nineteenth century moved into its third decade the last trail opened by Spaniards in America was about to change from a connecting link of missions into a self-sustaining road of wealth, to become truly a *Camino Real*—a Royal Highway. Here was no temporary jungle path through which men whipped mules laden with plundered treasure; nor was it a time-worn route divided by white-washed stones such as traders used to haul Eastern cargoes from the galleon mart at Acapulco. El Camino Real of California on the eve of great opulence stretched informally across six hundred miles of land so rich that livestock to the east and west bred faster than they could be slaughtered, and thousands of wild horses had to be drowned or driven off as nuisances.

The first man to envision an exploitation of that gold on the hoof was the shrewd and affable Bostonian, William Alden Gale, who came to the Coast in the early 1820s to secure pelts of sea otter for the Canton market. Because of his spectacles Gale was dubbed *"Cuatro Ojos"*—"Four Eyes"—by two Indian children, a nickname that bespoke extraordinary vision beyond the obvious. By mid-century homemade California *carretas* would have hauled five million hides and two hundred pounds of tallow.

Riding up El Camino ahead of rival agents Gale passed skeletons and carcasses left to vultures after barbecues. In valleys and on the slopes of rolling hills healthy range cattle grazed by the tens of thousands. The hide on each of the *novillos*—steers—and the 150 pounds of tallow one would yield should be worth about twelve dollars to the Californian, either in cash or credit.

Fathers at the missions showed eagerness to increase the Spanish doubloons cached under the tiles of their cells. From major-domos Gale learned the amounts of *diezmos* (contributions to the Church based on yearly cattle increases) paid by some thirty odd ranchos which belonged to descendants of Portolá's and Anza's men. Livestock on those vast holdings could not be seen from the highway. In the neighborhood of the presidios, and at the pueblos of Los Angeles, and San Jose, *Cuatro Ojos* entered *tavernas* to gossip and feel out the *vaqueros*. When he saw the false-bottomed ox horns used to serve two-bit drinks he was able to hint at fur trade and smuggling. On every hand there was an enthusiasm for an exchange of gold and luxury items for the "waste products" of the fast-breeding, self-tending herds. The people had nothing, and they knew less than nothing about business. Here lay a merchant's paradise.

Gale urged his principals to abandon the South Sea island trade in tombstones, drugs and iron safes to enter the California hide and tallow business that promised three hundred per cent profits. Bryant & Sturgis sent the brig *Sachem* round Cape Horn with a cargo of notions.

Circulars listing unbelievable articles were distributed up and down the road from Monterey to herald the arrival of the Boston ship. Priests, soldiers, *dons* and señoritas came from great distances to examine the merchandise displayed on the *Sachem's* deck: Chinese fireworks, satins, music boxes, mechanical toys, chicken-skin shoes, gilt spurs, exotic foods, new tools, ornate furniture,

65

stockings of red and black and flesh-colored silk. The simple *hijo de pais* gawked, much the same as Indians had three hundred years earlier when shown hawk's bells and Flemish beads on the decks of Vizcaíno's caravels.

Arms loaded with cheap gifts, wagons creaking under the weight of merchandise bought on credit, people returned to begin decorating barren adobe houses. The fathers who had paid cash, set up little stores where a modest profit could be extracted for the Pious Fund. The word spread along El Camino that more Boston ships would soon arrive.

Yankee ships followed by the hundreds to build a trade that in a quarter of a century reached the amazing total of twenty million dollars from hides, tallow and manteca; there were no records for the sea and land otter, and beaver smuggled aboard that fleet.

Richard Henry Dana, a law student who came out to the Coast in a Bryant & Sturgis ship for his health, and later wrote the famous book *Two Years Before the Mast*, described the customers lured to the hide ships:

> The Californians are an idle, thriftless people, and can make nothing for themselves. The country abounds in grapes, yet they buy, at great price, bad wine made in Boston and brought round by us, and retail it among themselves at a real (12½ cents) by the small wine glass. Their hides, too, which they value at two dollars in money, they barter for something which costs seventy-five cents in Boston....[1]

Appetites whetted by their first taste of luxury, eager for bolts of calico, green velvet, tooled leather saddles, silver buttons and a thousand other items, the Californians held larger and larger *matanzas* at the close of each summer to slaughter for the precious "California Bank Notes" as the hides were called. Tallow, and the more valuable manteca that lay near the hide, was melted down in large try-pots bought from whale ships, then poured into hide sacks to fetch two dollars per *arroba* (twenty-five pounds) in credit. Bullocks were prodded with iron-tipped sticks to drag heavy *carretas* whose axles screeched as they lumbered along on wheels four feet

66

in diameter, cut out of giant trunks. The sailors from down East carried green hides through the surf to waiting boats, then pulled out to trim brigs that lay off in open roadsteads, cables ready to slip in case of a sudden blow.

By the opening of the 1830s the commerce started by Gale had attracted ships from Peru, England and the Hawaiian Islands as well as Boston rivals of Bryant & Sturgis. The "drovers" followed a regular routine, working in pairs with each ship stationed for two years on the Coast. A vessel would gain Mexican customs clearance at Monterey before she anchored off missions and ranchos to trade. Hides were collected, cured at San Diego, and stowed in homeward-bound brigs.

THE BOSTON RIDERS

In the battle for business, merchants stationed their hide agents ashore to travel back and forth between Sonoma and San Diego. Fed, sheltered and provided with mounts by the missions, the rival brokers commenced deadly serious competition. Outwardly polite, pleasant to the point of fawning if necessary, they did not hesitate to castigate rancheros or priests who on rare occasions balked at paying, as an example, thirty dollars for a pair of three-dollar boots.

Alfred Robinson, a twenty-three-year-old apprentice brought ashore and shown the ropes by Gale, later wrote an account of his first trip up El Camino Real and indicated the attitude of the Boston men toward recalcitrant customers by his description of Father Francisco Ybarra of Mission San Fernando. That fat and jovial priest, jokingly called "Padre Napoleón" for his burlesquing boasts, prompted no friendly laugh from young Robinson when he attempted to strike a bargain. The Bostonian's usually mild narrative pictured Ybarra as:

> ...a short, thick, ugly-looking old man, whose looks did not belie his character...the niggardly administration of this place, compared with the liberality of other missions we visited, presented a

complete contrast; and the meanness and unpopularity of our host had gained for him the nickname of "*cochino*" or "hog." [2]

To a young man coming from the sophisticated East it was perhaps disturbing to encounter an exception to the general run of simple and even naïve people who lived along that pastoral road —people who spoke of their "fine bridge" when they referred to the 1½-foot stone crossing over the Santa Ines River, and had implicit faith in the San Francisco spring called *Polin* whose waters were certain to produce fecundity in childless women. Commercial shrewdness was not expected in a ranchero who, on being invited to drink tea for the first time, transferred leaves from the pot to his cup, sugared them and pretended enjoyment as he chewed.

Robinson showed his great affection for the last of the Franciscans: the "old father" Peyri, more interested in whist than in hides; Father Felipe Arroyo of San Juan Bautista who liked to watch his Indian children play and gave them the names of historical characters—Plato, Cicero or Alexander; and Father Zalvidea, too infirm to preach his sermons in dialect, performing a final penance by mixing meat, fish, tamales and dessert on one plate to make meals unpalatable.

New young priests came up from the Mexican College of Our Lady of Guadalupe at Zacatecas, educated to cope with the Yankee supercargos, agents and shipmasters. They kept themselves posted on prices, carefully checked ledgers, and even entered the profitable fur trade.

In the thirties *neophytes* for the first time mastered the sailing ship under the tutelage of the fathers in order to wrest the sea otters from Aleutian and Eskimo natives who worked for the fading Russian establishment at Fort Ross. The Zacatecan priests used Diego García de Palacio's early book on seamanship to construct miniature sixteenth century *naos*. The catches were hung in upper story "otter rooms" at the missions and sold for sixty dollars each to Yankees who preserved them in dried-out rum casks for resale at one hundred dollars in China.

The missionaries also branched out in the horse market, selling deck loads of the abundant animals for three dollars each instead of the once prevailing price of twenty-five cents. And to help the impractical Californians further, the fathers acted as advisors and bankers.

William Heath Davis, who penned a narrative of California, was a relative of Oliver Wendell Holmes and in many ways the most interesting of the Yankee traders. He regarded the priests as "first class merchants" and wrote:

> When they made purchases from vessels trading on the coast, they exhibited good judgement in their selections and were close buyers. ... I remember that our supercargo, Sherman Peck, spoke of the missionaries as shrewd purchasers, and strictly reliable men.[3]

The missions were still the centers of California gossip in the thirties. Sipping hot chocolate in the morning, or around the stables at night, the Yankees talked with major-domos and *vaqueros* to learn who had passed along the road. Of special interest were the Southern trappers—George Nidever of Tennessee who had killed two hundred grizzlies and rescued an Indian woman marooned eighteen years on San Nicholas Island; James Ohio Patti of Kentucky, released from the San Diego jail to vaccinate 22,000 Indians. Those men, and others who had come overland with the Joseph Walker and John Wolfskill parties might be regarded as "undesirable mountaineers" but they always had prime beaver and otter to trade.

Other mission news told of men who had deserted from the ships. Some followed the precedent set in the twenties by Joseph Chapman, captured from the pirate Bouchard's flagship, and William Richardson, mate of the British whaler *Orion*, by becoming Catholics and marrying into wealthy families. A number of Yankees followed that course, "leaving their consciences at Cape Horn," as Dana phrased the act of conversion.

Better dressed Californians appeared along El Camino while the hide trade boomed; more ranchos showed lights after eight o'clock and from them came the sound of music to tell of a *valecito casaro*—a little party for some visitor. Officious military people began to insist on seeing the *carta de seguridad* of well-known agents as though they were criminals not entitled to a passport. Soldier-couriers from troubled Mexico were more in evidence, and long before it happened the disbanding of the missions was rumored at every stop along the highway. To Boston men the anticipated secularization of the religious establishments meant little since cattle were unaffected by their owners. To greedy politicians who instigated the move there was the promise of spoils. For the Indian the act spelled death.

SECULARIZATION

In August of 1833 priests and their *neophytes* at the ten most prosperous missions heard administrators read the Governor's decree: half the holdings of each religious settlement henceforth belonged to the State; the other half—in land, cattle, equipment and stores—was to be divided among those Indians capable of living on their own. The Franciscans were to be curates and the missions turned into parishes. Political appointees would oversee the change and in time all of the twenty-one missions would disappear.

About thirty thousand *neophytes* were attached to the missions or on loan to adjacent ranchos when the largely unwelcomed news of freedom was announced. Had the Secularization Act been honestly enforced they might have survived, but political human nature gave them no chance. Bancroft summed up the debacle that was to erase the historic landmarks of El Camino Real:

> As to the comissionados, major-domos, and administrators who successively managed the missions, many were simply incompetent and stupid . . . exercising no restraint or influence on the ex-neophytes, and allowing the affairs of their respective establishments to drift. . . . Others were vicious as well as incompetent, always ready to sell any article of mission property, not only live-stock, but kitchen utensils, farm implements, tools from the shops, and tiles from the roofs, for money with which to gratify their propensity for

gambling. Still others were dishonest and able, devoting their energies to laying the foundation of future wealth for themselves and friends, oppressing the Indians, quarreling with such padres, officials, and assistants as they could not control or deceive, and disposing of the mission wealth without scruple, for their own interests. . . .[4]

The first reaction of the Franciscans was to salvage what they could for the Church and their charges. At Santa Barbara cattle were slaughtered by the thousands, carcasses left to rot, and hides sold for what they would fetch; grain in storage went to the first bidder. But the Governor's men moved swiftly to parcel out 200,-000 acres of mission land and burn new brands on 600,000 head of cattle, horses and sheep. In less than a decade establishments valued at $100,000 would be auctioned off for a few thousand dollars.

Since the dismantling process was slowed by cumbersome bureaucratic machinery, some of the Zacatecan priests managed to feather their own nests; and a few libertines among them went to the extreme of debauchery: Father José Lorenzo Quijos was notorious for heavy drinking and breaking the vow of chastity; Father Jesus María Vasquez del Mercado, another imbiber, was the parent of many half-breed children at San Rafael and Santa Clara; the charge was made against the padre at San Gabriel that he and the major-domo had converted the mission into a brothel.

Enemies of the Franciscans gloated over the scandals. Such gossip was of greater interest than the story of Father Vincente Sarría who had so long pestered people, begging food for Indian children, and then one Sunday morning, as he walked up the altar steps to say Mass at Soledad, keeled over, dead of starvation.

By 1839 plaster was peeling off church walls, weeds choked the vegetable gardens and irrigation aquaducts had crumbled. How low the greedy had sunk in the scramble for profit was dramatically shown when an old Indian *vaquero* rode in to Monterey on a stolen horse and asked that he either be shot or released from his service. So aged that he could remember Junípero Serra, the Indian had been forced into hard labor for which a politician received the meager wage.

The Governor appointed William E. P. Hartnell, a naturalized Englishman, as Inspector of Missions to listen to complaints and make recommendations. From two round trips on horseback came a report used to formulate additional regulations, most of them designed to increase revenue:

ART. 17. The major-domo shall, on presentation of proper credentials, furnish transportation and food to persons traveling on public service.

ART. 18. To aid private travelers charges shall be made for food and horses according to their means.[5]

The year of the Secularization Act would later be a statistical marker for critics and evaluators of the California missionary effort. From 1779 to 1833 the records show 29,000 births and 62,000 deaths, most of the latter from smallpox, syphilis and measles. The figures caused Dr. A. L. Kroeber to conclude:

The brute upshot of missionization, in spite of its kindly flavor and humanitarian root, was only one thing, death.[6]

Another student of the Indian, John Collier, observing that "death walked the mission compound" passed a condemning judgment and purported to fix the blame:

Many causes for the awful failure of the California missions have been assigned, but the significant cause for all time to come is plain. It was the total instantaneous suppression of the native societies, the willed destruction of those marvelous ecological complexes with which native life had gushed and bloomed in its millenniums.[7]

This classroom view of predestinated policy stands as pointless as the most syrupy of eulogies in judging the Franciscans. In an imperfect world perhaps the only fair comparison is with the missionary endeavors of other faiths, among the subjected peoples of Tierra del Fuego, the South Seas and parts of Africa. On that basis the California mission era was one of some lenity.

INDIAN RAIDERS

Nine out of every ten *neophytes* set free were to die in less than fifteen years. Wailing in protest, clinging to the long gowns of the fathers, many of the pitiful Indians refused to accept land or even drafts on the Mexican government; authorities obligingly relieved them of the burden. More enterprising natives were approached with liquor, offers of cash and threats. At San Luis Rey two hundred intelligent ex-*neophytes* moved into the Temecula Valley and flourished for twenty-five years, until the coming of the Americans.

One of the few individuals who survived that long was Rojerio Rocha, known for his skill as a blacksmith and silversmith at San Fernando. He prospered on twelve acres until Yankees evicted him one rainy night; by morning his sick wife was dead of exposure. Until 1902 Rocha silently nursed his hatred of the whites, until he was laid to rest in a grave beside his wife at the age of 112.

As mission lands were cut up into ranchos the natives hired themselves out, usually to masters far harsher than any priest; some sought employment at homes in the towns for three dollars a month; others served as guides. Travelers on the road were stopped by ragged Indians who begged paper for cigarettes or money with which they bought liquor; inflamed, they broke into stores and stole food.

Most of the Indians deserted to join gentiles between the Diablo Range and the foothills of the Sierra; many had been in the missions only a short time, victims of military raids organized when the labor quota dropped after an epidemic. Renegades, once chastised for abandoning *Chinigchinich* to embrace the white man's God, were welcomed after secularization, for the Indians were now waging war of a sort and needed information.

Since the days of Mexico's revolt against Spain there had been sporadic uprisings by *neophytes* and nuisance raids by gentiles. But when the Indian learned to ride, the forays became serious enough

73

to call for retaliatory expeditions of up to one hundred soldiers. And in the twilight of the missions a *neophyte* emerged as a war chief.

At Mission San José de Guadalupe, a half day's journey off the trail from Santa Clara, Estanislaus was regarded as the most intelligent Indian ever baptised. For a reward he was given the title *alcalde* with the power to govern his fellow *neophytes*. Thus inflated, Estanislaus decided to become a chief. He collected a number of followers, kidnapped two hundred young Indian girls, and made for the hilly country below Mount Diablo. Here he trained his little army, making practice raids on nearby ranchos to steal beef. The first expedition sent against Estanislaus met defeat; others failed to capture him until a large force sent out by Lt. Mariano Guadalupe Vallejo from Sonoma forced the chief and his men back into the forests of what is today Stanislaus County.

In 1837 at San Diego runaways and rancho house servants gave information to gentiles who swooped down on the hacienda San Ysidero. One hundred braves in warpaint took the scalps of Juan Ybarra and his two *vaqueros*, who were locked out of the gun shed by an Indian boy, sent his wife walking to San Diego naked, and captured two young white girls who were never rescued.

Three nights later, before presidial troops could be assembled, the same raiders approached Rancho Jesus María which was occupied by José Lopez, his wife and two daughters. All that afternoon Lopez had been sampling wine distilled from his fine vineyard and by nightfall was in a silly drunken mood that led him to light a dozen big fires and accompany himself in song by banging together tin vat covers as he marched back and forth away from the glare of the blaze. Indian scouts slithered back to their forest camp to report that a large force guarded Rancho Jesus María; the chief called off the attack.

The most renowned Indian rebel on the Southern California coast was Valerio, chief of *neophytes* who had fled the Mission Santa Barbara in 1826. This wily native and his followers hid out in caves of the Santa Ynez mountains near San Marcos Pass where between raids they painted pictures of their depredations. Valerio was never caught and Santa Barbara would honor his name with a street; the chief's forays were directed at property rather than lives.

Settlers to the north, on the stretch of El Camino between San Luis Obispo and San Jose, did not fare so well. In 1838, when a series of great quakes crumbled mission walls and frightened residents of Monterey and San Francisco, war parties rode down on isolated new ranchos to take scalps and drag off white women to "fates worse than death."

Chief Yozcolo, brother of Solano who ruled in the Valley of the Moon around the last mission, attacked at San Jose and Santa Clara; on one of his most daring forays he and his men snatched two thousand horses and a large number of Indian girls. Troops who were paid a two dollar bonus to leave Monterey tracked down Yozcolo whose head was raised to rot on a pole above the Santa Clara Mission.

On into the 1840s the Indians raided the several hundred ranchos granted after the disbanding of the missions. Hardened Indian fighters told sickening stories of tortures by fire or knife and mass raping of individual women. Orders were given to dispense with cutting off ears as punishment; all male Indians over ten years of age must be instantly exterminated, and women and infants taken prisoner.

To the ensuing slaughter in the field was added wholesale death on the northern frontier where a smallpox epidemic spread from Fort Ross to wipe out 70,000 natives. Despite this considerable dent in population the Indians continued to make raids to pillage and steal horses, urged on by American trappers who provided the tribes with experienced Canadian chiefs. But the Indian of the forties was doomed. The new rancheros, brought up in the saddle from the age of five, outrode the "thieves" and killed them as readily as *soldados de cuera* had butchered their grandfathers.

The *gente de raison* could tolerate no interference with stock raising, the still booming Yankee trade, and the building of elaborate
ranchos.

RANCHOS GRANDES

In sight of the Camino Real, joined to it by wide *avenidas*, were
built the great adobe ranchos. These rambling buildings with tiles
laid over timber roofs, iron-grilles on windows, and wide verandahs,
were usually one story high in the south, two stories from Monterey
northward. All were constructed with an eye to comfort, and homes
such as Don Manuel Nieto's at today's Long Beach needed to be
extensive to house servants and *vaqueros* who tended his 70,000
acres. The rancho *Cañada del Corte de Madera* in Santa Clara
Valley, owned by Don José Domingo Peralta, was another huge
establishment with chapel, bull ring, private dock and fleet of
barges. Even the lesser ranchos took on an air of luxury with pan-
eled floors, cushioned seats, double-hung windows and tapestries
decorating whitewashed walls. The cattle wealth of the Ortega,
Pico, Guerra y Noriega, de Haro, Estudilla and other old families
went into their ranchos.

Before Mexico lost California there would be close to eight
hundred ranchos varying in size from gargantuan holdings down
to grants of five thousand acres. Most of them thrived on range
cattle; a few raised sheep; and in the Sonoma, Santa Clara and San
Gabriel valleys vineyards were being expanded along with citrus
orchards.

No se abure—Do not be in a hurry—was the recipe of life that
produced a race of people notable for their good looks, gracious
manners and freedom from worry. Bald and prematurely gray heads
were seldom seen; only when dancing or riding horseback did Californians show any great energy. And the *hijo de pais* was renowned
for remarkable potency. José Ortega, eldest of the Portolá veteran's
twenty-one children, sired a like number; Juan Cota of Los Angeles
left more than five hundred descendants.

Davis wrote of his meeting with Don Antonio María Lugo of Los Angeles in the forties when that "eccentric old gentleman" was past his eightieth year:

> He had a wife aged twenty or twenty-two—his third or fourth. He introduced me, and in the same breath, as I shook hands with her, said, in a joking way, with a cunning smile, "*No se enamoro de mo joven esposa.*" (Do not become enamored of my young wife.) He had numerous children, grand children and great grand children. Los Angeles was largely populated from his family. Referring to this circumstance he said to me quietly, "Don William, I have done my duty to my country." [8]

It was into those wealthy rancho families that Davis, Robinson, A. B. Thompson, Thomas W. Robbins, William Dana and many another Yankee married, paying twenty dollars to become Catholics, and taking as brides the statuesque, dark-eyed girls who were often in their middle-teens. The aggressive businessmen enjoyed the strawberry gatherings, bear and bullfights, *meriendas* and *fiestas*, but they never contracted "California Fever"; instead they used their connections to build up profitable shore business.

As long as cattle bred, the rancheros could afford to support their large establishments and purchase spurs inlaid with gold and silver, and other equipment worth four thousand dollars, to bedeck a horse. Strong boxes filled with doubloons could supply any want, even at the ever-increasing charges fixed by the Boston ships. For soldiers, small businessmen and servants, buying from the Yankees was a different story.

The blond, blue-eyed John Augustus Sutter, a man whose fine military appearance lent credence to his assumed title of Captain —late of the Swiss Guards—and who was in and out of debt most of his life, commented on Boston prices in 1839:

> When I first came to California, articles on trading vessels were so high that he who went on board with $100 in money or hides could carry away his purchases in a pocket handkerchief. [9]

THE PEDDLERS

The narratives of early travelers published in the East and in Europe brought so many trading ships to California that prices dropped. And those accounts of open country and unlimited opportunity lured a trickle of immigrants over the old Spanish trail of Anza. By the early forties more than 350 foreigners lived on or wandered along the highway.

Jacob Primer Leese, a good-looking young Ohioan, was one of the first to arrive at Mission San Gabriel and then ride up to Monterey where he opened a store. Almost illiterate, but a shrewd bargainer, Leese's business acumen gained him a fortune. His devotion to profit was characterized by the decision he made when faced with starvation near the end of the overland journey: he killed and ate his pet hunting dog in order to save a spare mule.

One of Leese's business partners for a time was Nathan Spear, the uncle of William Heath Davis. Spear drummed up trade at the ranchos and pueblos by offering free his services as a physician. Having been a druggist clerk to his brother in Boston—who sent him supplies—Spear was in great demand between Monterey and the little town of Yerba Buena, forerunner to San Francisco. At the time one Army doctor cared for the ill, and so ignorant were most of the twelve thousand inhabitants that a deserter from a ship in Santa Barbara was able to start a "practice." That man's lone prescription was liquor, supplied by the patient and shared by the posing doctor until he passed into a coma.[10]

Spear, Leese, Davis, Able Sterns and other Yankees cooperated with the Boston skippers who made it a practice to enter San Francisco Bay as first port of call. Trim little brigs anchored close to the sandy beach to land the most valuable quarter of the cargo before paying customs duties at Monterey. Inspectors at Yerba Buena would be entertained in Jean Vioget's saloon while the contraband was stored in Spear's warehouse or loaded on wagons to be hauled south. Also carried in the smuggling wagons were specially constructed casks whose openings showed a false layer of hardtack (ships' biscuit); when they returned from the ranchos the *carretas* had secreted between layers of hides the primest of pelts.

Trappers from Kentucky, Tennessee and other Southern states were doing so brisk a business with the storekeepers and traveling merchants that the powerful British Hudson Bay Company sent representatives to scout the territory. Their agent, William G. Rae, settled at Yerba Buena with his lovely wife. Philandering and excessive drinking brought about his death before he could make good the boast that his company would "drive you Yanks from California if it costs a million." [11]

The evils of heavy drinking shadowed the history of that frontier out of all proportion to the number of imbibers. Californians, and even the Mexican soldiers, were as a rule temperate. They sipped the wines of Montecito, produced at Santa Barbara by Dona Marcelina Felix Dominquez, or those of the famous French pioneer Jean Louis Vignes whose 104-acre vineyard covered the heart of what would be downtown Los Angeles. Sober too were such hardworking men as the New Englander, Hiram Teal, whose wagons offered goods hauled all the way from St. Louis; and Peter Lassen, the Danish blacksmith who traveled out of San Jose. But numerous confirmed drunkards, together with a constant and ever thirsty population of above five hundred sailors, kept the jails filled. And in stopping places along El Camino Real that were a far shorter distance apart than the missions, grog could be had day and night.

At Navidad, in the neighborhood of Monterey, close to where Hartnell established California's first college, a combination distillery, grog shop and gambling place was opened in 1840 by Isaac Graham. This slovenly, quarrelsome "bummer," with his unkempt beard and loud voice, gathered about him an assortment of drifters and deserters who had been shunted away from ranchos and pueblos. The decent citizens of Monterey avoided the place; travelers were advised to give it a wide berth. In a few months Graham and his unruly cohorts would find themselves in serious trouble.

79

As disreputable as the still of Graham were the *bodegas* down at the bottom of the trail, for it was at San Diego that Boston ships lay longest to cure hides. Near old Deadmen's Point several busy oases flanked a brothel which had been in business fifteen years. Authorities attempted to control drinking by prohibiting sales on feast days, before Mass and after drumbeat; the fine was eight dollars and confiscation of all stock.

Enterprising liquor peddlers even went out on the highway to call on known nibblers like John Cameron, founder of Gilroy, and the carpenter Daniel Hill who built California's first all wooden house, on the Pajaro River. The swindler Gamboa y Caballero robbed Indians of their few coins by selling them brandy bottles containing water colored with burned sugar.

El Camino Real began to show a different character after 1840. For the traveler the missions had changed from friendly stopping places into "deadfalls" where mercenary major-domos offered scant rations and flea-infested beds at exorbitant rates. The ranchos had grown suspicious of visitors who came without an introduction. The once fine section of roadway lined with olive trees that led to Mission San Juan Capistrano had lost its neat appearance; weeds were growing over the one-hundred-foot-wide *alameda* between Santa Clara and San Jose, and many of the 16,000 bordering willow trees had died. Lone travelers rode hard to reach ranchos or pueblos before sunset.

THE PUEBLOS

While missions and then ranchos thrived, the three pueblos laid out by the early Spaniards were almost stagnant until the coming of foreign settlers. At Los Angeles, Santa Cruz and San Jose, plazas had been measured off, lots assigned to convict colonists, and main roads leading in and out of town graded for a few hundred yards over the trail. A chapel, a bar, and one public building faced each square, surrounded by huts.

Immigrants with Eastern concepts of cities headed for the pueblos and remained because there was no place else to settle except at the seaport capital of Monterey, already crowded with soldiers, government people, impecunious Indians and merchants. By virtue of numbers and a few loose dollars the pueblos slowly followed the ancient course of city growth.

Up at Sonoma a new pueblo was officially created by Colonel Vallejo when the mission closed. One of the most powerful men in California, Vallejo commenced his founding of the town with a huge plaza faced by a two-story *palacio*. Close by he erected a forty-foot watch tower. The fortress aspect of the town was to give warning to the frontier Indians and to the Russians who by that time were in desperate circumstances. A constant lookout manned the tower, soldiers and Indians spent hours drilling. Only twenty-five civilians could be enticed to take up residence, and there were few visitors for the ferry that extended El Camino Real to the north shore charged fifty dollars a round trip.

Santa Barbara, San Diego, Yerba Buena and half a dozen hamlets claimed to be pueblos, the owners of land, taverns, stores or rooming houses hoping to attract wayfarers with a few dollars. To give themselves standing the pueblos passed ordinances to prohibit such actions as excessive speed of riders in the streets, entering taverns on horseback, gambling, and leaving church when the sermon was about to begin.

MONTEREY

Regardless of where they eventually took root, the foreigners who began to arrive at the rate of one hundred each year were obliged to show credentials at the capital and apply for permission to settle in the Department of California. People without connections waited weeks as the red tape at Monterey reflected the jack-in-the-box change of rulers and their bureaucratic tails in Mexico. Most pioneers and Mexican immigrants suffered, for oak fuel cost

81

three dollars a cartload, rough pine in billets two dollars. And wealthy rancheros like Don Esteban Munras paid servants at his town house six dollars a month.

In the forties Californians and the Mexican officials were becoming alarmed at the number of Yankees who had invaded the country and took a cynical view of their embracing Catholicism. French and British visitors warned that the United States had designs on the Department; prominent among the intriguers was the Scot David Spence, a trader nicknamed *El Calvo* because of his bald head, and called other names because of his closeness in money matters.

With Yankees prospering while unpaid soldiers were forced to steal chickens, Captain José Castro of the Monterey garrison attempted to stir up anti-foreign feeling by voicing a popular complaint:

> ... for a Californian *caballero* cannot woo a *señorita* if opposed in his suit by an American sailor, and these heretics must be cleared from the land.[12]

Five   Road of War

THE DRAFT

Late one August night in 1841 an eighteen-year-old Californian, the son of a wealthy ranchero, pressed close against the damp adobe wall of the Blue Wing Inn at Sonoma. He stood perfectly still in the shadow of the long shingled roof when half a dozen soldiers reined up before the tavern door. Spurs jangled as two men dismounted and swaggered inside. From the coarse talk of the waiting horsemen the boy learned that Colonel Vallejo had ordered a sergeant to round up ten men for another surprise recruiting raid on the ranchos. The eavesdropper smiled grimly, waited until he had learned the direction the party would take, then slipped away to his horse.

Before moonset the young rider had reached the northern shore of Carquinez Strait where Indians ferried him across to the Contra Costa on a tule raft. He borrowed a new mount and spurred for Martinez to rouse a friend; the two boys stopped only to relay the alarm or get fresh horses until they reached El Camino Real near San Jose. Sleeping in the day, spreading the word as they galloped through the night, the draft evaders reached San Juan and safety; they had entered the province of Vallejo's Southern California rival, General Juan Bautista Alvarado with whom their parents had influence.

Along the line of ranchos youngsters avoided what they and their parents believed to be a senseless call to arms. A system of warnings had been set up so those liable for military service could be forewarned and sent away until they married. Boys impressed in the Army wasted months serving as mail carriers, messengers, servants, or guards of a few drunken Indians.

The rancheros had lost all patience with the Government. The head of the Department had changed every year since 1836 when Pio Pico led a revolt to declare the "free and sovereign state of Alta California" which had lasted eight months. Contentions between the north and south resulted in comic opera battles as ridiculous as the mother country's so-called "Pastry War" with France.

Talk of foreign invasion, the *alarma falsa* of half a century, no longer evoked a response. The Russians had abandoned Fort Ross in 1840, selling equipment to the manipulator, Captain Sutter. The Catholic ally France was not likely to permit Great Britain to seize the country despite Mexico's debt of fifty million dollars. As for America, Governor Alvarado had blundered when he seized and deported Isaac Graham and his cohorts for the Yankees were crossing the Sierra by the hundreds and had a powerful squadron cruising off the coast. But America was an affair for *mañana*.

Such was the temper of the people who held the largest stake in the future of California. Patriotism had reached a peak in 1842; rancheros were elated by news of an army being sent from Mexico to take over the defense responsibility.

THE CHOLOS

That August *caballeros* and their families gathered in festive dress and mood at San Diego to welcome the fleet of General Manuel Micheltorena, the new Governor, and his heralded *Batallon Fijo de Californias.* It was said that one thousand of Mexico's smartest troops would land from the ships.

Faces fell as slightly more than two hundred small, shifty-eyed, pock-marked men in slovenly uniforms scrambled from the boats, cheap cigars hanging from lips, bottles protruding from under wrinkled coats. Rough words reached the ears of the *gente de razón* as hard-faced soldiers leered at the women.

The defamatory name "cholos" passed along the beach, that synonym for a half-breed rascal first heard when unsavory characters came north in 1819 to defend against the Russians. Branded faces and cropped ears told that troops were former convicts. The proud dons muttered curses against one-legged General Santa Ana for this insult. Commenting on the arrival of the cholos, as the *Batallon Fijo* was thereafter known, Bancroft wrote:

> It was long before any considerable portion could be trusted with weapons; but from the first the *batallon* showed marked proficiency in foraging for supplies by night.[1]

On the slow march up El Camino Real—the gayest procession until then witnessed in California—the cholos showed greater stealth than foxes in raiding chicken roosts; with no money to buy clothing they extended operations to any wash left out to dry. It would take three years for the lethargic Californians to rebel against their unwelcomed defenders whose officers they were forced to billet in homes at Monterey. It was a tribute to General Micheltorena, whom the miserable cholos loved and obeyed, that serious trouble did not break out immediately and that after leaving San Diego their depredations were overshadowed by a holiday spirit.

THE GRACIOUS GENERAL

In Micheltorena the Californians recognized a kindred spirit. Handsome and over six feet tall, with a bearing that was at once military but not unbending, the new Governor instantly captivated both men and women through his charming manner. He showed a fondness for *fiestas, bailes,* horseraces and bullfights, and his habits were sensible: chocolate in bed every morning before a late rising; conversation that avoided affairs in favor of witty stories, compliments and chitchat. He endeared himself to older *hidalgos* by playing chess late at night. Best of all, Micheltorena, unlike most military men, moved always at an unruffled, leisurely pace.

At no junction did the General display his calmness to such advantage as at Los Angeles in October when a foam-flecked rider galloped to headquarters with news that Monterey was in the hands of the enemy. Commodore Thomas Ap Catesby Jones, commanding the United States Navy's Pacific Coast Squadron, had landed marines, spiked guns and run up the American flag.

Before retiring inland to San Fernando, Micheltoreno dictated encouraging messages to his northern commanders:

> I cannot just now fly to the aid of Monterey, for I am over 100 leagues away, nor should I leave Los Angeles unprotected.... You most therefore collect as many men as possible, sending me frequent reports on their number and movements in order to combine our operations. Triumph is certain; with my present force I should not hesitate to attack; but it is just that all share in the pleasure of victory ... Are there Mexican bosums [sic] which do not feel themselves boil with valor at seeing this effort to rob us of our territory? [2]

The Governor was soon able to return to Los Angeles, and accept congratulations for not having charged north. Commodore Jones, learning that he had been misinformed about the existence of a state of war, restored the Mexican flag and sailed south to offer personal apologies to Micheltorena.

The *Batallon* moved northward in easy stages, pausing longest at Santa Barbara where the General gave García Diego, the first bishop of California, advanced information that in 1843 he would order the missions returned to the Franciscans and predicted a revival of the chain; the decree was issued but the establishments proved beyond salvage.

A cool reception awaited the new Governor when he finally reached Monterey, the reputation of the cholos having traveled ahead of them. Unused to spending more than a few hours each day on business, Micheltorena found himself besieged with appeals, complaints and finally threats—most of them about the cholos. Pio Pico and José Castro needled him to send the convicts to Sonoma or execute a few as examples. "It is hard to shoot a hungry, unpaid soldier for pilfering food," Micheltorena replied, pointing out that the cholos had a perfect record in respect to rape and murder.[3]

With foreigners now overrunning the land, settling where they pleased, and Mexicans showing an arrogance not warranted by the amount of help their nation was giving, a group of hot-tempered Californians used the cholos as an excuse for rebellion. After a barroom brawl with some officers of the despised *Batallon* a dozen rancheros drove one hundred horses away from Monterey and advised Micheltorena that he must deport his cholos or face the consequences.

THE HORSE AND THE MULE

The suave Governor and his troops marched to the rancho of Juan Alvires below San Jose, negotiated with the rebels, and signed a treaty in which he agreed to deport his *malos* before three months had passed. He wrote Mexico for two thousand troops, drilled the cholos and enlisted the aid of Captain Sutter who promised to oppose the Californians with a force of one hundred foreigners and a like number of armed Indians. The Swiss feared a rebel victory and wrote in his *Diary:*

> I was well aware what we could expect should they succeed to do this, they would drive us foreigners all very soon out of the country now they have done it once....[4]

Sutter marched from New Helvetia on January 1, 1845, with a mixed company that included Isaac Graham, then back from Mexican prison trying to collect cash balm for his deportation. Inflated with the rank of colonel, elated at the promise of inheriting rebel land, the blond European adventurer chased the Californians down El Camino Real. A band played German martial music while he fabricated stories of his combat experiences and female conquests when serving under the French monarch Charles X. At Salinas the mercenaries waited for the Governor.

Micheltorena and his motley force, "each one worthy of a statue," [5] were forced to move at a snail's pace. The General, as he liked to be called in the field, was suffering from an embarrassing posterior ailment that prevented him from sitting a horse; even in an improvised carriage he could manage only four miles a day and often called a halt for two or three days. Some claimed he was not anxious to contact the enemy despite many bellicose proclamations which recalled former Governor Sola. With the foe one hundred miles away small detachments of cholos rode fearlessly in the van to return at nightfall blowing bugles; across their saddles hung chickens, shoats and pilfered clothing.

Around Santa Barbara local people offered to join Micheltorena on condition that he rid himself of his undesirables. Fearing reprisal in Mexico if he abandoned national troops, the General refused and after delaying as long as possible he pushed on for a showdown at Los Angeles. He was worried now at desertion by foreigners who resented being classed with the convicts.

Los Angeles Mexicans reacted to the return of the cholos by supporting the Californians. And foreigners who feared a victory that might place the arrogant Sutter over them joined the rebels. By the time the opposing forces came within artillery range at Cahuenga Pass on February 20th a junta had officially ousted Micheltorena; Pio Pico was named governor and José Castro *commandante general*.

At extreme range the California battery of two cannon opened fire; Micheltorena's gunners responded with three field pieces and after one hundred rounds blew the head off a horse, lone casualty for the day. The following morning a rebel ball creased the shoulder of a cholo mule and Micheltorena ran up the white flag of truce.

During the "height of the battle" Colonel Sutter disappeared;

he turned up later as a captive of the rebels with whom he soon was on the most friendly terms. Foreigners of both sides had tired of the mock cannonading and joined forces in a ravine to drink and scoff at the cautious combatants. To men like the Virginia mulatto Big Jim Beckwourth, Indian fighter, horse thief and one time chief of the Crows, the engagement was a joke. William Workman, pioneer Englishman and Taos trader, compared with ridicule the farce with the Texas battles of the Alamo and San Jacinto.

Micheltorena conceded defeat, was sent by ship to Monterey for his wife, and sailed home with the *Batallon Fijo*; smooth talk gained him exoneration in Mexico. Despite his obnoxious troops, bombastic pronouncements, and unmilitary abhorrence of bloodshed, the General lingered fondly in the memory of the people. In a sense Micheltorena belonged to the inevitable tide of history for Mexican sovereignty would soon be buried by the same vanquishing flood that washed over the Indian and Spaniard.

THE GRINGOS

Through the high-doored *taverna* of the Plaza Hotel at San Juan rancheros rode their horses up to the bar where they sipped *amontillado* in the saddle and openly expressed disgust with conditions. Pio Pico had made Los Angeles the capital, leaving the military establishment at Monterey. Discord between the north and south resulted in a rash of minor outbreaks as rival generals sought to oust José Castro from his position of *comandante general*. Messengers who slunk in and out of highway dram shops often carried a *carta gansa*—a decoy letter—and arranged to have themselves captured in order to spread false news.

While American and British squadrons ranged offshore, and hardy foreign pioneers reached the number of one thousand, the Mexican custodians of the land engaged in comic opera intrigues. At inns, and even whispered behind fans, was the "spy" story accredited to Monterey where an officer from the south arrived on the trail of a secret agent said to be hiding in the home of an official.

Lieutenant Tunis Craven, USN, of the *Dale*, recorded the search in his journal:

> It was early but the ladies had retired; the officer asked to look in their chamber, and assent was readily given. Two ladies were in bed; one of them sat up. . . .
> "Who is that between?" he asked *the husband*.
> "It is Juanita."
> "Good night," said the officer who was next day informed that the spy was the *happily situated* individual. . . . There is a picture, which needs no further embellishment.[6]

Spies, red tape and regulations turned many of the rancheros to favor the Americans who in that year 1845 had taken Texas under their wing. Mexico promised much and gave little: an army of two thousand, to be escorted by men-of-war, was swallowed in a revolution before it could embark at Acapulco. When the California deputy, José Castanares, was sent south to explain the desperate situation before an extra session he indulged in rhetoric:

> California is a rough diamond, requiring only application to the lapidary's wheel to adorn the aureola of Anáhuac with a jewel of the most beautiful splendor.[7]

Mexicans, military and civilian, sneered behind the backs of the proud rancheros but openly showed their hatred of the foreigners—"the gringos"—rough mountaineers and sailors who thought land and even women were theirs for the taking.

At Yerba Buena in the winter of forty-five drunken merchant sailors from the *Tasso* misused a Mexican girl outside one of the *pulperias* at the foot of Loma Alta. When they were jailed the ship's master, Captain Elliot Libbey, had the nerve to appear with Nathan Spear and demand the release of the seamen. Libbey and Spear were beaten and stabbed by ten irate Mexicans.

At every seaport and highway stopping place the Mexicans found cause for bitterness, sometimes from drunken abuses but as often through resentment of a growing invasion. Few of the newcomers showed respect or even consideration: squatters built shacks where they pleased; severe-looking heretics in black clothing who called themselves Methodists attacked the Church; down from Oregon came belligerent "Mexican-haters" like the Kentucky mountaineer Granville Swift, a tall, mean man given to bullying anyone who seemed to him a "furriner"; and the savage Rocky Mountain trapper Ezekiel "Stuttering" Merritt, ever spoiling for a fight. The *hijo de pais* could only curse or, like Feliciano Soberanes, proprietor of an inn at the ruins of Mission Soledad, overcharge the intruders and in the night see that their horses went astray.

THE PATHFINDER

Juggling the complaints lodged by and against the Americans was the United States Consul at Monterey, Thomas Oliver Larkin, a balding, frugal Easterner who worked hard for the annexation of California by his country. Dressed always in frock coat, stock and boiled shirt, with more than $66,000 in savings from his combination grocery-grog–dry goods store, Larkin bespoke Americanism: he never became a Mexican or Catholic; he married the widow Rachel Holmes who bore him the first all-American boy in California; and his two-story home was American.

To the Larkin residence came shipmasters, naval officers, travelers and a miscellaneous assortment of local Yankees seeking favors or redress. Among the callers were secret agents from whom he learned that the United States was trying to buy California and if unsuccessful might be forced to effect a conquest. He was urged to see that no overt act precipitate the country into the hands of the British to whom Mexico owed 50 million dollars. Larkin could do little more than watch the fuse during the opening months of 1846 as tension was increased by the conduct of drunks, overbearing merchants, ignorant backwoodsmen and such busybodies as Dr. John Marsh, the Harvard graduate then practicing illegal medicine, who sent out a call inviting Americans to make a hegira to his Mount Diablo ranch to discuss their rights.

The most troublesome caller was the "Pathfinder" Captain

John C. Frémont, U.S. Topographical Engineers, sent West by the War Department to make surveys of the Pacific Coast. In deerskin hunting shirt, wearing moccasins and a handkerchief bound around his head, Frémont had been dashing over the California trails with a force of sixty trappers, Delaware Indians and frontiersmen. Unwisely he had accepted the hospitality of Captain Sutter who now acted as a spy for General José Castro.

Through the influence of Larkin, the Pathfinder was given Castro's reluctant permission to camp briefly in the San Joaquin Valley and recuperate before heading back to Oregon. Instead of keeping his word Frémont led his men up El Camino Real a short distance then doubled back. To Monterey came protests from rancheros about stolen horses and an insult to the daughter of Angel Castro. When Frémont unfurled the Stars and Stripes above a camp on Mount Gavilan, in sight of the highway out of Monterey, Castro rallied two hundred indignant Californians.

Larkin urged Frémont to retire, warning that the result of an attack "either way may cause trouble hereafter to resident Americans." [8] Not understanding the action of Frémont, who appeared to be straying far afield from topographical work, Larkin sent a dispatch to Mazatlan asking that the sloop of war *Portsmouth* come to Monterey.

Frémont sensed that he had bitten off more than he could chew and retreated before he was closed in on by Castro. He rode toward Oregon, first stirring up the settlers around Sonoma. In the billiard saloon of Monterey, Castro posted a proclamation on March 13th that would spark a prelude to war:

> ...Compatriots, the act of unfurling the American flag on the hills, the insults and threats offered to the authorities, are worthy of execration and hatred from Mexicans; prepare then to defend our independence....[9]

THE BEAR FLAG REVOLT

On April 17, 1846, Larkin received a call from a vigorous, robust man who was using the ridiculous disguise of an invalid merchant in search of health. Lieutenant Archibald Gillespie of the United States Marine Corps had been on the road or at sea for six months with a confidential message from President Polk for delivery in person to Larkin and Frémont. War with Mexico was planned for that very month; the declaration might have already been made. The invalid moved on, making the mistake of pausing at Sutter's where his disguise was seen through and the intelligence passed along to Castro.

Late in April the *Portsmouth*, Captain John B. Montgomery, anchored off Monterey with no news of war. But from Mazatlan came disturbing reports that America might be too late in the race for California. The British were negotiating. And it was said that the Mexican government had tentatively approved the plan of an Irish priest to spot ten thousand colonists along the California coast. Father Eugene McNamara proposed "to put an obstacle in the way of further usurpations on the part of an irreligious and anticatholic nation." [10]

General Castro was rallying rancheros and conferring with Colonel Vallejo through the next month. Following his trip to Sonoma someone forged a proclamation in which Castro ordered all Americans to leave the country or be driven out, and instructed Indians to burn their wheat crops.

This piece of filibustering was enough to send Stuttering Merritt, Swift and half a dozen other squatters on the warpath. They left the Feather River camp of Frémont, who was returning south with Gillespie, and at dawn on June 14th swooped down on the sleeping pueblo of Sonoma. Colonel Vallejo, his officers, and all prominent men in the vicinity, including Jacob Leese, were made "prisoners of war" and sent back to Frémont.

After a night of drinking the revolutionists sought to dignify the act of capturing the fort. From the petticoat of Chepa Mathew, wife of the Sonora boarding house keeper, they cut out a flag and decorated it with a red stripe, star and the crude representation of a stalking grizzly. In black letters were outlined the words CALIFORNIA REPUBLIC. On Sunday, June 15, 1846, the "Bear Flag" was run up. Unknown to anyone at Sonoma, or elsewhere in California, Mexico and the United States had been at war since May 12th.

When two of the Bears were seized by Californians on the highway near Santa Rosa, and tortured before being put to death, Frémont stormed south from Sonoma to the Golden Gate and crossed to the ruins of Castillo de San Joaquin where he "spiked" some seventeenth century cannon.

On the march south the vaunted Indian scout Kit Carson made an ignoble entrance into California history. From Frémont, then being pressured by his rough followers, he received the direct order to take no prisoners. Carson and a Canadian were scouting the shores of San Pablo Bay when two boys and an old man in civilian clothes landed from a boat. Francisco and Ramón de Harro, and their uncle José Berreyesa, were murdered from a distance of fifty yards.

SAILORS ON HORSEBACK

The precipitate actions of Frémont came close to throwing California into the hands of the British. Neither the Pathfinder nor the three American naval captains at Monterey had any authority to act; pioneer English, and even Yankees, showed open resentment against the high-handed methods of the Bears who were crowing loudly, commandeering food, and insulting the people Larkin had tried so long to avoid offending.

When Commodore John Drake Sloat brought his flagship *Savannah* into Monterey July 2nd he was besieged by Americans to formally take the country. Sloat had been in the fighting frigate *United States* during the War of 1812, and had been the scourge of West Indies pirates, but he was near retirement and knew at first hand what would follow a repetition of Jones' premature landing. Finally, on July 6th, the Commodore wrote his decision to Captain John Montgomery for that officer's guidance:

> I have determined to hoist the flag of the United States at this place tomorrow, as I would prefer being sacrificed for doing too much than too little.[11]

With the Stars and Stripes flying over Northern California, and the movements of General Castro unknown, Sloat set up a messenger service between Monterey and San Francisco; after a few couriers narrowly escaped capture he was forced to pay $165 for the perilous ride. Frémont received orders to march down El Camino and engage the enemy.

At some time during his naval career Sloat had become an excellent horseman and with mounts available he decided to send out his own cavalry as a check on the erratic Frémont. Purser Dangerfield Fauntleroy was directed to select thirty-five able seamen from the squadron and purchase horses and necessary shore equipment; from the ships he was allowed six cannon, two eighteen-pound carronades and some old carriages. Sloat instructed him:

> Mind, sir, to so place those guns that the Enemy can't attack you without being raked.

Because it seemed lubberly for a naval contingent to be without a "Luff," passed-Midshipman Louis McLane became First Lieutenant of the California Dragoons. Rolling quids, directed by helm commands, the sailors shaped a course for San Juan to join Frémont who was chasing Castro. An English officer remarked with broad sarcasm that the Dragoons appeared to be first rate seamen, adding:

> As cavalry they would probably have been singularly destructive *to each other* . . .[12]

At San Juan Fauntleroy mounted his cannon as directed, sea watches were set, and man-of-war discipline made to prevail. Six Jacks who joined Frémont's followers in a drinking bout were sent back to Monterey in irons; two others were flogged with the cat-o'-nine-tails, then detailed to herd spare horses for couriers.

The seagoing Dragoons foretold the course of war in California. Mountaineers, Indian fighters, backwoodsmen, frontier cavalry and European veterans were to be defeated or checked whenever they faced the enemy alone; in the final battles it would be sailors —using makeshift adaptations of sea fighting—who gained the victories.

THE OCCUPATION

Commodore Robert Field Stockton, another officer who had seen action in the War of 1812, took over from the sixty-five-year-old Sloat. Frémont was commissioned a major and sent south with his California Battalion of 160 in the *Cyane*, occupying San Diego unopposed. Stockton landed 360 sailors and marines on the beach at San Pedro. The Yankee shipmaster, Captain William D. Phelps, described the naval approach to Los Angeles on August 11th behind a full band of music:

> ...a battery of four quarter-deck guns mounted on as many bullock carts; the carriages of the guns were secured by the breechings, and ready for instant service. Each cart was drawn by four oxen—the baggage ammunition followed in similar teams; the purser, doctor, and some other officers—part of them mounted on rather sorry horses, the others on foot.

Stockton considered the conquests complete in mid-August when the *Warren* made port to bring the reassuring news that a state of war existed. Pio Pico and José Castro had fled to Mexico; other officers were freed on parole. Frémont was appointed military commandant with orders to proceed north, garrisoning highway towns en route to Monterey. Former secret agent Gillespie, with the rank of captain, had the responsibility of ruling the south. Kit Carson rode east to report the fast victory.

At the beginning rancheros took stock in the commodore's proclamations, heartened by the promises of peace and justice. The assurance of a kindly occupation was seen in the treatment of twenty Indian horse thieves: the trembling natives were taken aboard the *Savannah* to face the portly, deep-voiced Captain William Mervine. Instead of punishment they received blankets and handkerchiefs while the band played "Hail Columbia." Stockton sailed up to San Francisco, filled with pride at having draped California with the mantle of "manifest destiny."

THE VAQUERO STRIKES

On the afternoon of September 30th a Swede sailor-adventurer named John Brown—known in California as Juan Flaco (Lean John)—stiffly dismounted from a sweating racehorse onto the beach at Yerba Buena. After some argument because of his bedraggled appearance he was taken in the commodore's gig to the *Savannah* where he presented a package of cigarettes. On the paper of each smoke was Captain Gillespie's seal and above it the message: "Believe the bearer."

Juan Flaco brought startling news: the Californians in the south had revolted. The commodore raised his brows when the courier declared that he had witnessed the first attack on September 24th—*six days ago!* It was difficult to decide which advice was least believable, the revolt or the ride. But both proved true.

Juan Flaco told of leaving Los Angeles at eight o'clock on the night of the 24th with a dozen *vaqueros* in pursuit. A bullet in the flank of his horse helped the beast clear a thirteen-foot ravine to let him escape. Delayed only by difficulties in getting fresh mounts, he had warned every garrison along El Camino. Five hundred miles in about five days—including some long waits and journeys on foot weighed down by spurs—gave the Swede a place in California annals. Some historians imply even faster riding but defame the character of Juan Flaco: he was said to have been found on the beach at daybreak the 30th, passed out and clutching an empty brandy bottle.

Messengers from the south confirmed the report of an uprising. Under General José María Flores and other paroled officers the Californians had at last been stirred to action, largely by a series of dictatorial edicts that came from Gillespie—the shutting down of amusements; making it an offense for two persons to walk together; unnecessary rules on wine consumption.

In two weeks Flores recaptured every town from San Diego to San Luis Obispo, including Los Angeles where his wild riding *vaqueros,* with *reata* and lance, repulsed a counterattack. The Californians were now using their natural advantage as great horsemen who could ride out of the saddle, showing the enemy only one leg as a target. To deceive and frighten the gringo they used such old tricks as running herds of riderless horses along dusty roads and sent a few dozen horsemen in an endless circle around some bend in the highway to create the illusion of great numerical strength.

Rebel scouts watched the Monterey road for signs of any southbound party; patrols between San Luis Obispo and Santa Barbara seized every foreigner who could not produce a pass signed by an official of their newly organized government. Indians came in off the old Spanish Trail with encouraging word that General Stephen W. Kearney at the beginning of October was 1,500 miles away and his "Army of the West" was merely a mule-mounted force of about one hundred.

Late in October Stockton sailed south with eight hundred men. Frémont was instructed to follow on the road when he had recruited additional troops which were being supplied by his new ally, Sutter, from immigrant parties. Fauntleroy's dragoons could guard the northern reaches of El Camino. The Territory's first newspaper, the *Californian,* sounded a warning to the area around the capital:

> The ringleaders will be apprehended and tried under martial law, and may suffer death; so much for an affair that can be of no benefit to anyone, and must entail sorrow on many. The people of Monterey are wiser.[13]

The owners of the *Californian* believed what they published. Reverend Walter Colton left active duty as a Navy chaplain; his six-foot, eight-inch partner, Robert Semple of Kentucky, gave up fighting, dentistry, farming and wife-hunting to concentrate on setting type.

The editorials of the newspaper made little impression on Northern Californians who were outraged more than ever after Stockton sailed. Eulogizing Frémont and a few officers of high caliber in the California Battalion did not place a halo around the red-headed, dirty-mouthed Bluford Thompson, a much hated professional gambler, or the many other marauders.

It was against a party of "Hell-roaring" Thompson's men that the Northern Californians first struck—at Natividad, scene of Frémont's defiant flag raising eight months before. Swift horsemen surrounded the mountaineers and through a series of maneuvers made them empty their rifles, then swooped down to discharge pistols at short range before riding away. The casualties were a dozen on each side.

The Delaware scout Tom Hill, a tall and handsome brave with heavy black hair that reached to his knees, emerged as lone hero of the brief skirmish. Tom had fought Comanches on the Cimmaron and knew the buffalo country of Montana so he did not hesitate to travel back to Monterey alone with news for Frémont. When three Indian *vaqueros* surrounded him he sought cover until taunted, then came out into the open calling:

"You come here, me kill you. You fight like one woman."

The Delaware ducked a *reata* and felled a *vaquero* with a rifle shot. A lance pierced his hand but he opened the second attacker's head with his tomahawk; the third man fled.

On November 17th, the day after the Natividad skirmish, and before Hill staggered into Monterey, Frémont was on the move again, leading the California Battalion toward action in the south. To Captain Phelps he looked like "the King of the Rocky Mountains," but many were glad to see him depart. The Navy secured the north in a matter of weeks.

THE RAVISHED HIGHWAY

The Pathfinder's trek down El Camino Real was strikingly similar to the march of Micheltorena one year earlier. Both winter journeys were slow, plundering, non-combatant and ended safely beyond range of fire. The leaders bore some resemblance in martial affectation: Frémont looked every inch a fighting man in his blouse, leggings and rakish felt hat, flanked by the fierce Delaware body-guard; the Mexican general sounded fearless and unbeatable in his proclamations. Each officer headed men that had no business in uniform. But Frémont's was the heavier responsibility for the ragtag in his battalion were no mere menace to poultry.

In the ten companies, numbering five hundred men, the Path-finder had forced upon him so many malcontents, unruly spirits and drunks that enforcement of strict military discipline would have meant establishing a stationary prison. When an Indian servant of one of the Pico family was captured Frémont allowed the man to be shot without a trial to appease his ruffians; a detached party at Paso Robles raped three girls; in San Luis Obispo the bell-ringer was killed for tolling the Angelus; and Rancho Los Ojitos was razed because the owner had two sons thought to be in the California Army.

Stockton's couriers kept Frémont posted on developments in the south. On December 6th the small Army of the West had come off the desert to be soundly defeated; some fifty casualties marked America's heaviest battle loss since the War of 1812. The commodore rescued Kearney's force and escorted them to San Diego where his sailors were shaping up for an all-out attack after the first of the year.

The Pathfinder had nothing to send south with returning messengers. His riflemen had defeated twenty-six grizzly bears; supposedly wily frontiersmen were panicked by a mirage in which a *madroña* tree appeared to be the enemy army; the Sonoma black-smith and Bear Flag hero Captain John Sears led a night attack on a house filled with women and children; they scaled an adobe wall, fell into the mire of a sheep corral, and made themselves ill devouring pumpkins and *frijoles* that had been sparingly rationed out to hungry babies.

It seems likely, as some historians claim, that Frémont had orders to move slowly despite the disgraceful forays. The battalion might have been slaughtered at San Pasqual with demoralizing re-sults. While the Pathfinder was more a topographer than soldier, he was no coward. Just before leaving San Luis he showed his disregard for personal safety by refusing to execute the captive Jesus Pico; perhaps he was shamed into the decision by Señora Pico who came with her fourteen children to ask: "Is your fight with these?"

Frémont averted an uprising over Pico's release by getting his men and their livestock on the road. Grievances were soon forgotten when a rumor reached them that Californians had set up an ambush at Gaviota Pass. The old English sailor Benjamin Foxen, whose cattle brand was an anchor, was forced to show the battalion an Indian trail that would avert contact with the enemy. Cannon were knocked down and swung across chasms along with wagon parts in order to reach the summit. There a violent storm made the descent precarious; lightning and thunder stampeded one hundred horses to death in swollen ravines; the ten companies were covered with mud by the time they entered the deserted town of Santa Barbara on Sunday, December 27th. A "capture" was effected while women, children and old men were attending Mass.

The battalion rested and inspection tours were made of old Spanish homes with an eye lifted for hidden gold or any other loot. On January 7th Frémont received a dispatch from Stockton who on that day was about "to close with the enemy." The commodore warned:

> If there is one single chance for you, you had better not fight the rebels until I get up to aid you. . . .[14]

THE SAILOR ARMY

Commodore Stockton was then in his fifty-second year and known throughout the Navy as an exceptional gunnery officer. The men called him "Fighting Bob" and "The Sailor's Friend." Brigadier General Kearney, suffering from a lance wound received at San Pasqual, reluctantly turned the command over to the commodore but looked with misgiving on naval preparations up to the eve of battle. There being few horses the seamen trudged along wearing canvas shoes and carried boarding pikes; officers in blue flannel shirt-jackets had pistols, cutlasses and swords fixed to leather belts. That army used ship's time, struck every half hour on a bell, and "steered" by compass. Into a "rough log" went entries on wind force and direction; anything "sighted" was reported in relation to port and starboard flanks. Stockton envisioned the clash ahead as being comparable to a number of frigates—in the person of horsemen—attacking a ship-of-the-line which was the shape he had dictated the army would take, fighting from a hollow square. Finally, the men had been trained as though they were at sea.

Ordinary Seaman Joseph T. Downey of the *Portsmouth* described Stockton's methods:

> "Fighting Bob" was a gassy old Cove, and would have "his bullies" as he termed them out every day, drilling, charging, forming hollow squares, and putting themselves in the best possible discipline. He would collect a crowd around him, and commence a harangue, and chalk out to them the exact . . . way in which the Californians were to be whipped.[15]

Approaching the San Gabriel River, scouts of the enemy were seen near sunset January 8th. Thirty horsemen showed flashing lances decorated with red flags then retreated to join Flores' army of five hundred on the far shore. That night the commodore rounded up a number of California ladies and held a pre-battle hop which he personally "secured" at eight bells—midnight.

The next morning Stockton turned over command headquarters to Kearney while he led the dragoons to the water's edge and called a halt to let two columns and the rear guard form a square around cattle, mules, carts and wagons bearing the one-ton nine pounders. At the order "Forward!" the "corral," as they called the square, moved into the knee-deep water for the one-hundred-yard crossing.

On a bluff that rose fifty feet inland from the other shore the Californians opened fire with round and grape shot. Stockton and the dragoons forged ahead. But when they had crossed the San Gabriel they were alone. The commodore sloshed back to find that the cautious Kearney had ordered the guns unlimbered for a distant artillery duel.

"Limber up again! I want those guns hauled across!" Stockton bawled orders to his bluejackets and with them tailed on drag lines. "Pull for your lives, men!" he shouted. "Your commodore is here. Don't desert him. Don't for the love of God lose those guns!"

Amid the hail of gunfire cannon were dragged along the river bottom, threatening at times to be sucked under by quicksand pockets. Young Downey wrote:

> The Guns once crossed, the Commodore took charge of them himself and soon 'twas seen that fame had not overrated his powers with a Big Gun. He was as sure of his mark as if he held a Rifle in his hand, and in less than three discharges, a loud cheer from the Artillery men and Dragoons announced that he had capsized one of their Guns . . .[16]

Kearney led the square across the river, remaining calm when his mule balked. The tall general dismounted with pistol in one hand, riding whip in the other, and trudged ahead. From distant hills the corral loomed like some kind of ship; it had no sooner moved ashore when the California Cavalry dashed down in a single line, bright lances glittering in the sun ahead of the black hats and red saddle blankets. It was then that Stockton's strategy went into operation.

As wild-riding horsemen circled the square the front line of men knelt, muskets ready to fire a broadside, while the Americans behind them were prepared to double the force of the discharge. All hands remained cool as the cavalry thundered close. The "Fire!" order dropped horses in every direction; dismounted rancheros fled and those unharmed wheeled away to organize another charge. The California Artillery resumed its bombardment. Downey continued his narrative:

> . . . while Round and Grape were flying as thick as Hail about him, stood "Fighting Bob" here and there and everywhere with his telescope in his hand, sighting first this Gun and then that, and

giving the order to fire at the proper moment, his face glowing with animation, and showing plainly by his every action that he was half wild with excitement.[17]

After repulsing two more cavalry charges, and suspecting that the enemy was running low on his poor powder, Kearney and Stockton together gave the order to advance. With fixed bayonets and pikes at charge the army swarmed up the hill, yelling madly, eager for hand-to-hand fighting. But one look at the wild sailors sent the Californians into a retreat. The Battle of San Gabriel had ended and while the band played "Life on the Ocean Wave" the surprisingly few dead were buried.

The Sea Battalion and a scattering of soldiers marched the next morning to enter Los Angeles without resistance. Frémont brought his battalion down and since he was slated to become governor signed the provisional treaty.

The despised California Battalion was awarded $130,000 for its "services" and the government footed a $235,000 bill presented by Frémont for beef. In time historians glossed over the shoddy record of the rabble-ridden companies for they did include some able and later distinguished men.

ENDS OF THE TRAIL

The international treaty of Guadalupe Hidalgo, signed on February 2, 1848, gave the United States all California north of the stone line which Father Francisco Palou's Indians had set ten miles down El Camino Real from San Diego. Before the official peace enough Americans entered their conquered Territory to guarantee sovereignty: two parties of Mormons; covered wagons from Oregon, Missouri and Salt Lake; adventurous young men of Colonel Jonathan D. Stevenson's New York Volunteers, smartly uniformed in blue scarlet-trimmed coats, gray pantaloons and "new-style French caps."

The last shot of the war was not fired until March 23 when the sloop of war *Dale* stood into Todos Santos Bay near the tip of

Baja California to relieve a contingent of forgotten Navy men long under siege.

Thus a war started at Sonoma, Spain's northernmost stronghold in the New World, ended on the shores where the *conquistador* Hernán Cortés first landed in his search for gold more than three centuries earlier. Strangely, that dream of early Spaniards was about to be dramatically realized. And as though to recall every evil of gold there came a horrible prelude to its discovery in California.

Six   The Gold Rush

"BRAINS MAKE GOOD SOUP"

In the spring of 1847 "Fighting Bob" Stockton used the victory at San Gabriel as a gangway ashore and traveled overland to become a United States senator. General Kearney had Frémont arrested and took him to Fort Leavenworth to face a court-martial. The Pathfinder was found guilty of insubordination but pardoned; in his agitated wake he left the enduring name Golden Gate, a prophetic christening for the entrance to San Francisco Bay. Amid historically familiar squabblings Colonel Richard B. Mason became military Governor of California and more soldiers came to swell the non-Indian population to almost twenty thousand.

By early March those people ceased to talk about politics, war or the increased scarcity of women: out of the high Sierra came reports of a grisly tragedy whose sickening details emphasized a potential peril for all who traveled West. The horrible experience of the Donner party loomed as the harbinger of a jungle epoch.

On Christmas Day the Illinois farmer George Donner, with

his own and three other families that included twenty-one women and thirty children, found the way across the Sierra summit blocked by a raging blizzard. With cattle lost and supplies gone the party divided, seventeen struggling west in home-made snowshoes, the others remaining at cabins on what is now Donner Lake. Members of both groups were soon dying of starvation and survivors turned cannibals. Murder accompanied the savage feasting.

Those who lived through the ordeal testified against companions and to give accusations more weight they supplied revolting anatomical particulars. Edwin Bryant, one of Frémont's several high caliber officers, was among the rescuers of the Donner people and wrote of the last survivor to be taken out, a demented old man found

> reclining on the floor of the cabin, smoking his pipe. Near his head a fire was blazing, upon which was a camp-kettle filled with human flesh. His feet were resting upon skulls and dislocated limbs denuded of their flesh. A bucket partly filled with blood was near, and pieces of human flesh, fresh and bloody, were strewn around.[1]

William Fallon, leader of the rescue party, asked why a partly buried horse and bullock, preserved by the cold, had not been eaten. "Too dry," the old man answered, saying that he had grown fond of human flesh. "And," he added with an insane grin, "brains make good soup."

The lives of the forty-eight Donner party survivors were shadowed through the next few years by a morbid notoriety, and those who settled along El Camino Real had to tolerate the curiosity of travelers. But one couple capitalized on the experience by running the "United States Tavern," the only eating place in San Juan; profits on meals ran high, for the man and his wife diminished appetites with their unsolicited recollections.

After the Donner catastrophe westbound pioneers made certain to be guided by men like the great mountaineers Captain Joe Walker, Elisha Stevens or Colonel Joe Chiles. Every wagon train hoped to avoid such charlatans as Lansford Hastings, the "four-flushing" temperance lecturer, who had advised the Donners.

KEEPERS OF A SECRET

All kinds of books, newspaper articles and government publications about the West were being read in the months before the discovery of gold. Two thousand hopeful settlers were moving along the Oregon and Santa Fe trails, many with visions of a promised land whose soil was rich and where there was no winter. Mule-drawn Conestoga wagons lurched into the Santa Clara Valley, bodies weathered to a faint blue, mud encrusting once red wheels, and bows visible through rents in their canvas covers. Men wearing wide-brimmed felt hats, dungaree jackets and thick boots viewed the red-tiled, white-washed buildings of sleepy pueblos that lined the wide dirt highway south to San Diego; only at the town of ramshackle houses called San Francisco was there much to recall the east. Women dressed in bodices and skirts of linsey-woolsey stared at the lace *mantillas*, satin sashes and silk shawls of vivacious señoritas.

Pioneers who came before the Treaty of Guadalupe Hidalgo were shunted north and south in a vain search for land where they could permanently "light" to build, fence and plant. Mid-western farmers learned of 50,000-acre ranchos and heard themselves called "North American Adventurers" or "gringo squatters" by Californians who had not forgotten the Bears and Frémont's plundering battalion. Eventually those families would make a demand out of the words in a popular song, "Uncle Sam is rich enough to give us all a farm."

More concerned about his land than any Californian was John Sutter. In January of 1848 a discovery at his sawmill on the south fork of the American River promised to rid him of debt at last. It was even possible that the gold dust and pellets found by his employee, James W. Marshall, on the afternoon of the 24th, might make the Swiss a wealthy man.

Secrecy was all important. Sutter warned, cajoled and threatened the Indians, Mormons and immigrants of his settlement. But he knew the word must eventually get out so the trustworthy Charles Bennett was sent to Monterey to obtain a complete American grant for Fort Sutter and adjoining lands.

The secret was too big for Bennett who carried a buckskin bag containing six ounces of gold. At San Francisco he showed it to Isaac Humphery, a Georgia miner. In Monterey when Governor Mason said he was not authorized to give Sutter a deed, the messenger repaired to John Robertson's saloon and after a few drinks the gold was on display. Bennett traveled home by way of several more places of refreshment.

Others who left Sutterville, as some called the fort, found themselves powerless to keep quiet, for the gold area was spreading every day. In February mill workers scraped up pellets with their fingers or dug ounce slivers out of crevices using pocket knives. Some had panned $250 worth one week in an Indian basket. The discovery was talked about all through March at Leidesdorf's City Hotel in San Francisco and at inns and saloons down to Donnelly's gambling and grog shop in Santa Barbara.

Strangely, little attention was paid to the gold talk. Even after the *Californian* and the two San Francisco weeklies reported Marshall's find, few bestirred themselves. Mission Indians were known to have brought bits of gold to the padres at San Jose and Santa Clara; near San Fernando Francisco Lopez, a sheepherder, discovered the metal in 1842; it had not made him rich although it was said to have helped Abel "Horseface" Stern, the Yankee hide and liquor trader. Most people were content to agree with Mexicans who said: *"No es oro todo que reluce."* ("All that glitters is not gold.")

One man did act, and in a way that foretold how the greatest fortunes were to be made from the Gold Rush. Elder Sam Brannan, dressed more like a gambler than a leader of the Latter-day Saints, had been in close touch with Mormons on the American River. The tithes they paid went into merchandise for several stores Brannan opened in the gold country.

After the stores were ready to handle a flood of customers, and when Brannan judged the people of San Francisco ripe for a dramatic announcement, he made a noisy entrance into town and a crowd followed him to Portsmouth Plaza on May 11th. As soon as he had everyone's attention Sam whipped a bottle of gold dust from inside his long coat and with a flourish shouted: "Gold! *Gold!* GOLD from the American River!"

The Gold Rush began.

THE FORTY-EIGHTERS

More than one hundred people left San Francisco a few days after Brannan's display—almost one-fourth the male population. Men without money could borrow up to $2,000 by giving some merchant an order on a mine not yet found; the price of mules, horses and small sailboats skyrocketed over night. Shrewd traders dispatched orders East for every kind of merchandise.

Even soldiers could not resist the lure of gold and one of them, James H. Carson, described his feelings:

> ...a frenzy seized my soul; I was soon in the street in search of necessary outfits; piles of gold rose up before me at every step; thousands of slaves bowed to my beck and call; myriads of fair virgins contended for my love—were among the fancies of my fevered imagination. The Rothschilds, Girards, and Astors appeared to me but poor people; in short I had a very violent attack of gold fever.[2]

Mounted soldier-postmen carried the mail down El Camino to San Diego and spread the word that San Francisco would soon be evacuated. Fifty new buildings were left half finished as laborers departed for the diggings; servants, including one Chinese, refused the then fabulous salary of ten dollars a day. The two newspapers shut down, the *Californian* printing a farewell fly-sheet:

> The whole country from San Francisco to Los Angeles ... resounds to the sordid cry of *gold!* Gold!! GOLD!!! while the field is left half planted, the house half built, and everything neglected but the manufacture of shovels and pickaxes, and the means of transportation to the spot.[3]

110

Through the summer months the fever raged. When four Mormons stopped at Monterey on their way to Los Angeles and showed one hundred pounds of pure gold, a thousand people surged north in a wave. Lieutenant Edward Ord's entire garrison deserted; ships of the Pacific squadron canceled all shore leave and Commodore Thomas Ap Catesby Jones, returned to the West Coast, wrote:

> For the present, and I fear for years to come, it will be impossible for the United States to maintain any naval or military establishment in California . . .[4]

Jones offered $40,000 for the return of 164 deserters from the *Warren*. Some of those men almost delivered themselves by getting drunk after taking "French leave"—they followed a circular course and made their first camp back on the Monterey beach, awakening just before dawn to escape. It was rumored that the bluejackets had been roused by John Swan, the old English seaman, before he closed his shop and empty sailors' boarding house to head toward the mines.

For any who needed proof at hamlets and inns to the south the four Mormon travelers willingly showed their $20,000 worth of gold. But before the end of summer the evidence was overwhelming.

Among the ten thousand men at the diggings in the fall of '48 there were only a few who did not scrape up twenty dollars worth of gold a day, and hundreds could truthfully tell of fabulous strikes. Jacob Leese and four partners made $75,000 in three months on the Yuba using picks and shovels. William Daylor dug $15,000 in one week; at Parks Bar the *average* yield per man was $100 a day; and for a while knife and crowbar miners at Wood Creek cashed in $300 worth of chunks every evening.

It was only a short time before a businessman found a way to increase profits by hiring help. The German merchant Charles Weber promised the Walla Walla Indians cheap trinkets if they brought him gold. Chief José Jesus produced a kidney-shaped nugget that weighed 80½ ounces and sent his men to the Stanislaus where new and richer diggings were opened.

Another forty-eighter who used the Indians was James "Oregon" Savage, one of the malcontents in Frémont's battalion. He paid the *Tulareños* whiskey for their gold and "married" half a dozen young daughters of different village chiefs.

News of the "easy pickings" had almost depopulated coastal towns by the end of the year. The aged and the crippled came from the south in *carretas*; parents brought their children to help; Henry Bee, the San Jose jailer, herded his ten prisoners—including two who awaited trials for murder—to continue sentences at the gold fields.

During the first seven months of the Gold Rush only a dribble of outsiders reached California—from northern Mexico and Oregon in response to the news; from the sea and overland trails with no knowledge of the strike. For the most part the surface scraping and gouging had been the frantic work of amateurs yet the yield was an astonishing 4 million dollars. And that was a mere fraction of what would be taken from the mother lode.

THE ARGONAUTS

President James K. Polk's message to the Congress on December 5, 1848, sparked an East Coast and world-wide rush to the California gold fields. A courier from Governor Mason had arrived after four months' travel and assays of the lumps he brought showed the gold to be worth more than eighteen dollars an ounce. The Chief Executive stated:

> ... Recent discoveries render it probable that these mines are more extensive and valuable than was anticipated. The accounts of the abundance of gold in that territory are of such an extraordinary character as would scarcely command belief were they not collaborated by the authentic reports of officers in the public service ...[5]

The offices of steamship and packet lines thronged with gold fevered people seeking passage round Cape Horn or to the Isthmus of Panama from the Atlantic and Gulf coasts. Out of Europe one thousand emigrants were sailing every day for America; Hawaii, South America, China, Russia and the Marquesas sent ships.

Associations formed in every state to purchase prairie schooners, animals and supplies for the overland journey, people heedless to the known hardships and dangers they must face. By April 20,000 impatient gold-seekers were camped on the Missouri waiting for the thaw that would let them cross the Rockies.

Impatient, too, were the forty-eighters who had returned to their homes or to San Francisco when snow blanketed the diggings. Many had gambled their money away; some like the unfortunate discoverer Marshall had miraculously found no gold. A number who "struck it rich" decided to leave future digging to others and increase their fortunes supplying the hordes that would arrive in late spring.

The Kentucky trapper Job Dye, a resident since thirty-two whose distillery and mill at Santa Cruz had failed, was wise enough to enter a partnership with Thomas Larkin before investing the $40,000 he took home from the mines. Dye chartered a ship and brought a cargo from Mazatlán, then went down to Sonora and returned with a drove of mules.

The hide and tallow trade had ceased but rancheros were on the verge of even greater profits; for a time they would sell beef on the hoof for *one dollar a pound*. Horses commonly sold for $6 were to fetch as high as $300; flour $800 a barrel; eggs $3 each; butter $6 a pound.

With help scarce and wages high, owning a restaurant was risky even though forty dollars could be charged for a meal. Investors bought town lots on the highway, erected buildings, and rented them for $500 a month to hopeful landlords. Small stores built up inventories of items each to carry a $100 price tag: a shovel, pick, gallon of whiskey, pair of boots, on through the list of necessities that prospectors might have lost, pawned or forgotten on the journey.

The first customers for those roadside merchants were southern

Californians getting an early start to be near the hundred-mile stretch of diggings at the end of winter. Joining larger parties as they passed numerous hiding placcs were men who had slipped ashore from whalers and other vessels, together with army deserters.

Fifty mule trains led by a bell mare filed up from Sonora, the small animals weighted with 300-pound packs of mining equipment, rice and beans. The unpopular Mexicans cut inland to the southern diggings around the Tuolumne. Even before the Treaty of Guadalupe Hidalgo these little men with dark skin were being called "greasers."

In April a continuous stream of Argonauts hurried down the San Francisco peninsula, stopping to eat and ask directions at Andy Whistman's Inn. Orientals, South Sea Islanders and heavily-armed, clerical-looking men mingled with sailors who had deserted from more than one hundred ships; the crowds pushed on to the noisy, shanty-lined street of San Jose, raucous voices singing:

> *Oh! Cali-fornia,*
> *That's the land for me!*
> *I'm a-goin' to Sacramento*
> *With my washbowl on my knee.*

The forty-niners were first seen on El Camino Real in August when a party reached San Diego over the Gila route. These travelers had been too impatient to wait for spring and dared not risk the fate of the Donners; instead they heeded the words of the Houston *Democratic Telegraph* recommending that from Texas to San Diego "is emphatically the emigrant's route to California." [6] The southern crossing was at the time also lauded by the *Arkansas State Democrat* which assured a direct passage through country "whose valleys wear the warm smile of an eternal summer."

The traveling writer, Bayard Taylor, heard a different version at San Diego:

The emigrants by the Gila route gave a terrible account of the crossing of the Great Desert, lying west of the Colorado. They described this region as scorching and sterile—a country of burning salt plains and shifting hills of sand, whose only signs of human visitation are the bones of animals and men.... There, if a man faltered, he was gone; no one could stop to lend him a hand without a liklihood [sic] of sharing his fate.[7]

The path of Father Kino and Captain Anza was as hard in its way as the northerly California Trail from Independence that passed above Great Salt Lake. But it was an all-year way to gold; on it a man was always moving westward. The principal complaint of the ragged and exhausted sufferers, once they had gulped water and food, was disappointment: "Did you say *six hundred more* miles to the diggings?"

Almost ten thousand wild, sunburned gold pilgrims reached San Diego and Los Angeles from the southwestern desert, often on foot after having animals stolen by Yuma Indians. In the wake of Texans came foreigners who had reached New Orleans by ship; Southern gentlemen attended by Negro slaves; people in the strange garb of Eastern deserts; Georgia and Florida "crackers"; West Indies fishermen.

Easterners who studied maps and plotted "average" day journeys through short cuts usually met with grief. Charles A. Paul and his New England pioneers found no easy path from Vera Cruz to San Blas and the schooner chartered there was beached before it sank off Cape San Lucas. The Yankees underwent terrible suffering on a march up Baja California; others who later were lured to that old route of the eighteenth-century Spaniards barely survived on the still desolate wasteland.

Up the road they trudged by the hundreds, pausing only to ask for information. Southbound travelers were stopped by companies eager for "golden news." There were tales of nuggets weighing fifty pounds; of $3,000 being sifted from two pans of dirt; of $36,000 made in four days. Strangers received advice at every highway hamlet: go to Rich Gulch, Murderer's Bar, Frytown, Cut Eye Foster's Bar, Iowaville, El Dorado City, Yankee Hill, and fifty other favorite spots.

Dreams conjured by the promise of unbelievable wealth spurred on weary travelers. And each month companies from out of the southwest would be more and more in need of such stimulation: water holes along the route were drying up; forage had become scarce; Apache attacks caused the loss of supplies and animals; trade-wise Pimas soon raised prices on food and ferry service. By fall prospective miners, and the first homesteaders, were near death when they entered California.

Broke and hungry, but revived by yarns of gold, the Argonauts were so destitute that many could not afford to pay a *real* for three pears. Instead they foraged, stripping orchards and breaking into barns.

Bayard Taylor reported the extremes resorted to on the property of Thomas Blanco near Monterey:

> There is a fine garden on the Rancho but during his absence at the placers in the summer all the vegetables were carried away by a band of Sonorians, who loaded his pack mules with them and drove off. They would even forceably have taken his wife and her sister with them, had not some of her relatives fortunately arrived in time to prevent it.[8]

THE DANGEROUS JOURNEY

Californians began to bar doors and animals were corraled under guard. At the crumbling missions caretakers slept in the old otter rooms; roadside innkeepers hired protectors. Honest farmers gave up trying to settle the land and brought families and possessions to the highway towns. A greater peril than scavengers soon threatened the people.

From the Gila came companies of New Orleans gamblers, cutthroats, thieves and disheveled women accompanied by their French pimps whom they called *maquereaux*—a name miners shortened to "macks." The criminals stopped at the growing Los Angeles tenderloin of *Calle de los Negros*, then rode up to the more flourishing deadfalls of San Francisco's "Sydney Town" where they joined the sweepings of the world. Ruffians who were driven from those shanty-town nests sought hideaways near the road.

No wise man traveled alone after the summer of '49. High prices and the influx of ruffians brought a wave of robberies and assaults. Hardy emigrants who had escaped cholera, Apaches, starvation and death on the desert soon found they trod no peaceful path to the mines.

J. Ross Browne, riding a burro from San Francisco to San Luis Obispo as a representative of the United States Postal Service, narrowly escaped with his life after encountering American brigands on the road near San Miguel. Breaking away from his attackers, Browne fled on foot for two days and nights, closely pursued, and found shelter in an abandoned house where he dropped into the sleep of exhaustion without looking around the dark room. A shock awaited him when he awoke after daybreak:

> A ghastly spectacle was revealed—a ghastly array of room-mates lying stiff and stark before me. From the general appearance of the dead bodies I judged them to be an emigrant family from some of the Western States. They had probably taken up a temporary residence in the old adobe hut after crossing the plains by the southern route, and must have had money or property of some kind.... The man was apparently fifty years of age; his skull was split completely open.... The woman was doubtless his wife. Her clothes were torn partly from her body, and her head was cut nearly off.... The two children had evidently been cut down by blows of an axe.[9]

The brutality described by Browne was no more noticed than reports of violent deaths on the overland trails and mass slaughters when new Sacramento River side-wheelers exploded. The few law enforcement officers and the crowded, disreputable courts were unable to cope with crime at Los Angeles, San Jose and San Francisco, let alone bring order to the road. The tide of immigration defied peace.

THE SCOURGE OF GOLD

Even in its third and fourth year the Gold Rush showed no sign of slacking. The largest part of the billion in precious metal to come out of the mother lode was mined in that period but because

100,000 emigrants went to the placers—about the same number as did not go—many returned disappointed.

Stories of luck were more fabulous than ever before in the fifties: Major Pierson Reading, late of the California Battalion, was said to have struck a vein that brought him $80,000 in *one week*; from Sierra City came a huge nugget called "The Monumental" which weighed 148 pounds, 4 ounces! Frenzied men gambled high wages to get a "stake" so they could go back and try again; criminals at the towns, especially sprawling, rowdy San Francisco, waited for "flush" miners.

The American writer Hinton Helper visited California in the opening years of the rush to find "degradation, profligacy and vice" confronting him at every step. From his survey of gambling places, deadfalls, grog shops, brothels and saloons he concluded:

> I have seen purer liquors, better segars [*sic*], finer tobacco, truer guns and pistols, larger dirks and bowie knives, and prettier courtezans here, than in any other place I have ever visited.

Helper, best known for his anti-slavery writings, assured readers that "California can and does furnish the best bad things that are obtainable in America" and by way of illustration described a phase of tavern activity:

> ... nearly one-fourth of the bars are attended by young females of the most dissolute and abandoned character, who use every device to entice and mislead the youthful and unsuspecting. Women being somewhat of a novelty here, saloons are always thronged with customers. . . . What a base prostitution of her destiny and mission! Woman has come here not only to pander to man's vitiated appetites but also to create and foster in him unholier desires.[10]

The shortage of marriageable women which had dogged California since its discovery was never more acute than in Gold Rush days. In large towns most daughters of young married couples were still children. Females arriving in the fifties were, in the Victorian words of Hubert Howe Bancroft, "only the fallen image, the center of gyrating revelry and discord." [11]

The ladies of easy virtue represented about every nation on the globe. Hispano-Americans, Africans and Indians were imported for the mines; Chinese brothel masters bid for "Daughters of Joy," recruited from the flower boats on the Yangtze where they had been sold by starving parents, and sent them from Dupont Street—San Francisco's teeming Chinatown—to San Jose and Los Angeles; kidnapped girls from the Marquesas Islands and waifs picked up in Mazatlán were sold at coastal towns to the highest bidder. The "high-class" prostitutes from France and the East Coast—who made as much as $50,000 a year—often married and helped build California's first American society, giving birth to children and the embarrassingly truthful jingle:

> *The miners came in forty-nine,*
> *The whores in fifty-one;*
> *And when they got together,*
> *They made the Native Son.*

Among those who objected to the unholy traffic in women were the respectable cultivators of vineyards in Los Angeles who every Saturday night paid their Indian laborers with *aguardiente* rather than cash; the ex-*neophytes* were then left alone to drink up their wages until Sunday. Major Horace Bell, the California Ranger, described the weekly aftermath:

> About sundown the pompous marshal, with his Indian special deputies, who had been kept in jail all day to keep them sober, would drive and drag the herd to a big corral in the rear of Downey Block, where they would sleep away their intoxication, and in the morning they would be exposed for sale, as slaves for the week.[12]

The vineyard men, and others operating businesses that required slave labor, bought peons for from one to three dollars, a third of which was paid the next Saturday in brandy to the slave. Bell recorded the "legitimate" sacrifice of the San Gabriel Mission Indian:

> ... the slave at Los Angeles was sold fifty-two times a year as long as he lived, which did not generally exceed one, two, or three years.

... Those thousands of honest, useful people were absolutely destroyed in this way. ...

Three enterprising American grog shops were opened by squatters in Mission San Gabriel to sell the Indians their brandy on the week-end. On Sunday mornings a "qualified Justice of the Peace" would drink and play cards, ready to order the hanging of any drunken native who became obstreperous.

In 1851 the United States government made a gesture of recognizing the Indian's right to "Life, Liberty and the pursuit of Happiness" and attempted to rescue him from enslavement at Los Angeles and elsewhere. Commissioner G. W. Barbour proposed "a treaty of peace and friendship" [13] that would give the remnants of the Indian nation some 8½ million acres—about one per cent of the newly admitted state.

Screams of California state legislators in behalf of the "energetic and zealous miner" [14] reduced the grant to *thirty-two acres*. Natives who could not escape were led away to bull-pen reservations.

Indians found dubious sanctuary at the mines: as long as they would labor for nothing miners used them; petty theft or malingering meant quick death at the end of a rope. Before long the same treatment was accorded all foreigners—Mexicans, Negroes, Hispano-Americans, Chinese and even the rancheros—for the complexion of mining had changed.

In 1855 powerful syndicates formed to underwrite four thousand miles of canals worth 6½ millions; quartz mining companies built costly crushing mills and sank deep shafts. The day of the lone prospector at the rich placers had passed.

Chinese driven from even poor diggings opened laundries or restaurants; to California from China came strange foods—cuttle fish, duck liver, seaweed, lily seed and bamboo shoots. Dark-complexioned Frenchmen were driven down to San Francisco from the mines; many joined countrymen of the *travailleurs associés—La Californienne* and *Le Bretonne*—which had sent emigrants to establish agriculture colonies.

One Frenchman who left the mines when it suited him, and sneered at the hypocrisy that made him acceptable, was Marquis Charles de Pindray. A man of tremendous physique, the marquis could bend a Spanish doubloon with his fingers; it was known that dueling caused him to depart from France. To show his scorn for those who would make a mockery of Abbé Sieyès' rights of man, de Pindray wore a Mexican sombrero and old serape.

The marquis joined drovers who would buy cattle on the hoof for $15 a head from Isaac Williams or other rancheros at Los Angeles for sale in San Francisco at $48 each, paid in six-sided gold slugs worth $50.

The route of the drovers in the fifties was through unfenced fields on each side of El Camino Real where they could get one-dollar meals at small American inns. Those cowboys were the nemesis of Swiss, Portuguese, German, Irish, Dane and French squatters as cattle trampled through truck gardens and mixed with herds of dairy cows or sheep.

Suffering with other oppressed groups were the rancheros. Brigands were slaughtering their cattle and stealing horses; trespassers and squatters defied them; panderers had forced their daughters into brothels; crooked gamblers were cheating them in the towns. They had even become the object of patronizing ridicule by foreign vagabonds: the French wanderer, Ernest de Massey, had written:

> We passed one fine rancho, owned by a rich Californian who, like most of his associates, is uneducated and unable to read or write. Riding, gambling, playing, drinking, swaggering and brutality take the place of this elementary knowledge and seem essential to the happiness of these isolated ranch owners.[15]

To the proud *hidalgo* the injustices brought by the Gold Rush would be a mere scourge before his crucifixion. In the five years since California became a state, land commissioners had been demanding proof that Spanish and Mexican grants were valid. Crooked and greedy politicians, lawyers, and speculators hovered like vultures over the dying rancheros.

THE VIGILANTES

The plight of Indians, prostitutes, oppressed foreigners and the victims of crooked gamblers, shyster lawyers or assassins was tolerated or ignored in the lure of gain. With millions of dollars invested or circulating in towns from Sonora down to San Diego even such disasters as five devastating fires that leveled San Francisco, cholera which spread to San Jose, and the 1855 earthquakes at Los Angeles were passing misfortunes.

A round-the-clock struggle for second-hand Sierra gold was the great common denominator of 200,000 persons settled in California in the mid-fifties. With the honest frugal people from all over the world were crooks who ranged from Henry "Honest Harry" Meiggs, the amiable San Francisco businessman who bilked friends and neighbors out of one million dollars, to the imaginative faker Frank Ball of Los Angeles.

Frank bought a mustang which he decked out in ornate blankets and tethered in a large stable. He then placed Spanish and English advertisements in the newspapers and tacked up posters announcing that he would voyage to Catalina Island on the great and unique Kanaka swimming horse *Hippopotamus*. The public was invited to view the remarkable animal which had recently swum all the way from the Hawaiian Islands to San Francisco. Thousands paid fifty cents each to see the amphibious wonder that looked no different from an ordinary horse. On the eve of the Catalina swim *Hippopotamus* disappeared. Ball was last seen in a boat, following the logical course of pursuit.

There was no extreme to which a man would not go to make money. Pontifical capitalists used legal devices to strip close associates; politicians dipped into the public till to put California $3 million in debt after only five years; Peter Biggs, the Negro barber and part-time pimp, snatched more than three hundred cats from the dark streets of Los Angeles and sold them for $100 each to owners of rat-infested homes and hotels at San Francisco.

In 1856 property in coastal towns and along El Camino Real,

where the far-sighted believed a railroad would be built within ten years, became more important than human life. At San Francisco merchants proclaimed theft a greater crime than enslavement, vice or even murder. War was declared against house-breakers, shop-lifters, safe-crackers, arsonists and any others who sought to violently storm the walls of business.

Again that stormy petrel Sam Brannan came forward to rally seven hundred merchants who were suffering from the antics of Sydney Town ruffians. Sam reviewed the losses sustained through a drop in real estate values, numerous robberies and fires set by incendiaries. He demanded action and urged that the Vigilance Committee of 1851 be recalled.

Armed patrols of merchants roamed the streets on the night of June 10th and into their net was gathered John Jenkins as he attempted to make off with a safe stolen from Long Wharf. Fire bells called the Vigilantes to City Hall the next day and thousands watched as Jenkins was hung from the verandah.

Quickly eight thousand persons joined the committee in San Francisco; as many more formed in Sonoma and San Jose and the movement spread to the south. Warnings were issued to criminals. The Army, Navy, city police, state officials, and even Washington, were defied by marching Vigilantes who wore white ribbons, exchanged pass-words, and had medals struck off for the veterans of three more executions.

Twenty-five criminals were deported and one thousand others fled the towns. To still the murmur that the action was no more than a brazen chamber of commerce scheme, the Vigilantes took under their protective wing the Chinese—whom they would soon renounce.

When the Committee of Vigilance adjoined August 21st simultaneous parades were held at coastal towns; in homes and taverns parties celebrated a victory over crime. Real estate values began to climb, trade improved, and municipal expenditures soon showed a drop: at San Francisco in the first year of the new order the decrease was from $3 million to $300,000.

The Vigilantes brought no abrupt end to crime. The threat they posed segregated vice, driving evil-doers into the Barbary Coast at San Francisco and to satellite tenderloins elsewhere. But no longer did arrogant assailants intimidate merchants; "fixers" used caution in approaching judges.

The aroused citizens not only forced hundreds of criminals into the hills along the coast but conducted a "witch hunt" among men who objected to the so-called "popular tribunals" on constitutional grounds. Industries were urged to hire "loyal—and cheap—John Chinaman" to replace undesirable "niggers" and "greasers."

Up at the placers American miners seized the Vigilante movement as an excuse to wage renewed warfare on the swarthy people from Sonora and made arrangements for them to be given brief sanctuary at highway cities. Since a $20 a month head tax, chastisement and frequent lynchings had failed to push all the Mexicans from the diggings, vigilance committees began a wholesale operation. Bancroft—who had started his profitable bookstore in a threatened area of San Francisco—included in his history of the miners the observation that they "achieved most gratifying results." [16]

The Mexicans were ruthlessly hunted down by bands of uncouth Americans who knew they faced no penalty and stood to acquire further claims. Beatings, rapings and lynchings took on the fury of the righteous and that terrorizing forced the "greasers" to the coast towns. Then came the financial panic of 1855 and after "Black Friday"—February 23—the recent owners of all California were again evicted.

The little sons of Castile and Anáhuac, never able to unite, beaten down by the Anglo Saxon conqueror of land and owner of gold, made their final bow as desperados. The Gold Rush whose herald was cannibalism had its ending marked by the birth of a vengeful legend and a splurge of terror along the skeletal way of El Camino Real.

Seven The Highwaymen

WHAT ROAD?

The battle between Vigilantes and highwaymen from the early fifties until the end of the Civil War was fought largely along the old mission trail. In those days of robbery, violent death and lynching the historic route was seldom designated as El Camino Real; in fact it had temporarily lost its identity altogether as a continuous thoroughfare.

Yankees accustomed to stage travel on the Boston Post Road behind teams of German coach horses, or fast Cleveland bays, poked fun at the rude paths that connected San Francisco with San Diego. Some Easterners talked of their planked highway from New York to Buffalo—built at a cost of $10,000 per mile—while Englishmen had long known the smooth pavements of John McAdam. Those sophisticates, and even emigrants who had bumped over the crushed stone National Pike westward to Missouri, asked sarcastically, "What road?" when directed to California's main artery.

The forty-foot, planked toll road that led out of San Francisco's muddy business district gave false assurance to travelers arrived from sea; even when it ended abruptly at 16th Street there seemed to be promise of comfort in the hard-packed avenue which continued. Ahead lay those popular roadhouses, "The Grizzly Bear," "The Nightingale," and "The Mansion House"; in a valley sprawled George Treat's "Union" and "Pioneer" racetracks. But civilization ended abruptly at "The Red House," so widely advertised for "bird, chicken and wine breakfasts, served at all hours of the day and night."

Horsemen, wagon drivers, pedestrians and early stagecoach passengers viewed a pastoral scene from the outskirts of the city. Wheel ruts along with the prints of animals and men disappeared into grass fields or dunes studded with chaparral; cattle grazed for miles between peninsula foothills and the wide southern arm of San Francisco Bay. The starting traveler could see little to confirm the stage company advertisements which had appeared in the *Alta California* since Gold Rush times:

> There is no more charming drive in California than that from San Francisco to San Jose and as one is whirled rapidly through the oak openings and across the level plains ... he finds that pleasure is united with business and wonders why he has never made the trip before.[1]

Those who braved the 3½-day (and night) trip to Los Angeles agreed that the first leg of the journey could be called the most "charming"—but only by comparison with stretches of road along mountain sides, through swollen streams, and across miles of parched semi-desert country. Steep climbs and descents in the years before the Civil War were "perfectly awful" according to Mrs. D. M. Bates who could be called something of an authority: before riding a California stagecoach she had survived three consecutive fires at sea, an open boat voyage in the Pacific, and was castaway on the bleak and wintry Falkland Islands.

During the decade that followed the Gold Rush, old El Camino Real changed but slowly: country inns, saloons and stage stops between the missions were as a rule the houses of farmers or squatters; small towns such as Salinas and San Luis Obispo showed the traveler windows and doors protected by ominous iron shutters; Santa Barbara, still the main town between San Jose and Los Angeles, was distinguished by its many saloons, gambling halls and billiard parlors.

In the hope of attracting settlers through more easy access, the Santa Barbara *Gazette* in 1855 urged that the northern approach at Gaviota Pass be cleared of boulders. It was suggested that citizens

> . . . tear themselves away from the blandishments of keno, billiards and cards long enough to examine the route for a post road.[2]

South of the city the "road" disappeared at high tide as it always had since the march of Portolá. Unchanged also was the broad trail through the beautiful San Fernando Valley and the arroyo-scarred country below the wild, alcohol oasis of Los Angeles. A sea-facing path from Emerald Bay widened at the disreputable settlement around the ruins of San Juan Capistrano, made tortuous bends over Torrey Pinos and the mountain of Soledad, finally coming to an end in the Plaza at San Diego. Near the site where Junípero Serra founded his first mission stood the Exchange Hotel, presided over by diminutive George "Two-bits" Tibbetts.

The roughness of the road, that evoked ironic remarks from urban Eastern and European pilgrims, was a mere inconvenience after Vigilantes drove Mexican desperados from the mines and cities. Then commenced the era of highway crime that for long seemed impossible to combat. Bandits struck in passes or canyons and vanished to mountain hideaways; murderers and robbers caught their victims going through redwood forests.

Posses were frequently riding out of Los Angeles and San Diego but on the near-deserted reaches of the road there was little protection. Sometimes a horseman of the express or postal service would rein up in time to save an unwary traveler; more often he would bring in the news of another stripped corpse. The State Legislature was prodded to action as early as 1853 when the annual killings reached five hundred; it authorized two Ranger divisions to protect the north and south parts of the highway. But even those tough, hard-riding lawmen could not be everywhere.

"DEATH TO THE GRINGOS!"

The first *vengador* to gain notoriety was Solomon Pico, of the numerous progeny left by the old soldier José Dolores Pico who had come to California in 1790. In '49 Solomon had been whipped and threatened with lynching, then banished from his Sierra claim. He headed for the mountains twenty miles below Santa Maria where his father once commanded.

The word spread along the highway: Mexicans who drove *carretas* to Monterey with kegs of butter returned with followers; from "Sonora Town," the Mexican criminal settlement at Los Angeles, came fugitives wanted by the Rangers. Hideouts were established in the hills below a peak that could be seen for seventy miles and would be known as Mount Solomon.

Cattle buyers en route toward Los Angeles were the earliest victims of the Pico gang. Then assaults were made on miners returning from small placers discovered in the fifties through Ventura and Santa Barbara counties. Bodies left at the roadside—always Americans—bore the terrible mark of Solomon Pico: the ears had been hacked off. Mexicans said their avenger vowed to collect enough gringo ears to make a rosary for the girl he loved; they added that the hero was a man who loved many women.

Always practical, Solomon sacrificed one señorita for whom the grisly gift may have been intended. She was at his side when he led the band into San Luis Obispo in 1853 to pawn valuables taken from a party of slain gringos. Surprised by a posse, the bandit chief used the girl and half a dozen men, including his aide, Manuel Vergara, as decoys while he escaped. When the girl was lynched along with the men, Solomon pledged greater slaughter.

Pico continued his career for almost a decade. When the land of his father became too crowded with lawmen he escaped to Baja California. Across the border he died at the hands of his own people: for merely defending himself in a knife fight against a man as vicious as himself, Solomon Pico faced the firing squad on the order of a *sub-jefe político*.

Throughout his career Solomon had been the bane of the southern Rangers whose headquarters was the Montgomery Bar in Los Angeles. In the hope of capturing him the Rangers would stage surprise raids on *Calle de los Negros*—called *Nigger Alley*—and from the dragnet take a few suspects. Those unfortunates were "cat-hauled" up and down the filthy drainage ditch. Unsavory-looking fellows who refused to reveal the whereabouts of the bandit might be taken to the Plaza for a public whipping, administered—to give it added sting—by an Indian.

Mexicans responded to the Ranger treatments by forming gangs throughout the Southland. When posses rode out to hunt them down, leaving the city protected by a few policemen, desperados appeared in pairs. It was a favorite trick to ride down a peace officer, each horseman holding the end of a *reata* which would be jerked taut under the victim's jaw.

In one of those forays the sheriff was murdered at midday before a large gathering. The infuriated people helped the Rangers "string up five greasers," and it seemed to make little difference that one of the men executed—by accident—was the innocent San Gabriel cobbler, Cipriano Sandoval. Late in 1853 the Mexicans retaliated with a well-organized and unique raid.

THE BAGNIO BANDITS

Scene of the bold attack was a plush brothel which celebrated its opening with a much talked about *soirée*. The vice chiefs and principal gamblers of Los Angeles were being entertained by a bevy of "young, beautiful and newly arrived" prostitutes. Revelry was at its height about midnight when a dozen armed Mexicans barged through the door. Major Horace Bell described the event from the time the masked leader of the raiding party raised a hand for attention:

> He informed the gamblers that the house was surrounded by a hundred armed men, and if they offered the least resistance they would be murdered without mercy.... The robbers then went through and plundered the house, finding most of the gamblers' overcoats and revolvers in the adjoining wineroom. After which they then passed the gamblers out of the ballroom, searching and robbing them one by one until the last man was fleeced, when they proceeded to search and rob the frail sisters, stripping them of their valuable jewelry and money. They then bade the household *"buenas noches,"* mounted their horses and rode away.[3]

Leaving town the Mexicans paid a call on a wealthy Frenchman. He was robbed of jewelry, money and a valuable gold watch; as a parting gesture several of the gang raped his wife.

Mystery surrounded the raid and there came rumors that individual Mexican outlaw leaders—Solomon Pico, Juan Soto, Manuel "Three-fingered Jack" García, and several scoundrels named Joaquin—were uniting to invade Los Angeles. Many believed the murder of all gringos was imminent in December for another law officer had been stabbed to death in broad daylight by a Mexican who leisurely cursed the slain man before riding away.

Then, at the height of nervous and fearful expectancy, a hero rode into town to tell how he had wiped out the ringleaders of the band that robbed the Main Street brothel and the home of the Frenchman.

The "white" and respected Mexican merchant Atanacio Moreno, who disappeared from Los Angeles when his business failed the previous summer, returned to declare that he had been kidnapped and in making an escape managed to break up the organization of his despicable countrymen. As evidence he uncovered a cart to show five stiff corpses, one of them the murderer of the marshal for whom the town had been offering a $1,500 reward.

The hero of the hour collected the bounty money and re-opened his old shop. Crowds of well-wishers seemed to insure success but it was only two weeks before trouble shrouded the one-man gang-buster. Captain Alexander Hope of the Rangers arrested him for attempting to pawn the gold watch recently stolen from the Frenchman.

Moreno then made an astonishing confession: he had masterminded operations on the night of the brothel robbery, and claimed other "non-murderous" coups. He had been unable to resist the $1,500 temptation and so murdered his own men, lifting the watch from one of the betrayed victims. Moreno received a light sentence because he had acted in the public interest and had killed only Mexicans.

THE PICKLED HEAD

Los Angeles and Santa Barbara newspapers hailed Captain Hope and his men for the capture of a *real* criminal, mostly as a salve to regional pride. At the time the Los Angeles Rangers were greatly overshadowed by the northern division. In a race to capture a desperado and collect rewards totaling $6,000, Hope's men had lost to the Rangers under Captain Harry Love, a transplanted Texan.

The original storm had been raised by the State Legislature in an effort to rid California of the growing number of Mexican murder rings, and charged the Rangers to capture "dead or alive" the party or gang of robbers commanded by the five Joaquins— surnamed Carillo, Valenzuela, Ocomorenia, Botilleras and Murieta. Out of the directive would come the legend of Joaquin Murieta, bandit extraordinary.

After a long search up and down the highway and into many suspected hideaways of the Coast range, Love and his men turned up in Sacramento to report their mission accomplished and claim the bounty: in a jar of alcohol they showed the severed head of "the notorious murderer and robber, Joaquin" and as additional proof of eradicating the gang Love exhibited the similarly preserved hand of Manuel "Three-fingered Jack" García. With considerable modesty the Rangers told of a violent fight. And before reaching the capital Love collected affidavits to identify the head as that of Joaquin Murieta, one of the five wanted bandits.

For the next year the head was on exhibition at saloons and museums around the state but since highway robbery increased many suspected that Love and his men had decapitated a Mexican who would pass for a bandit in order to collect the money. The editor of the San Francisco *Alta* stated as much in an editorial:

> ...although I will not say that interested parties have gotten up this Joaquin expedition, yet such expeditions can generally be traced to have an origin with a few speculators.[4]

The grisly traveling exhibition inspired town liars to fill in gaps about the life of the virtually unknown Murieta and when Mexicans were hauled up for hanging they were sometimes identified as the cousin, brother-in-law or close friend of "the famous bandit, Joaquin, whose name is associated with a hundred deeds of blood," as the San Francisco *Herald* described him.

The growing, haphazard tale of Joaquin Murieta took solid form in 1854 with the publication of a little papercovered book, *The Life and Adventures of Joaquin Murieta, Celebrated California Bandit*, by John Rollin Ridge. The author was a part-Cherokee journalist and poet who previously had written under his Indian name "Yellow Bird." His book sold widely, was pirated in four languages, rewritten and made into a "biography," then a movie. The pickled head took on a new personality that recalled Robin Hood rather than any composite of local Mexican gang leaders.

In his book *Bad Company*, Joseph Henry Jackson, an understanding and warm historian, summed up Ridge's picture of the Joaquin nobody really knew:

> Murieta, as Ridge depicts him (and as the legend to this day devoutly insists he was), is a young man of excellent reputation, "gracefully built and active as a young tiger." He has turned outlaw because a party of American miners (a) raped his lovely young wife, Rosita, before his eyes, (b) hanged his brother in his presence on a trumped-up charge of horse-stealing, and (c) tied Joaquin

132

himself to a tree and whipped him—a series of events which might well have soured the sweetest character. It was no more than natural, Ridge feels, that Joaquin should swear "an oath of the most awful solemnity, that his soul should nevermore know peace until his hands were dyed deep in the blood of his enemies." [5]

From the swearing of the oath until his decapitation, Ridge had Murieta rob and murder at a fearful pace, the while rescuing ladies in distress and spreading largesse to the poor. The ridiculous fiction in time approached the status of fact, for California needed a romantic hero to give some dignity to the shabby, money-grubbing post Gold Rush era and to strike back at the injustices it bred. When the giants of state history—Bancroft and Theodore H. Hittle—used Ridge's book as "documentation" for their ponderous reference works, Joaquin Murieta became a stable figure of the past. Hittle wrote:

> Notwithstanding various stories that the real Joaquin was never taken ... there can be little or no reasonable doubt that the man killed was the right one or that the right man was killed.[6]

To Rangers, town police and sheriffs much of Ridge's invented dialogue was offensive. Lawmen who had looked upon the mutilated bodies of ambushed Americans now saw insult added to murder; to them the itinerant head emphasized the slur coined by the half-breed Indian writer: "these *very* superior specimens of the much-vaunted Anglo-Saxon race!" [7] Joaquin Murieta, whoever he may have been, precipitated a temporary surge of law enforcement that created California's first large state prison.

SAN QUENTIN

Every highway town of any size had its *calabozo*, usually a relic of Spanish colonial times and always crowded with prisoners whose crimes ranged from murder, rape and embezzlement down to the common offense of drunkenness. The adobe walls of those *juzgados* (hoosegows) were so weak that when an inmate was thrown the end of a *reata* he and his friend outside could "saw" an opening in the easily crumbled mortar. Moderately strong men could pull out prison bars. A jail that was full by midnight would be empty and in need of repair before dawn.

Men refused to accept employment as prison guards against the growing horde of marauders who took pride in imitating Murieta, Pico and a dozen other *asesinos*. Citizen groups formed under the names of "Rifles," "Fusiliers," "Lancers" or "Cadets" and for a time drove criminals to cover. Some Mexican and Spanish Californians left for Baja California in 1854 to fight the *yanqui* filibuster, William Walker, who sought to "conquer" for the United States the still untenable peninsula. When the "grey-eyed man of destiny" was defeated—mostly by the bleak littoral—the renegades came north again, bringing friends to join the highway carnage and glut the jails.

Pressured by decent citizens, the State Legislature authorized the purchase of twenty acres at Point San Quentin, a lonely headland near the northern section of El Camino Real where it arched around San Pablo Bay not far from the ruins of Mission San Rafael. The state also bought the Gold Rush prison ship *Euphemia*—once operated so profitably by William Heath Davis—and anchored her off the point. Into the bunk-lined hold went three hundred convicts which relieved town jails and provided labor to build a brick prison.

Records of the prison under construction, from 1853 to 1860, show a predominately Latin population of highway murderers and rustlers. Americans and Europeans were incarcerated mostly for manslaughter or embezzlement. An occasional Oriental "made" the *Euphemia*—for tunneling under a street toward the basement of a bank; or for passing lead-filled twenty-dollar slugs which had been hollowed out by one of the ingenious Chinese circular sawmills. Negroes crossed with the law over knifings or theft, and one of them became San Quentin's first cook. Few Indians were committed since the law allowed that they could be taken from jail to work on bridges and highways; their principal crime was drunkenness and San Diego had set the pattern of punishment—a whipping over the old cannon, *El Capitán*, set muzzle down in the Plaza.

An emergency not anticipated by the state prison founders is described by the California writer, Miriam Allen DeFord:

> When prisoner No. 87 checked in a new problem arose for she was a woman, Agnes Reed, sentenced for aiding her husband to escape from jail in San Francisco. Within the next year five other women, three of them Mexicans, were added to the list. They bunked in the after cabin and were said to work as laundresses. Most of the women were in for grand larceny. The one half-Indian girl, Dolores Martinez, was serving a year sentence for manslaughter.[8]

Out of San Quentin came stories that every woman committed was forced into prostitution, that liquor flowed freely and that the authorities permitted open gambling. There were other tales of brutal guards who used bull whips and thumb screws, and of turn-keys beaten or strangled to death.

Marin County ranchers protested that their lives and property were endangered by fugitives who escaped at the rate of fifty a month before dungeons and cells had been completed. In 1851, and again in 1856, Vigilantes rode up the highway from Sausalito during those two periods of mass retribution against crime. But the San Quentin escapees did not linger in the Marin hills; most of them did not stop their flight until they had gained the sanctity of coast hideouts, many settling at Santa Barbara.

The channel city in the mid-fifties was headquarters of a new bandit lord, the handsome, hard-riding and suave Jack Powers who lifted brigandage to near-corporate heights and gained the title "The Devastating Angel of the King's Highway."

THE LION AMONG RATS

Jack Powers had first come to Santa Barbara as a sergeant in Stevenson's New York Volunteers and even before his discharge the best riders on the De la Guerra Rancho accounted him an exceptional horseman as well as an uncanny gambler. The dashing Powers won a $5,000 bet that he could ride 158 miles in 8 hours: his time, including 15 minutes of rest, was 6 hours, 43 minutes and 31 seconds. He used twenty-five mounts and ended with a characteristic flourish, galloping an extra mile to show the *vaqueros* he was far from exhausted.

After his regiment mustered out, Powers settled for a time in Los Angeles to gain more scope for his talents as gambler, horseman and politician. A newspaper reported that Jack "made many friends among the sporting men," adding the opinion that the moral worth of the company was "nothing to speak of."

Through the fifties Powers extended his influence. He became the friend of governors, the confidant of San Francisco underworld chiefs who rode in $4,000 Brewster coaches, and the ruler of Los Angeles' four hundred gamblers. Newcomers gawked at the dandy Powers, seen usually after dark with some overly pretty woman in crinoline on his arm, and were told that he was worth $250,000— in *cash*. Among the denizens of the tenderloin he carried himself, in the words of Major Bell, "like a lion walking among rats."

Some unrecorded change of luck, or whim, caused Jack to abandon the gambling dens of Los Angeles and set himself up in business as the "bandit lord" of the Coast Highway. He chose Santa Barbara as an ideal headquarters: gringos and the *hijo de pais* were at odds over land grants; juries could be bribed or plied with liquor; the topography of the country was exceptional for ambushes.

Powers was given a reluctant welcome because of his known connections with crooked office holders and went to work as a horse wrangler on the De la Guerra Rancho. He spent his free time circulating among the town's thirty-odd saloons to recruit Mexicans. A camp was set up in Montecito where robberies could be planned; picnickers were discouraged from using Tucker's Grove in nearby Franklin Canyon by bullies who started fights.

When the sheriff, Russell Heath, and his deputies began lurking around "headquarters" Powers leased the Arroyo Burro Rancho from Dr. Nicholas Den who soon regretted having taken in such a tenant. Extensive highway brigandage commenced between San Buenaventura and San Luis Obispo; many of the five hundred annual murders and robberies committed in California through the fifties originated at Arroyo Burro. And Jack Powers even swaggered into town flaunting his power.

The dapper bandit appeared to aid the notorious drunken street fighter, Patrick Dunn, late of Stevenson's Regiment, when the Irishman murdered a citizen who had merely refused to part with a hat. Witnesses were intimidated; Dunn was released. Growing lawlessness at Santa Barbara brought down the price of town lots to one dollar and prospective settlers avoided the channel shore. Business people advised Dr. Den to get rid of his undesirable tenant when the two-year lease expired; they formed a Vigilance Committee after Powers refused to leave Arroyo Burro.

Confronted by force, the bandit responded in terms of "squatter's rights" and backed his legal talk with elaborate preparations for a siege. Stocks of food, liquor and ammunition were hauled eight miles out of Santa Barbara; dancing girls and several musicians arrived from Los Angeles to insure high morale. When blood had been shed by both sides, and Judge Charles Fernald threatened to call in federal troops, Powers made a jaunty surrender; volunteers enlisted by the Vigilantes were treated to drinks.

Businessmen were forced to tolerate the arrogant but somehow always likable Powers until 1856 when they caught him without his usual alibi: that year he made the mistake of believing he could intimidate an honorable doctor. The indignant physician appeared before the authorities with a slug removed from what Powers had instructed him to regard as a boil.

Vigilantes announced that the slug had been fired from the gun of a defiant Basque sheepman who met death when a gang swooped down on his large flock grazing in Ventura County. Fifty citizens dressed in new white straw hats and red flannel shirts rode out of town to lynch the bandit lord. And Jack Powers rode out of California history, escaping to Mexico where he bought a ranch and settled down to a life of ease.

In the year of his forced departure from Santa Barbara Powers helped save the life of another fugitive from Vigilante justice, and that piece of ingenuity would be more resented than any murder or robbery credited to Jack. The man rescued from the committee was the notorious Judge Edward McGowan, under a Grand Jury indictment for complicity in the murder of the newspaper publisher James King of William, and on whose head rested a total of $15,000 in rewards.

THE UBIQUITOUS FUGITIVE

At lamplight on the evening of June 3, 1856, Ned McGowan, deposed judge and before that a Philadelphia cop, boldly left a house in San Francisco and shouldered his way through a crowd, unrecognized. His moustache and beard had been dyed with pomatum and shoe blackening; French stays held in the large paunch developed through years of good living; a wide brimmed hat and large overcoat, weighted by two derringers, completed the disguise. Undetected, Ned reached a hideaway provided for him by friends—a small house near Mission Dolores owned by "a pious old lady, a member of the Baptist church." [9]

Enemies of the Vigilantes—of whom there were far more than later popular history would acknowledge—began to circulate reports of Ned's presence at different spots while the flabby judge made preparations for an escape to Philadelphia via El Camino Real and Mexico.

For one month the fugitive's cohorts diverted the "law and order" men from the proposed escape route by reporting the quarry at points to the east and north; newspapers were soon jocularly referring to "Ubiquitous Ned" and chided the pursuers for being unable to run down the bloated judge who then carried 182 pounds of soft flesh on a smallish frame. Ned tried to reduce while he waited, eating plain food and taking gin instead of brandy.

McGowan was far from fit when he embarked on the perilous journey with James Dennison, the Halfmoon Bay butcher, and

Ramon Valencia who had charge of six horses. The ride almost ended in disaster the first night when Ned sustained a bad fall— after having stopped to have a few politically expedient glasses with William Shear, proprietor of the Nightingale Inn.

The stout fugitive suffered as the party kept to the rough hill country for the Bay Area towns were still unsafe, Vigilantes having spread the word of the large reward. Whenever a halt became imperative Ned assumed different disguises: Father Eduardo, an American priest gathering material for a book on the old missions; a retired magistrate traveling to Los Angeles; a cattle drover bound for Texas.

At San Luis Obispo a blacksmith recognized the former judge and the party rode day and night to gain the wilderness of the Santa Ynez mountains; Dennison would not halt even after his charge was again thrown and almost had an eye skewered by a sharp branch. When the cavalcade reached Refugio Rancho below Point Concepción late on July 3, 1856, after five hard days on the road, the fugitive dropped exhausted in the corral and fell asleep before he could remove his spurs.

Two days of heavy brandy drinking revived McGowan but impaired his sense of caution. He rode into Santa Barbara and was recognized before he had gulped a second drink in the Fond Hotel. Presently a dozen men were chasing him along the street. The dreaded cry "A lynching!" sobered Ned who backed to the wall and drew his derringers, believing that the end had come.

From out of the mob dashed Jack Powers. He hauled the quaking McGowan into an alley and shoved him through the door of an adobe house with orders to roll up in a large rug. Powers then led the mob on a false scent until dark when Ned escaped to the hills.

For the next month McGowan hid in the brush behind Mission Santa Barbara, coming near the highway only to scrounge food and brandy. The Vigilantes then at their crest sent a ship from San Francisco with irate bounty hunters; Captain Selim Woodworth, the former naval officer, had warrants issued at every southern town to cut off escape. But neither posses nor the hirelings of McGowan's political friends caught up with Ned until Jack Powers located him through one of his gang. The wanted man was taken to the house of Dr. Den who by that time had come to hate the moneylenders and land-thieves among the Vigilantes; the Irish physician may also have hoped for a favor from Sacramento.

During the ensuing eight months McGowan was in touch with his political organization. And he wrote letters to the San Francisco newspapers giving a Mexican address. In those letters of a clever politician the groundwork was laid for "a fair trial" away from the influence of the "stranglers."

The ubiquitous Ned, reduced by forty pounds, traveled the coast road again with a strong escort when his friends in Sacramento had arranged for a trial at Napa. After ten minutes' deliberation the jury there found him "not guilty" and he leveled his guns at the San Francisco Vigilance Committee. In a skillfully written book and a vitriolic newspaper, McGowan bitterly elaborated on the opinion expressed by the Sacramento *Union* June 2, 1857, regarding his trial:

> This case should teach the people of California the gross injustice, tyranny and cruelty of which masses of men may become guilty, when under excitement.[10]

Even the dullest of readers recognized Ned as a practical politician which in the fifties was almost without exception the equivalent to being a scoundrel. But if McGowan was an unwelcomed ally of those with real grievances against the Vigilantes he at least confined himself to the printed page and was in every way preferable to a butchering self-appointed champion who entered the lists in the autumn of 1856.

THE RUSTLERS' REVOLT

Twenty-two-year-old Juan Flores came out of solitary confinement at San Quentin at the time when McGowan's Sonora letters were appearing in the San Francisco *Bulletin*. He had been disciplined because he led a revolt soon after being sentenced on the charge of rustling in Southern California. Ranger Bell described the youthful desperado as being "young, lithe and graceful" with "the most cruel and vindictive eyes ever set in human head." [11]

Flores teamed up with crime-hardened Jim "Red Horse" Webster for a second and successful break out of San Quentin. They led a group of fellow convicts to overpower officers and men aboard a vessel discharging bricks at the prison. Slipping the anchor cable and making sail, the men proceeded to Contra Costa, beached the stolen craft and scattered.

Flores stole a horse and rode to San Luis Obispo where he gathered around him fifty men and told them of his plan to wrest California from "the gringo bastards" forever. It was decided that San Juan Capistrano would be headquarters because it commanded the San Diego to Los Angeles road and lay in a country being peopled by ranchers.

The only man in the gang that rode south who had not pledged himself to revolution was Andres Fontes; but that ex-convict held the esteem of Flores for he had sworn to kill Sheriff J. R. Barton—a blood oath grown strong since the time Fontes went to prison for defending the honor of a Mexican girl.

At Capistrano more outlaws joined Flores' revolution. Riders in groups of ten scoured the country stealing horses and exacting tribute from travelers and at ranch houses. When opposition flared up in Anaheim—a communal settlement of Germans—a hostage was dragged back to headquarters and shot—"for treason"—in the San Juan Plaza.

Anticipating retribution, Flores deployed his gang to set a trap. Sheriff Barton and ten men were ambushed and quickly cut down—Andres Fontes pumped bullets into the body of the sheriff from safe cover, then deserted the gang and headed for Baja California to enjoy his revenge until he met death at the hands of Solomon Pico. Flores and his followers gathered up the weapons and horses of the dead, letting it be known in Los Angeles that a new regime would soon begin.

The southern city responded with a new call for volunteers. All able-bodied men were issued arms; drills prepared those unfamiliar with the weapons; into the defenders ranks came sailors and skinners who had recently driven camels across the desert from Texas.

The Angelenos did not wait for an attack. Strong forces blocked off passes and swept down the cliffs of *arroyos* to rout and capture the main body of the Flores gang, including the leader.

When a lenient court began to free Mexican captives the Vigilantes rallied. The jail was broken into and the insurgent, or bandit, chief found himself being hustled to a scaffold. His last request—to be dressed in black coat and white trousers—was granted before the noose went around his neck on February 14, 1857. A clumsily-rigged plank caused the lynching to become a prolonged torture; many hurried away, sickened, before Juan Flores ceased his contortions.

MANHUNT

Flores, Powers, Murieta and Solomon Pico were followed by a dozen ambitious chiefs, each hoping to make his star shine brighter. Around campfires in the high fastness of the Sierra de Santa Lucia, and in abandoned adobe ruins off the southern highway, leaders who were called "The Avenger," "The Cock" and "José California," goaded the brethren of the road. Were they to be peons on the land of their ancestors? Let the once wealthy Californianos grovel in the reeking courts of the *yanqui*, sombrero in hand while they politely begged for crumbs from shysters, shylocks and bureaucrats, but not so the *vaquero*. How nice that Abraham Lincoln had returned the mission lands; how very noble were the land commissioners who could read no Spanish yet passed judgments on documents in that language! A much used thorn was John C. Frémont for the Pathfinder had returned to the land of his predilection— and the 10 million dollar La Mariposa holding which had caught his fancy while in government service before the conquest. Frémont had evicted Mexicans.

With revenge their sanction the Mexican bandits—and others of mixed nationality—waged highway war until the last *vengador*, Tiburcio Vasquez, was jerked aloft at San Jose. But that vain little man, with his unaccountable attraction for women, was not erased until the seventies. Like Narcisso Bojorques, the sadist, and Juan Soto, the maniacal half-breed Indian giant, Tiburcio was driven off the coast highway to inland killing territory before the end, even as his forebears had shunted Indians away from El Camino Real.

Posses usually rode down such men as Vasquez, Bartolo Sepulveda, Pancho Ruiz and a host of others; often Vigilantes took over, as in the case of Manuel Cerradel who was snatched from custody aboard a ship off San Pedro in 1863 and hung from a yardarm for the highway slaying of John Rains, popular son-in-law of Colonel Isaac Williams. But from the late fifties onward the law and order groups played second fiddle to the lone enforcer—the agent, detective and sheriff whose persistence located the criminal chiefs.

One of the better known of California's manhunters was Sheriff Harry N. Morse, relieved of his Alameda County duties in the heyday of brigandage and made a free agent. His orders to "clear the road" sent Morse into the Coast Range where he painstakingly collected information that led to the downfall of a dozen ruffians.

A dull man in speech and appearance, with the look about him of the plodder, Harry actually was as sharp, brave and resourceful as any legendary western hero. Some claim he was faster than any man who ever drew a gun.

Morse revealed his identity to few people while he ferreted out the lairs of highway gangs. He would leave messages of his whereabouts with such trusted friends as George Dutton, owner of the little hotel and stage station at Jolon, close to the ruins of Mission San Antonio. Occasionally he rode down to San Jose for a warrant or to organize a posse when he was ready to strike.

From the pages of his memoirs Harry emerges as a man whose sense of humor sometimes carried bravery to the brink of recklessness. He tells of one outlandish disguise he used going into the camp of an outlaw band:

> I wore an old pair of ragged pants, a gray woolen shirt, a great broad-brimmed hat that flopped about my ears like a dilapidated umbrella in a rainstorm. A pair of dark green goggles covered my eyes, and the lower part of my face was hidden by a long shaggy beard.[12]

Morse used no such "mail order detective" technique when he beat Narcisso Bojorques to the draw or put a bullet into the head of Juan Soto. Often he fought against odds; in any posse he rode well ahead. Fearlessness was never thought remarkable in men like Morse, and there were scores of them—James B. Hume and John N. Tucker, the Wells Fargo detectives; Sheriff Russell Heath of Santa Barbara who defied Jack Powers; Sheriff Barton who was shot down in ambush by the cowardly Fontes; Sheriff Don José De la Guerra, called *"El Chato,"* at San Luis Obispo.

California history would have a better memory for its desperados than for its lawmen. Murieta, Vasquez and Powers took on Robin Hood qualities while there seemed to be no "good" sheriffs of the caliber found in the fictionalized history of the mother lode, the "Badlands," and various locales "west of the Pecos." But the little-known lawmen of El Camino Real were too tough for the most notorious of the gun slingers who became legends.

Jesse James laid very low when he came to visit his uncle, D. W. James, who was part owner of Paso Robles Rancho. He did no more than carve his initials in the adobe of the Huer Huero ranch house. Bill Dalton, of the fabulous gang, had scarcely taken off his spurs for a night's rest on the Estrella, near San Miguel, when the Express detective Bill Smith made the territory too uncomfortable for any daring activity. And the Flower brothers, wanted in Missouri for bank robbery and murder, were routed from La Honda in the redwood country above Santa Cruz.

Sheriffs, special agents, Vigilantes and Rangers performed as well as any lawmen on that frontier road that was the Coast Highway in the fifties. Perfumed and painted women in towns, and gay señoritas riding sidesaddle, still carried little derringers in their bodices; gamblers and "dandies" were never without an Apache gun—a combination pistol, brass-knuckles and spring-dagger; and the strongest men toted a Smith & Wesson revolver. But those were unruly times even within the law: dueling was common and arguments were often settled on the street with firearms.

For the Pacific Coast even a rough semblance of law and order awaited a stronger tie to the urban East than ships and covered wagons. This came in '58 with the arrival of John Butterfield's Overland Mail.

Eight   The Coast Stages

BUTTERFIELD'S OVERLAND MAIL

In 1858 the hodgepodge of paths, trails and graded toll roads that followed the trace of El Camino Real was about to begin shaping up as a regular American turnpike. The pre-Civil War courting of western states had already started Jim Birch's "Jackass Mail" from San Diego to San Antonio, Texas; in September inaugural stagecoaches of Butterfield's Overland Mail were racing to the west and east along the "Ox-bow" route between St. Louis and San Francisco. The impact of those continental mails, especially the latter, would have a dramatic effect on the Coast Highway.

For ten years—since Kit Carson rode East with news of the conquest—Congress had turned a deaf ear on California demands for a railway, post road and pony express; every proposal was considered overly expensive, too hazardous or unnecessary. Growing secession talk loosened the government purse strings, first with the mule service, then a $600,000 annual mail contract for a semiweekly, six-horse coach to bring the Mississippi within twenty-five days of the Pacific. As an added inducement to remain in the Union the continental stages were scheduled to connect Los Angeles and San Francisco by way of the San Joaquin Valley, with a feeder line along the coast.

Much criticism attended the awarding of the mail contract to a syndicate of wealthy New York express and stage men headed by fifty-seven-year-old John Butterfield. To Southerners the bluff chief of Overland Mail—who had risen from stage driver to line superintendent of American Express—was "too thick" with such Yankees as William G. Fargo and Henry Wells. Northern politicians charged that Overland was breaking trail for a secessionist railroad. Unsuccessful bidders were quick to point out that Butterfield was a close personal friend of President James Buchanan.

On one point there was a general agreement—north, east, west and south: Overland Mail was doomed to be swallowed by the "Seven Deserts." A widely quoted Washington pamphlet predicted:

> Human ingenuity cannot devise a plan for such an unheard-of achievement. . . . It never has been done. It never will be done.[1]

Sharing that sentiment, San Francisco held only a perfunctory ceremony on September 15, 1858, when the eastbound stage rolled out toward El Camino Real and the Mississippi. Following coaches —with mail possibly destined for Apache or Comanche fires— aroused no great interest. But by the end of the first week in October bets were being laid. Butterfield's initial westbound stage was due no later than eight-thirty on the morning of the 10th. Shipping people from Montgomery Street covered all wagers on the Overland Mail; they also offered attractive odds that mail which left St. Louis at the same time as the stage—to go east by rail and via Panama steamer to the Golden Gate—would be received first.

Since the transcontinental telegraph and Pony Express did not start until 1861, gamblers had no way of knowing that the delayed westbound stage reached Fort Yuma on the California border twenty-seven hours and fifteen minutes late. Time was gained, then lost, dipping into Mexico and pushing north through a dozen stations into Los Angeles where the sixth mail out of San Francisco had just arrived.

Leaving the new brick depot at Los Angeles it seemed certain that Overland Mail had little chance of getting back on schedule. At Fort Tejon the lag remained almost a full day but the stage, traveling at nine and sometimes fifteen miles an hour, gained steadily. At Firebaugh's Ferry, twenty miles from Gilroy on the Coast Highway, six hours still remained to be made up.

The only passenger aboard on the 2,800-mile journey was young Waterman L. Ormsby, special correspondent for the New York *Herald*, whose dispatches gave a detailed account of the race against contract time together with bits of human interest. At Gilroy Ormsby and the driver gulped supper and answered questions: "Have you got the States mail?" "Meet any Injuns?" "What, slept in the wagons?"

The stage tore along through the night, neither driver nor passenger mentioning the common thought that even a minor accident would disappoint their backers. At one o'clock in the morning, almost on schedule, the driver reined up in San Jose, blowing with vigor on the coach horn. The *Telegraph* reported that "People were aroused by the unusual noise at such an hour." [2]

In his diary entry for Sunday, October 10, Ormsby wrote that the city of San Francisco hove in sight over the hills just after sunrise. He perched on the box with the driver, referring frequently to his timepiece:

> Soon we struck the pavements, and, with a whip, crack, and bound, shot through the streets to our destination. . . . Swiftly we whirled up one street and down another, and round the corners, until finally we drew up at the stage office in front of the Plaza. [3]

The time was 7:30 A.M., beating the announced schedule by one hour! Actually the scheduled—and betting—time gave Butterfield one day of leeway. The time from St. Louis was 23 days, 23 hours and 30 minutes. The competing mail steamer did not dock for another six days!

In the flourishing style of the day the San Francisco *Bulletin* reported the enthusiasm that greeted the stage:

> As the coach dashed along through the crowds the hats of the spectators were whirled in the air and the hurrah was repeated from a thousand throats responsive to which the driver, the Lion of the occasion, doffed his weather-beaten old slouch and in uncovered dignity, like the victor of an Olympic race, guided his foaming steeds towards the Post Office.[4]

The *Bulletin* covered a mass meeting the following night at the Music Hall—the largest ever held in San Francisco—where speakers hailed "a new epoch" and "the end of the steamship monopoly." Newspapers made light of the joggling and bouncing aboard the stage; the long journey was even called "a health restorer." Ormsby, traveling on a pass and being a healthy and adventurous twenty-four years of age, was able to ignore various hardships:

> To many Americans who travel for pleasure this route will be a favorite. Relieved from all danger of seasickness and the dull monotony of a sea voyage, they can travel by comfortable stages, stopping at such interesting points as they may choose for rest . . .[5]

Frightening stories that came from the Ox-bow trail—Indian massacres, the burning of stations and a man gone insane from lack of sleep—did not dissuade prospective passengers; soon Overland had a waiting list. When the stages began arriving either on or ahead of time express companies and correspondents favored them over the steamers: the Christmas mail out of Los Angeles in '59 included 10,000 letters sent by a single coach.

The remarkable continental line set an example for future Coast staging. To handle the Pacific operation Overland had hired as superintendents the most able men. Marcus L. Kenyon, a New York partner, had under him such Western stagecoach veterans as Warren F. Hall, once a famous "whip"-driver; and Charles McLaughlin, California's best known stageman.

It had taken about one year to set up relay stations and regular scheduled stops across the wilderness terrain. To the 750 conductors, agents, drivers and employees who cared for 1,500 animals and kept one hundred coaches rolling, Butterfield issued a list of "Special Instructions" for operation. The first of nineteen items stressed time which was the essence of stagecoaching:

> Have teams harnessed in ample time, and ready to proceed without delay or confusion. Where the coaches are changed, have the teams hitched to them in time. Teams should be hitched together and led to and from the stable to the coach, so that no delay can occur by their running away. All employes will assist the Driver in watering and changing teams in all cases, to save time.[6]

Butterfield first used coaches made by James Gould who also designed the light thorough-brace "Celerity Wagon" which was hitched to teams on rough stretches of the route. Eaton, Gilbert, builder of the rugged *diligencias generales* for Mexican roads, supplied other vehicles but most famous of all was Abbott, Downing and Company's "Concord Coach," a $1,050 vehicle that seated twelve travelers inside and came equipped with leather boot, deck seat, brake, lamps and ornamental sides.

The stage hauled five hundred pounds of mail in addition to a bag of newspapers and up to forty pounds of baggage for each passenger, who paid one hundred dollars to make the continental trip, and a varying fare between San Francisco and Los Angeles. The baggage allowance cut unnecessary gear to a minimum; it had to include warm and light clothing for almost one month plus emergency rations and cooking utensils if the traveler exercised the option of preparing meals. But Overland passengers were permitted to carry rifles, revolvers, Bowie knives and spare cartridges in case of Indian attack.

FEEDER LINES

Months before the arrival of the first continental stage Marcus Kenyon had set up stations, bought horses and hired help. With

McLaughlin and Hall he went over the route from Warner's Ranch to San Francisco by way of the San Joaquin Valley and again via the ocean highway.

A temporary horse mail offered competition to the San Antonio–San Diego mule line. Los Angeles and Santa Barbara were persuaded to vote a joint indebtedness of $15,000 to grade and fill some seventy-five miles of bad road between them; Santa Barbara County was urged to spend another $30,000 on a passage through the Santa Ynez and San Rafael mountains into the valley of the Santa Maria River that led to San Luis Obispo.

Kenyon and his aides stopped at free-lunch saloons, billiard parlors and taverns. They urged that bridges be built to replace ferries, that bogs be laid over with logs, rocks and earth. At the "mile" houses—inns that took their names from rough estimates of the distance to some town—the Overland representatives sold the "stagecoach era." They told of New England "one-horse" towns that had mushroomed; of plush-lined coaches that would be patronized by women; and offered figures to prove that prosperity followed the stage. In the more populated north the San Bruno Turnpike Company was hired to smooth the San Francisco–San Jose Highway, cutting down the number of stages, or relay stops, for the through mail.

Along the improved pike farmers' houses and abandoned inns of Gold Rush days spruced up to vie for Overland trade. At San Jose, a city of 3,000, Abe Beatty's hotel and stables became the exchange point from Concord Coach to Celerity Wagon; Mountain View had James Campbell's inn; Redwood City the Grand Hotel under John Crowley; San Mateo the tavern whose heavy oak framing had come round Cape Horn in '49. Then there was the 17-Mile House at Millbrea and John Cumming's place twelve miles from Portsmouth Plaza.

The old Plaza was the terminus for a dozen new lines of stages and omnibuses during the first year of Overland service—feeders from Sonoma, Napa, San Rafael, the Sausalito and Contra Costa ferries, and coast villages down to Halfmoon Bay. There were also local coaches to San Jose over the oldest route in California.

Since '49 there had been one or more stage companies whose owners were among the renowned whips of the time: Jim Birch, Warren Hall, Jared B. Crandall, John Dillon and, earliest of all, John Whistman. Small outfits changed hands, consolidated, and were finally absorbed by the monopolistic California Stage Company which in its turn was pushed off the peninsula and coast by Charley McLaughlin who came to own all or large parts of every San Francisco stage. One of his properties feeding to north Monterey Bay was advertised that year in the *Bulletin*:

> STAGE NOTICE—To and From San Francisco and Santa Cruz in Twelve Hours! McLaughlin & Co's. Stages are now running DAILY as above and are enabled, owing to the completion of the San Bruno Turnpike and Santa Cruz Mountain Road, to make the following quick time—
>
> San Francisco—depart 8:00 A.M.
> Monterey   —arrive   7:30 P.M.[7]

So well-known was the name McLaughlin, that Overland Mail retained it after buying a half interest in his Coast Line. Kenyon made that arrangement sixty days before the first Butterfield stage came in from St. Louis and offered a tri-weekly service south out of the continental junction at Gilroy.

SIX-HORSE CLIPPERS

The one-time hamlet of Gilroy, founded by the pioneer sailor who adopted the name after deserting his ship, stood as forceful evidence of what the stagecoach could do to a town. By 1859, when Overland completed a large office and stables, the population had risen to more than six hundred residents; on mail days many more came in from Santa Clara Valley farms and ranches to shop at half a dozen stores or drink and play pool in J. Houck's hotel.

Children from three schools were excused to meet the stage and ran alongside with their barking dogs from the outskirts of town to the depot. Boys hung around the stables and the depot to pick up bits of lore. They spoke knowledgeably of *off leaders, near swing horses* and *wheelers* with much the same pride as youngsters on the San Francisco waterfront who learned to name properly the ropes and spars of the three-skysail clipper ships that captured the imagination of the world in the fifties.

From heyday to sad decline the stagecoach and the sailing ship shared a common effect on people—both spectators who enthused over their personalities, records and arrivals, and the men who sailed or drove with such skill. Like the old salt, able to cast a lanyard knot in stiff four-stranded hemp and set a course by picking out a star "a point to wind'ard of the main t'bowlin'," the stage driver maintained great pride that took exception to ignorance of his profession. Captain William Banning, a great California driver, set down the attitude with the aid of his nephew:

> The word coachman does not exist properly in the West-American stage-coach world. It was used only by a few passengers, usually foreigners, who didn't know any better. A stage driver, though he could tolerate the affectionate or poetic expressions of "Jehu," "whip," "whipster," "Charlie," "knight of the ribbons," etc., could accept the appellation of coachman no more than he could accept a "tip." [8]

The rank of admiral came ashore in '59 when the tobacco-chewing whittlers on the verandah of Gilroy's hotel spoke with respect of "Admiral" John Butterfield, the genial worker of the continental miracle that had rejuvenated their town. Not only had Butterfield brought prosperity but his stages provided some of the best stories ever heard along the coast; there was never any telling what exciting or gruesome tale would come in with the next mail.

Passengers on one stage told of being held up for almost half a day by six hundred Comanches in warpaint. Instead of being massacred they were made to stand in the sun while each brave in turn made a careful examination of pole, couplings, trappings, box and seats of what the Indians called the "swift wagon."

In the first year there came other reports that were without humor: travelers had found the remains of an emigrant party burned alive; the personnel of one remote Texas station was found staked out on the plains, ripped to pieces by coyotes; William Willis, conductor of a westbound stage, took the reins when a band of fifty Apaches attacked and put an arrow through the driver; Willis miraculously reached Tucson.

Dr. J. C. Tucker of San Francisco entertained listeners at Los Angeles, Gilroy and San Jose with snatches of a violent romance that commenced and ended on the westbound. The stage picked up a party of French gamblers—two men and two women. One of the men kept a jealous eye on the younger woman whom the doctor described as "handsome with bright, black eyes, evidently fresh from some rural province in France." Trouble commenced when the coach was boarded by "a tall young fellow in boots and buckskins, bound for his ranch in Texas." [9]

The flirtation between the girl and the Texan led to a duel with pistols in which the American received a shattered wrist and the Frenchman was shot dead. The girl and couple were left behind to bury their companion while the stage raced on to make up time.

More women used the stage once Admiral Butterfield's fame had spread. Gossips gathered at the stage depots to stare at an occasional tired mother carrying a baby, young wives come out to join husbands, school marms, or some lady of questionable occupation headed for the *café chantants* of Los Angeles and San Jose, or San Francisco's new Barbary Coast.

At the Gilroy junction loafers now and then were rewarded by a look at celebrities—such personages as the cigar-smoking, spider dancer Lola Montez, and the Reverend Thomas Starr King, then intent on saving California for the Union.

So firm a hold did the Overland Mail take that merchants in San Francisco and Los Angeles sold "overland hats," "overland boots" and "overland coats." Swing stations offered "overland eggs" and inns had "overland chickens" on their menus. Perambulators with the lines of a stagecoach came on the market along with toy horns and whips.

Butterfield brought Overland Mail to its peak of efficiency by 1860 and had laid the groundwork for the coast stage route. Then, on April 14th, the first Pony Express raced into San Francisco, 10½ days from St. Joseph, Missouri. Postage was five dollars per one-half ounce and the ponies offered no competition to passenger carriers, but John Butterfield wanted to beat them at their own game—running saddle horses over his southern route where he had a complete string of relay stations. When recently acquired partners balked, the Admiral resigned to continue staging farther north and east.

The Pony Express to San Francisco, and another between Arkansas and Los Angeles, were put out of business in November of '61 by the overland telegraph. Stagemen scoffed at the telegraph —and the rails that crept westward in its wake—much as deep-water sailors had ridiculed the early steamships. Those romanticists of the whip and long splice were no more correct than California Indians who mistook countless telegraph poles for great crosses that signified a mass conversion of Americans to the Catholic faith.

The secession of Arkansas and Texas near the start of the Civil War brought guerrilla warfare to the southwestern trail and ended the southern transcontinental stage. On March 2, 1861, Congress ordered rolling stock sent north to operate on a new Overland Mail line under Ben "King" Holliday.

Overland Mail's coast line had already passed into control of the partners who forced Butterfield to retire. These were his old associates in American Express—one of them an early member of Overland—whose names together symbolized the very essence of the West: *Wells Fargo*.

"BY GOD & BY WELLS FARGO!"

Henry Wells and William G. Fargo, backed by Eastern capitalists with political connections, launched their express and banking business at the height of the Gold Rush. They weathered "the great express panic" of 1855 that ruined the big competitors, Adams,

Page, and Bacon, took business away from the Government Post Office, and before the close of the fifties had shipped $58 million in gold on California stage lines alone. Fast, dependable service along the best routes, and a policy of promptly paying loss claims, made Wells Fargo the most popular institution in the West.

Until 1859 Wells Fargo paid heavy charges to lease space for its messengers, sacks and chests, but that year, when the tremendous rush started to the Comstock mines in Nevada, it purchased the Pioneer Stage Company. In 1860 a controlling interest was bought in the Pony Express which had ruled out John Butterfield's scheme to compete when Wells Fargo took command of Overland. What was left of that line—the coast division—soon felt the effect of a vigorous enterprise whose gross annual profits were $250,000 and whose stockholders received eighteen per cent a year on their investment.

At sixteen main stops along the Coast Highway, Wells Fargo became even more famous than Overland. People gathered around the iron-shuttered express offices to read the daily list naming those for whom mail was being held; they patronized the green Wells Fargo mail boxes in preference to the government's red ones, using the inexpensive "franked envelopes," stamped and imprinted: *Paid, Wells Fargo & Company over our California and Coast routes.*

Anyone with a loss claim knew he would receive "cash on the barrelhead" and that almost any kind of shipment—from iced oysters to diamond bracelets—could be arranged without red tape. Agents frequented the saloons and billiard parlors as well as the churches; Indians, Negroes, Chinese and Anglo-Saxons received the same treatment. Pride in its reputation for speed and reliability kept Wells Fargo from ever slipping to the level of the Government Post Office service which the *California Chronicle* called "proverbially slow and uncertain" and guilty of "provoking delays." [10]

Lucius Beebe and Charles Clegg, those unique historians of the West, have set down an embracing definition of the powerful express:

Wells Fargo, too, was an empire, a vast domain of wealth and wealthy properties, of gold and coaches and horses, of banks and bullion vaults and stagehouses and, above all else, of the elimination, or at least of the abatement of time and distance.[11]

Speed of stagecoaches increased over better roads as Wells Fargo continued the prodding started by Butterfield superintendents. In April of 1861 a cannon boomed and gaily dressed townspeople gathered at Santa Barbara to welcome the first up stage over the new Los Angeles road. A larger crowd was on hand when the down stage came in from San Luis Obispo for the channel city was proud of the trail through Gaviota Pass and over the Santa Ynez mountains. That road even met with the approval of Professor William Brewer, the Yale scientist who was inclined to find a great deal of fault with California during his travels in the sixties. On April 7th he noted in his diary that the highway was "well engineered, built over and along high hills and through deep canyons at great expense and labor."

At the new stage stops of Santa Barbara and San Buenaventura, Wells Fargo tacked up reward posters on recent robberies near Virginia City, thinking fugitives might not have heard that Jack Powers no longer held sway along the channel coast. The only culprits the sheriff sought at the time were some boys under ten years of age who had broken into the Presidio church and carried off organ pipes to play in the woods, together with violins they gave to musicians at a saloon. Stagecoach holdups around Santa Barbara and elsewhere on the highway did not come until the seventies.

South and north of the pivotal depot at Santa Barbara stagemen yarned with Wells Fargo agents. Big A. L. Seeley planned to run a line up from San Diego when the end of the Jackass Mail left that town stranded. Phineas Banning wanted to improve the Wilmington–Los Angeles route where Dana, returned to California for a visit twenty-four years after his hide-droving voyage, rode the box of a coach drawn by "six little less than wild California horses." [12]

Over the Parajo River that emptied into mid-Monterey Bay a four-thousand-dollar toll bridge did away with uncertain fording. Since the opening of the Comstock, toll bridges and roads had become popular and gatekeepers day-dreamed about tending something like the Folsom to Carson Valley gate which collected $3 million in 1862.

Settlers discouraged by the dreary rains of Oregon and Washington reached the newly-opened Wells Fargo stations at Sonoma, Santa Rosa and San Rafael to hear talk of secession, the Comstock, public land and local gossip. At Petaluma they boarded Charlie Minturn's horse-drawn railcar for the down slough trip to Haystack Landing where steamboats plied to San Francisco.

With provincial pride the people of the trail erected signs— "Eat at Thompson's," "Dine with O'Farrell," and bragged of having entertained Rhodolphus Hall, the "New Hampshire Minstrel," when the champion bugler of America made the circuit of El Camino Real. The pot-bellied, likeable Hall played "Home, Sweet Home" and "The Last Rose of Summer" on the trumpet, accompanied by the tin whistle of his wife Katie.

The point of view of what people then called "croakers" was recorded by Professor Brewer:

> I find it hard to realize that I am in America—in the United States, the young vigorous republic as we call her—when I see these ruins [*the missions*]. They carry me back again to the Old World with its decline and decay, with its histories of war and blood and strife and desolation. . . .

At the time Brewer was setting down those notes the vigorous republic had commenced its devastating War between the States. In April of 1861 Abraham Lincoln used the new telegraph to send his call for volunteers. Thereafter people waited for San Francisco papers that carried Civil War battle reports.

By 1862, when the first of California's five hundred combat-bound volunteers sailed to join the Massachusetts Cavalry, fund raisers, politicians and recruiters rode the stages. Warnings were issued that Southerners and their sympathizers had formed a secret society to take over the state. Confederate raiders were said to be lurking off the coast, in wait for Panama steamers on which Wells Fargo was transporting Comstock bullion.

To Indians and Mexicans over sixty-five years of age the Civil War, with its rumors, alarms and saloon fights, followed a pattern grown familiar since the days when they had awaited attack from the Russians. Again no enemy hove in sight but more than three hundred volunteers fell in twenty-three bloody battles.

Along with the numerically small contribution to battlefield slaughter California sent express shipments of about $1,250,000 in gold. War underwriting, business banking and silver cargoes from the Comstock saw Wells Fargo's San Francisco office handling 3,000 pounds of treasure every day; before the assassination of President Lincoln directors were wealthy men and even superintendents could afford to splurge.

By the end of the sixties Wells Fargo had spread its net over virtually every stage and express service west of the Mississippi, gobbling small operators and in 1866 all of Ben Holliday's lines. But no monopoly had so endeared itself to the public; the expostulation "By God & by Wells Fargo!" held more the warmth of good feeling than of humor.

The express giant was so mighty in post–Civil War days that it could remain aloof from land shuffling, a terrible drought in Southern California, and the westward crawl of the railroad. With the over-confidence of too great power the directors of the original company assumed that any landowner provided customers, and that railroads in the West meant another mode of transportation which as a matter of course would come under the protecting wing of Wells Fargo. A sad surprise for those financiers was in the offing.

THE DUST-CHOKED ROUTE

The important-looking former Sacramento grocer, Governor Leland Stanford, officiated at ground-breaking ceremonies in 1862 that began the titanic struggle to lay rails across the high Sierra.

A preview of what transcontinental trains would do to California came two years later when the state's first railroad opened between San Francisco and San Jose.

Numerous "misunderstandings" and "differences of opinion" arose over right-of-way land in the path of the rails; real estate boomed and speculators at San Jose anticipated a great splurge of travel by building new hotels, including the $150,000 Anzerais House which was called "California's Best." The little San Francisco–to–Alviso steamboat that connected by coach with San Jose laid up. The fate of the fifteen-year-old stagecoach route was plain in an issue of the *Alta California:*

> Staging Outfits for sale—California
> Stage Company—
>> 25 Concord coaches
>> 25 11-passenger wagons
>> 25 14-passenger wagons
>> 30 sets, four-horse harnesses
> A complete set of blacksmith and wood
> worker's coach making tools. Saddlers'
> and Ironers' tools
>> *Cheap* [13]

While the San Francisco Bay Area talked of progress in terms of railroads from 1862 to 1864 Southern California thought only of survival: in those years the most devastating drought of its history blighted the land from the Salinas Valley to the Mexican border.

Instead of steady and heavy rains that were counted on during the winter months, Southern California received only four inches in two years! The cold statistics of what resulted were startling and tragic: on a drive of 1,500 cattle from Cuyama toward water at San Julian only 36 head survived; out of 300,000 head on the Santa Barbara County assessor's books 295,000 perished—98 out of every 100 animals! Visitors at the springs of Paso del Robles in 1864 saw famished cows crowd around the hotel verandah to devour old mats in which Chinese rice had been shipped.

South of Los Angeles only the highway town of Anaheim remained green, because of its irrigation system. In his memoirs Harriss Newmark, a Los Angeles merchant, described the cruel scene at
the German settlement where horses, sheep and cows lay dead:

> Thither the lean and thirsty cattle came by thousands, rushing in
> their feverish state against the great willow fence.... The Anaheim
> people were summoned to defend their homes and property and
> finally they had to place a mounted guard outside the willow en-
> closures.[14]

In April of '64 the Los Angeles *Semi-Weekly News* told sub-
scribers that "nothing can save what few cattle remain on the desert
California ranches." [15] In the county—with a $2 million assess-
ment—not one cent of taxes was collected. Merchants refused to
extend credit; notes bearing heavy interest were peddled for pennies; moneylenders moved in on hapless rancheros.

Louis Schlesinger and Hyman Tishler foreclosed on the Ri-
cardo Vejar property near Los Angeles; Able Sterns mortgaged his
26,000-acre *Los Alamitos* to Michael Reese of San Francisco for a
paltry sum; a four-thousand-acre slice of *Rancho San Pedro* went
for thirty-five cents an acre to speculators who sold parcels at five
dollars an acre to a church organization pledged to teetotalism.

For many *hijo de pais* the whim of weather was a final blow
in the battering that had been given him throughout thirteen years
by United States courts and their accredited hangers-on, the lawyers. In the words of the historian Bancroft the *Californianos* "were
virtually robbed by the Government that was bound to protect
them." [16]

LAND GRABBERS

In 1851 a board of three commissioners appointed by the President
commenced taking testimony from holders of Mexican and Spanish
land grants, most of which lay along El Camino Real. To their
astonishment the rancheros learned it was up to them to prove
ownership of family lands. And they must present a proper docu-

ment to define boundaries—not the kind of description previously found adequate: "from the highest ridge of the mountain to the sea, and one day's ride north and south." [17]

Rancheros who spoke no English were taken in hand by shyster lawyers, loan sharks, and crafty speculators, to be charged outlandish fees, taken in land and cattle. Owners of valid titles went before a succession of bureaucratic courts. Moneylenders advanced sums to pay the lawyers, at exorbitant interests, then pounced on the land.

The author Cameron Rogers, whose forebears were early residents of Santa Barbara, summed up the judgment of later generations:

> California wrote no blacker page in her history than that which records this shameful business unless it be one which deals with her treatment of her Indians. [18]

Stripped of land, homes and even possessions women sought work in towns; *hidalgos* hired out as *vaqueros*, sometimes on the very land stolen from them; proud old Castilians were known to die of starvation. When Mexican grants did get clearance from the courts owners found themselves overrun by squatters, many being shiftless migrants from the southwest. Those drifting families were called Pikes—whether they came from Pikes County, Missouri, or some other southern state. Pike had the same derogatory inference as the deep South's "white trash."

Squatters, and earnest settlers who believed they had located on public land, came into the legal maw but often they fought back: at San Jose in the sixties one thousand angry homesteaders defied a notice evicting them from houses along the highway and stormed the city, dragging along a cannon; in Ventura County Thomas More, who had in good faith bought *Rancho Sespe*, was murdered by a squatter gang in the seventies. Men hired out as squatters and groups formed associations such as "The Squatters League of Monterey."

The tough league opposed a notorious Monterey moneylender

named David Jacks who had grown wealthy since '51 by snatching virtually all the land around the first capital. When a court ruled that squatters on the Chualar grant—which he foreclosed—held just claims, the League wrote Jacks calling him to task for the expense he had caused:

> Now if you don't make that account of damage to each and every one of those settlers within ten days, you son of a bitch, we will suspend your animation between daylight and hell.[19]

Robert Louis Stevenson who was visiting at Monterey wrote of Jacks:

> ...the man is hated with a great hatred. His life has been repeatedly in danger. Not very long ago I was told the stage was stopped and examined three evenings in succession by disguised horsemen thirsting for his blood.[20]

THE OCTOPUS

Behind the vicious land-grabbing that generated so much hatred and misery lay speculators' plans to reap huge profits once the Southern Pacific Railroad pushed south from San Jose to San Diego. Big operators, the few remaining rancheros, squatters and even men with single highway plots grew excited as railroad surveyors looked over the route; when estimators appeared to count stage passengers and gauge cargo hauled in wagons, property owners felt certain they stood in the path of prosperity. Lot prices in Santa Barbara jumped to $5,000; roadside land previously sold for 75 cents an acre was on the market for $100. Then the bubble of hope burst.

To California in 1869, with the completion of the transcontinental railroad, came the corporate monster soon to be known as "The Octopus"—the Southern Pacific which was controlled by a quartet of former Sacramento shopkeepers, "The Big Four."

Coast highway towns and individuals hoping to fatten on the largesse of the railroad were among the first to learn that the Big

Four—Collis P. Huntington, Leland Stanford, Mark Hopkins and Charles Crocker—expected to receive, not give, when their rails served any area. Instead of building down the coast Southern Pacific announced it would follow the route of Butterfield's first stages through the San Joaquin Valley. Civic leaders joined speculators in a howl of protest. The State Legislature approved the decision of the railroad and the government hurried to present the Big Four with 7,500,000 acres of free valley land.

Southern Pacific bought newspapers, state legislators, congressmen and judges to facilitate the absorption of all transportation in the West and that included the mighty firm of Wells Fargo. Top echelon railroad financiers arranged the coup by stock manipulation and use of a front express concern. Caught in a stranglehold, Wells Fargo directors surrendered and were replaced by railroad men at whose head was the Kentucky gentleman, Lloyd Tevis, the man who would sell John D. Rockefeller the Great Anaconda Copper Mine for $10 million.

Staging along the coast highway steadily began to shrink in extent as Southern Pacific laid rails or forced independently-built roads to join its unpopular family. When the Iron Horse reached Gilroy, Soledad and San Luis Obispo, those towns in their turn became the northernmost terminals of the stage on the through road.

The historian Zoeth Skinner Eldredge described the rapine process of the many-tentacled combine:

> The sinister influence of the railroad was all over. It controlled judges; it owned legislatures; it invaded the halls of Congress and sought to undermine the very foundations of government and society... this creature, generated and nourished by the people, grew and became so powerful that it pervaded all, crushed all opposition, and laid a heavy hand upon the industry of the State.[21]

THE SAN JUAN EXPRESS

Because the mighty railroad was not at first interested in crumbs to be swept up along the coast south of Monterey, staging flourished for almost a decade at the common man's level of competitive enterprise. The West's most skillful Jehus came to hold the ribbons and shout "Hoop-La" at blacks and bays of seven stagecoach lines that made San Juan Bautista the last great hub of the Concords.

More than seven hundred people lived close to San Juan which lay forty miles from Monterey, on the Coast Highway at the foot of Mount Gabilan where Frémont had prematurely raised the American flag in 1846. Valley sheepherders and fruit farmers came in to the Wells Fargo office or the barroom of the Plaza Hotel, the famous two-story inn built over the Spanish barracks. Drummers from San Francisco, Los Angeles and the East—smoking "two-fer" cigars—stayed over at San Juan and hired buggies from the big hotel stable to make day-long selling trips through the valley and over to the coast. Gypsies and circuses pitched camp across the spacious plaza near the ruins of what had once been the largest of the Franciscan missions.

Owner of the Plaza was Angelo Zanetta, who had come from New Orleans in the Gold Rush, leaving a job as chef at the St. Charles. He put his stake into a small taproom that expanded with the stages and built up a reputation among gourmets for his Italian and French cooking—and his specialty, which was beefsteak smothered in onions. The demand for his meals became so heavy that Angelo retired to the kitchen and left innkeeping to a partner with the reassuring name, John Comfort.

The stage companies that picked up and deposited passengers at the Plaza were led by the Coast Line which Amasa Bixby and Benjamin Flint operated after the coming of the railroad. With forty new Concord coaches purchased from Wells Fargo the "San Juan Express," as it was known, hauled the bulk of mail and through travelers to San Diego.

Up and down the line in those dying years of the stage, outfits could hire such men as John Waugh and Jim Meyers out of San Luis Obispo; Dave Berry at Santa Barbara; Bill Sproul, William Banning and John J. Reynolds from Los Angeles. And for their $125 a month, and keep, those whips drove the one ton Concord

165

coach at ten miles an hour over the frightening ledges at Cuesta, Santa Ynez and Torrey Pinos as well as through pounding surf below Santa Barbara. The spirited teams were trained not to stop on flat ground, so at places like Foxen's Rancho Station that served the Santa Ynez Valley, stages and teams would tear around in a 200-yard circle for half an hour while passengers ate and mail was sorted.

Handling the horses was an art that had reached perfection by the mid-seventies. Captain Banning tells of the intricate exercises practiced by Reynolds in his youth and offers a little exercise for the automobile driver to test himself against the likes of old John J.

> ... flatten out both hands, fingers together, then suddenly command a certain two fingers of one hand and a different two of the other to spread—to do so simultaneously and immediately without affecting the other members.[22]

With his great skill handling the ribbons Reynolds—who ended his career as a hack driver in Los Angeles—was a courtly, good-looking man who swore infrequently and never drank whiskey. He told Major Ben C. Truman: "I delighted in fast driving and in making myself solid with the ladies." [23]

An opposite to Reynolds in manners was Charlie Parkhurst who out-swore, out-drank and out-chewed even the Monterey whalers. Loud on the box and at Santa Cruz elections, with unpredictable spells of gentleness, Charlie presented a fearsome appearance, with a patch covering one eye that had been blinded by the kick of a horse.

What gave Charlie enduring fame among whips was the startling news that came after death: Charlie was a woman! She had also been a mother and the first woman to vote in California—by almost half a century.

Far more gentlemanly in every way were drivers of the San Juan Express, especially the Jehus in dark, form-fitting clothes and cream-colored felt hats who handled the reins of the "Great Eastern" and "Great Western." Those crack coaches maintained a rough decorum, and before departure from San Juan passengers read advice clipped from the Omaha *Herald* and tacked up along-side Wells Fargo's WANTED posters:

> Onboard the stage a lady never speaks unless spoken to—properly.
>
> The best seat inside a stage is the one next to the driver. Don't let any sly elph [*sic*] trade you his midseat.
>
> Don't keep the stage waiting. Don't smoke a strong pipe inside the coach. Spit on the leeward side. If you have anything to drink in a bottle pass it around.[24]

THE ROUGH ROAD

For their nine cents a mile stagecoach passengers of the seventies and eighties still traveled a rough road, for at nineteen stops to San Diego only a few inns approached the Plaza's cuisine and comfortable feather beds. One of those was Shepard's Inn at Carpinteria, run by the Iowa farmer James Erwin Shepard, where many celebrities signed the guest book; another notable hostelry was opened at New Town, San Diego, by Captain S. S. Dunnells. New Town had been founded by Alonzo Erastus Horton, the San Francisco furniture dealer, whose $267 investment would one day be valued at $2 million.

Most travelers were glad to get clear of Los Angeles after buying an ice cream or tamale at the depot from old Nicholás Martínez, for there was no end of trouble at that slow-growing shantytown. In one of the early uprisings against the Chinese, whom the Big Four imported as cheap labor for railroad building, twenty-five of the Orientals had been massacred. And the town already was suffering from a condition that would later be blamed on automobiles and factories. A San Francisco newspaperman was pleased to write that "the atmosphere is so filled with smoke as to confine the vision within a small circumference." [25]

People expected little at the American Hotel in San Buenaventura or J. B. Butchart's Caladonia House in San Miguel; they were glad for only a short stop at Capistrano with its Chinese vendors, gamblers and drunken Indians. The posted advice to travelers read: "Don't imagine for a moment that you are going on a picnic."

Passengers were made aware of the unpicnic-like character of almost any trip long before they reached a station. Good roads had been built, and rebuilt, but never fast enough to keep up with rains and the damage caused by such vehicles as the twenty-ton wagons hauled by forty mules—the "jerk-line" teams. Stage companies agitated for a government road from San Juan to Los Angeles that would improve on what could be done with the two dollar head tax and periodical bond issues of state maintenance.

Since the stage road was not a railroad, little could be accomplished. In wet weather a horseman accompanied the coach with a shovel to clean mud from the wheels; time was lost on winding country roads that were too narrow to let six horses pass some covered wagon. In 1874 the Santa Barbara down stage was forced to wait in February rain while a line of prairie schooners lumbered past with 150 Campbellites who had been eight months on the trail from Missouri.

The road above San Buenaventura was literally a sore spot. In the seventies Josephine Clifford crossed it at a bad time:

> ... the rest of the night was passed inside the stage though of sleep there was no thought, such jolting and jumping over rocks and boulders; I ache all over to think of it.[26]

Newspapers poked fun at stage advertisements that urged people to "avoid the risk of Ocean travel." On the ride south of Santa Barbara coaches had more than once been waterborne. A typical news story in the *Press* read:

> The down stage from Santa Barbara upset at Punta Gordo on Sunday night, throwing passengers, baggage, mail, etc. into the surf. Everything was thoroughly drenched, the way bill lost and one man was thrown clear over the driver's head into the breakers, but luckily no one was injured.[27]

At Santa Ynez River, Paso Robles Creek and Arroyo Grande, on the road from Guadalupe to San Luis Obispo, stages and wagons foundered like hulled ships. On March 11, 1876, at Paso Robles Creek the brave young Indian, José Luis, used his *reata* to drag the driver and passengers of a sinking stage to the safety of a sand spit, then rode for food. The stage line rewarded that *vaquero* with one hundred dollars. And the venerable Don Luis Estudillo showed in 1875 that he was still master of the *reata,* heaving it eighty feet out into Arroyo Grande, dropping the loop over the head of a boy who was being washed seaward on the ebb in a wagon hitched to four horses.

A final hazard on the rain and rut-harrowed trail was the masked man with the double-barreled shotgun, the self-styled road agent, come to wage a Robin Hood war against the Southern Pacific by holding up its Wells Fargo stages. This new bandit was no murdering Murieta or crusading Flores; he merely sought money and often had been forced to lawlessness by some railroad injustice.

THE ROAD AGENTS

Up in the Comstock country express detectives and shotgun messengers had etched the legend "Wells Fargo Never Forgets" on the headstones of hold-up men they sent to "boothill," back in the days before the company was grabbed by the Octopus. But the new outfit—said to be hauling Southern Pacific mail free—provoked less fear than resentment along the coast. People had even made a hero out of a mysterious hold-up man who for almost ten years eluded the combined forces of Wells Fargo and California lawmen. This was the then unnamed Charles Bolton, a broad-shouldered, gentlemanly robber and sometime poet who was known as Black Bart. Joseph Henry Jackson wrote:

> Between 1875 and 1883, twenty-eight California stage drivers saw the masked man and knew him for the most famous bandit California ever boasted. All twenty-eight halted their sweating horses as they were bid and listened for the four words in which Black Bart invariably announced the reason for stopping the stage. *"Throw down the box!"* he used to say in a voice his victims unanimously declared to be both resonant and deep. Most drivers threw down the box.[28]

With the empty box the impressive highwayman left bits of verse scrawled on way bills which he signed "Black Bart, the PO8," the appendage standing for poet. Wells Fargo published some of his work—on circulars offering eight hundred dollars' reward for his capture:

> I've labored long and hard for bread,
> For honor and for riches,
> But on my corns too long you've tred,
> You fine-haired sons of bitches.
>
> BLACK BART, the PO8 [29]

Subsequent publicity given the poet—who never stole from women or killed—caused Wells Fargo to cringe. They received no response to their circular on Black Bart, or on other offers such as one of a $500 reward for two men who robbed the San Juan Express between Soledad and San Miguel; small boys penciled dirty words on the posters and town jokers wrote anonymous "tip-off" notes. On December 20, 1876, Superintendent John J. Valentine announced:

> Wells, Fargo & Company have withdrawn all rewards for the arrest of highwaymen offered by them previous to January 1st of this year.[30]

Wells Fargo drivers were no longer permitted to carry guns and had strict orders never to fight: if a highwayman shot the driver horses would stampede, turn over the coach, and the resultant death or injury might lead to damage suits where judgments might be greater than the loss of the box.

Encouraged by this cautious policy, and with a measure of tacit public approval, gentlemen bandits adjusted masks and went to work. Dick Fellows, a two-time loser, left his teaching job to hold up the stage between San Luis Obispo and Soledad; two stages were robbed the same day at the foot of San Marcos Pass and when a lady wept over the loss of every cent she owned a gallant bandit returned the cash. At the divide below La Graciosa a highwayman simulated force by rigging two dummies with guns in the path of the stage and calling to them to hold fire while he emptied the box and then fled. For half an hour the stage waited, the "guards" refusing to answer hails asking for clearance; finally the wind toppled one of them.

The prince of road agents, Black Bart, ended his reign in 1883 when an informer turned him in at Sacramento. The dignified, moustached bandit, looking like some prosperous, retired miner, served four years in San Quentin and then disappeared. Newspapers charged that Wells Fargo "made a deal" with Bart that if he did not attempt to escape, and swore off stage robbery after his release, he would be given a lifetime pension.

The vigorous denials of the express company were laughed at by stagemen. John Waugh, the Santa Barbara whip, once admitted that he had a stand-in "with one of the boldest and most successful of the stage robbers" who had been his schoolteacher at Ukiah. The highwayman was captured and given three years to serve in San Quentin, according to Waugh:

> When he came out Wells Fargo bought him off. They gave him a pass and a pension. He used to enjoy riding over the company's lines with the drivers. And he stuck to his bargain and held up no more stages.

With the railroad already through the valley to Los Angeles, and pushing south on the coast route toward San Luis Obispo, shortened stage lines and too few unpopulated areas drove out the road agents. Old-timers spat with disgust at the change from the rough, big-hearted men who once laughed from behind Wells Fargo counters where a bottle was stashed, to the querulous, job-worried clerks who obediently read circulars on the evils of alcohol when their president "invited" consideration and observation

> ... of the immense advantages that would accrue in the aggregate to the 6,000 employes of this company in economy of time, saving of money, health, nerves and character by abstinence from the use of liquor in any form.

THE VANISHING STAGECOACH

Wells Fargo was richer than ever in a staid regime that emphasized banking; its hoggish guardian, Southern Pacific, in 1864 had a

$37,000,000 surplus, and the mass snatching of pennies from the poor gave the Octopus an income of three million a year. The advancing Iron Horse, dedicated to amassing personal fortunes of about fifty million dollars *each* for the Big Four, pushed the Concord coach before it; when the narrow gauge from San Luis Obispo pulled into Los Olivos in 1887 only forty miles of mountain road to Santa Barbara remained without track along the entire San Francisco to San Diego coast route.

For almost fifteen years the daily stages used the San Marcos Pass road going up and down from Pat Kiniven's relay station on the sea-facing ridge. Drummers stopped in the Cold Springs Tavern to drink and play poker at the big table whose many colored chairs gave a man the chance to shift his seat and luck. Veteran drivers reined in at the town named for W. N. Ballard, an old whip, and Ted Whitney, Tom Coe, Harry Cook and "Uncle George" Heller yarned of runaways, washouts and road agents.

At Felix Mattei's a crowd gathered every year to see the schoolmarms with their long full skirts, leg-o'-mutton sleeves and dust veils when those ladies traveled to Santa Barbara from the north for Teachers' Institute.

The narrow-gauge from Los Alamos, and the up stage out of Santa Barbara, brought news of the few remaining feeder lines on the Pacific Coast—the Halfmoon Bay stage that "Buckskin Bob" Rawles had driven years before; stages into the lumber country at Woodside and the redwoods farther south, along with short runs branching off Seeley & Wright's San Diego to Los Angeles line which went out with the coming of the California Southern Railway.

There was a new type of traveler being hauled now, along with the old-fashioned heavy sole-leather mail bags—Eastern gentlefolk who were pouring into California to see the sights or regain health. Railroad publicity had been working hard to populate areas served by its coaches and Pullmans.

Nine   The Tourist Wave

THE SONG OF SOUTHERN PACIFIC

No spontaneous inflow of adventurers, settlers or tourists followed the opening of the transcontinental railroad. Instead, after the novelty had worn off, coaches arrived with only a trickle of passengers—Union generals, drummers, European rustics, entertainers and politicians.

The news that came from California throughout the seventies offered little inducement to make the three-thousand-mile journey: the collapse of the Comstock silver boom; severe earthquakes in Owens Valley; the Modoc War in the northeast; Chinese massacres; Vigilantes and labor riots at Coast cities. Pikes, foot-loose Confederate veterans, religious colonists and other destitute drifters with nothing to lose came by foot and covered wagon—unwelcomed by the Big Four and its servants, the 300,000 residents of the state. When Easterners of substance wanted a vacation they turned to Florida, balmy wonderland of alligator teeth, sea beans, egret plumes and pink curlew wings. Investors shied away from the feeding place of the Octopus.

The Big Four had weathered the panic of '73, but faced probable disaster unless it could reap gains from its millions of acres of government gift land, and utilize the costly machinery of monopoly. So thin was California's population that statistically it amounted to *one person for every three hundred acres of land!*

To the Southern Pacific tentacle was given the job of dragging in a population that would sustain the voracious railroad. The tool selected to accomplish that considerable task was publicity, so designed as to minimize or ignore bad news while featuring the undeniable charms of the "Golden State." Onto the payroll of the Big Four came writers, lecturers, artists and preachers; broadsides, books, pamphlets, circulars and advertisements showered the cities of the East and Europe. The outpouring of superlatives smothered the antagonistic California press—including the caustic pen of Ambrose Bierce, the famed columnist on wealthy young William Randolph Hearst's *Examiner*. The song of S.P. was to start an influx that before the century changed would bring more than one million people to the shores of the Pacific, and turn El Camino Real into a truly Royal Highway of luxury hotels, crowded excursions and tourist activity.

First of the railroad canticles was written by Charles Nordhoff, a mild-mannered, able journalist who had been a sailor in his youth and whose grandson would gain fame in the twentieth century writing historical novels. For his boosting efforts Nordhoff gained some measure of wealth and the honor of having his name temporarily given to the coast resort of Ojai.

Excerpts from Nordhoff's book, *California: For Health, Pleasure and Residence*, set the Garden of Eden pattern that ever after would be followed by state eulogists:

> There are no dangers to travelers on the beaten track in California; there are no inconveniences which a child or tenderly reared woman would not laugh at....
>
> They dine in San Francisco rather better, and with quite as much form and a more elegant and perfect service, than in New York....

The cost of living is today less in California by a third than in any eastern state. . . .

Santa Barbara and San Diego have become . . . favored winter resorts for invalids from the colder eastern states. The climate of both places is remarkably equal and warm all winter. Observation, as well as the experience of consumptives, shows that it is far superior to Mentone, Nice, or even Aiken in South Carolina.

The Chinamen . . . do not drink, do not quarrel, are not idle or prone to change, give no eye-service, are patient, respectful, extremely quick to learn, faithful to their instructions and make no fuss. With these qualities a working man is cheap at almost any price.[1]

With its glowing account of fertile farms, fourteen-dollar-a-week boarding houses, brilliant poppies, lupin and jacaranda, and other "exquisite and unalloyed pleasures," Nordhoff's book swept the East, outselling such titles as *Thirty Years in the Harem.*

S.P. fanned the flame with circulars that led midwestern farmers to believe its so cheaply offered grant land in the desolate south San Joaquin Valley was no different than acres pictured by Nordhoff —property along the Coast Highway with "wheat growing luxuriantly almost to the seashore . . . roses grown in masses . . . and the pomegranate, the fig, the almond and a great variety of flowering shrubs"[2] plus vegetables and the eucalyptus, or Australian gum, which grew fifteen feet in a single season from rich soil watered out of artesian wells pumped by windmills.

When Southern Pacific opened a new transcontinental line through Yuma, and the rival Atchison, Topeka and Santa Fe came in from Mexico, more fuel was heaped on the publicity fire. The railroad urged land companies, chambers of commerce and merchants to join the crusade. An appeal to every bracket of society came from the publicity mill with special emphasis on bait to hook wealthy invalids.

Invalid, in the mid-eighties, meant anyone in search of health, and physicians were hired to opine that California climate would benefit those who suffered from consumption, phthisis, asthma, catarrh, rheumatism or almost every common ailment that plagued the crowded East. Dr. Walter Lindley wrote:

Still another health-seeker, whose joints no longer respond to the mandates of the will, who is harassed and tortured with pains at every change in the weather, looks to the genial climate and the healing waters of the springs of Southern California for relief.[3]

Millions of words and thousands of pictures started the westward flow of curious, hopeful people. It built steadily until the mideighties when about fifty thousand Easterners were aboard the emigrant and excursion trains of the "rival" Southern Pacific and Santa Fe lines. Then began what knowing observers of the day regarded as a "contrived rate war."

WESTWARD HO!

The historian Glen S. Dumke told of the price slashing that in 1887 had reduced fares from the Mississippi Valley to Southern California from $125 down to $15 and reached a climax March 6th,

> ... when both the Southern Pacific and the Santa Fe settled down to a finish fight over the fares between Kansas City and Los Angeles. In the morning the Southern Pacific met the Santa Fe at twelve dollars. The latter then dropped to ten dollars, and the Southern Pacific followed suit. The Santa Fe cut again to eight and was met. ... Finally, shortly after noon, the Southern Pacific announced a rate of one dollar.[4]

Southern Pacific, which later steadied rates at twenty-five dollars, predicted that 120,000 people of "high quality" would come to California by the end of the next year and the Pasadena *Daily Union* declared that the estimate was "too low." [5] Extra trains poured bargain travelers into depots on both ends of the Coast Highway. Many carried copies of Major Truman's railroad-inspired book, *Homes and Happiness in the Golden State,* which explained the colony method of settlement—a small down payment plan for cooperative farming. Prospects were met at the depot by representatives of The Illinois Association, The California Colony of Indiana, and various groups interested in cultivating oranges, lemons, cotton and silkworms.

With the "high quality" travelers came the very poor, carried by Southern Pacific in miserable, ancient coaches. At the end of the slow trip families agreed that their luckiest member had been the one chosen to ride the "zulu car"—cars that operated in freight trains to carry the livestock and possessions of people who were coming out to buy and farm the railroad wastelands. Those who could not stand the treeless, waterless Tulare Basin trudged to the Southern California coast.

Los Angeles began to grow at the rate of two thousand a month; San Diego about half as fast. And other thousands swarmed over the six southern counties until two million acres of arable land seemed inadequate. Then professional boomers moved in from the East and Midwest to show the crowds how hot air could be changed into money.

THE PAPER CITIES

"Never were more apt scholars found," wrote the contemporary historian Theodore Strong Van Dyke, "and they soon became dizzy with the rapid installation of wisdom." [6] Farmers put aside thoughts of crops; tourists ignored the sightseeing excursions; businessmen who had come out to "appraise the situation in California" became speculators.

The "Escrow Indians"—promoters, swindlers, boomers and part-time real estate salesmen—set up offices where tract maps outlined the sites of future cities. Extravagant claims went into advertisements that heralded those paper towns where luxury hotels, country clubs and golf links would soon appear. Acreage worth fifty dollars sold for as high as ten thousand dollars on sand hills, cow ranges and even sheer cliffs—sight unseen! Van Dyke noted:

> At many a sale of the merest trash buyers stood in line all night and fifty dollars or even a hundred were often paid for places in the line in the morning. [7]

Los Angeles ended its pueblo-shantytown days as brass bands led parades of elephants, clowns and hay wagons past rows of shacks, tents and hastily built lodging houses to the outskirts of town where high pressure salesmen thrust barbecued chicken and contracts at fevered buyers. Lotteries, moonlight excursions, and free lunches lured San Diego buyers out to the Cajon Valley and down to Baja California; lavish promises sent people up the Coast Highway beyond Santa Barbara to Santa Maria, San Luis Obispo and Paso Robles.

One hundred new towns were platted and flag-bedecked with the assurance of smooth-talking tricksters that each was "Gilt Edge Real Estate," and definitely "Not a Paper City!" Persons who once felt that "Lucky" Baldwin had been skinned by Harriss Newmark on the purchase of the Santa Anita horse-breeding acreage, no longer thought $100,000 an unreasonable profit; transactions in '87 approached the astonishing annual figure of $500 million!

With the boom rose a wave of disorder that shocked straight-laced midwestern visitors. At the new coast town of Santa Monica the Los Angeles *Times* complained of the "hoodlums, male and female, who resort thither by the hundred every Sunday."

> These toughs committed some of the most atrocious outrages against law and decency, both at the beach and on the homebound train; and their actions were fast scaring off the thousands of respectable people.[8]

From mushroomed San Diego down into Baja California the boom lawlessness was described in the history of Walter Gifford Smith:

> ... the desecration of Sunday was complete, with all drinking and gambling houses open, and with picnics, excursions, fiestas and bullfights, the latter at the Mexican line, to attract men, women and boys from religious influence. Theft, murder, incendiarism, carousals, fights, highway robbery, and licentiousness gave the passing show many of the characteristics of the frontier camp.[9]

Southern Pacific's publicity, and the rate war with Santa Fe, had more than accomplished the task of bringing people to California when the boom ended suddenly in the spring of 1888. From a corporate standpoint the following depression was not bad; and even the common man did not suffer if he could handle a hammer to work at building for his fellows. Dumke summed up the result, comparing the boom in the south to the Gold Rush that developed northern counties:

> Where once the "cattle of the plain" had grazed in silence over rich acres, now the American citizen built his trolley lines, founded his banks, and irrigated his orange groves. The boom was the final step in the process of making California truly American.[10]

RESORT HOTELS

Throughout the boom, and on to the end of the century, "tourism" grew to be one of the mainstays of California prosperity. While the railroad, recessions and epidemics held back agriculture and business, the luring of tourists was the means of a livelihood for thousands. "Boosters" at highway towns erected signs and sent out brochures whose superlatives defined mineral springs, perfect weather, boating, fishing, hunting and every variety of amusement.

On the peninsula one mile from San Diego was the famed Hotel Del Coronado, "Mecca for the Eastern visitor." The huge white building, its red tile roof broken by turrets, spires and towers, rose beside a city of campers' tents. The travel writer Kate Sanborn—in her book *A Truthful Woman in Southern California*—told readers that

> The dining room may safely be called roomy as it seats a thousand guests and your dearest friends could not be recognized at the extreme end.[11]

The winter excursion circuit offered by tour companies proceeded from Del Coronado up to the Ramond Hotel on the outskirts of Pasadena. The vacationers frequently complained of having to pay one dollar for having their trunks moved between the resorts—a distance of some ninety miles. Emma Hildreth Adams voiced the objection of gentlewomen having to wait in a stage station when making the transfer at Los Angeles, but that unpleasantness did give her the opportunity to deliver a righteous thrust at degeneracy:

> I had the pleasure of seeing no end of money set fire to, in little slender rolls of tobacco, during the hour I watched for the stage.[12]

Tourists who did not want to get too far away from the friendly bustle and familiar things of home—the Odd Fellows, Knights of Pythias, or the Woman's Christian Temperance Union—stayed at the imposing Arcadia Hotel, its four stories rising from a bluff at Santa Monica. There too was that novelty, The Gravity Railroad, a mild forerunner of the roller coaster.

To the veteran winter visitor—one who knew the comforts of the St. James Hotel in Jacksonville, Florida—there was no place in Southern California quite like Santa Barbara's Arlington, with its running water, gas illumination, billiard tables for ladies, men's Grill Room, and ninety rooms each having its own fireplace. Suites were even equipped with speaking tubes that connected to the main desk.

Many regarded the principal charm of the Arlington to emanate from its genial manager, Dixie W. Thompson, a former shipmaster, rancher, sheepman and connoisseur of both beautiful women and fine horseflesh. He took over at the Arlington in 1887, ten years after it had been built by Colonel W. W. Hollister, the Ohioan who came down from San Juan Bautista to become a benefactor of Santa Barbara.

The hotel was a "white elephant" even before the colonel's death, but Captain Thompson had not been long at the helm before a change was noted. Horseback picnics, lawn tennis, tally-ho excursions and moonlight riding parties kept the visitors busy; Dixie urged invalids to use the ocean as well as the hot springs and convinced them that sea bathing was a sovereign remedy by asking, "Did you ever hear of a sailor with a cold?"

Dixie Thompson was a seemingly endless source of information, yarns and humor. Driving parties around Santa Barbara, he pointed out the giant Sailor's Sycamore on which seamen had taken bearings coming into port. He told Easterners how Modoc Road, out by the Hope Ranch, had been so named after the northern war when an Indian employed by Thomas Hope was ordered to kill Surveyor J. J. Barker for "trespassing." And the genial manager would rein up at the spot where Nick Covarreuias and John J. Forster arrived on May 25, 1883, to set a record for a two-horse team on the 105-mile road from Los Angeles, via Conejo Rancho. Fifteen and one half hours had been their time, the final eighty-five miles without changing horses.

The fame of the Arlington spread to the East and three successive Presidents stopped there—Benjamin Harrison, William McKinley and Theodore Roosevelt. Southern Pacific thought to build a rival hostelry at the paper town of Naples, a few miles up the coast, but abandoned its plan after considering the popularity of Dixie Thompson. To insure that the city remained the "Riviera of the Santa Barbara Channel," and that Arlington guests saw no unpleasantness, the mayor addressed a special edict to the marshal:

> Sir: You will use every effort and means in your power and at your command, to keep out of Santa Barbara all confidence operators, thieves, thugs, house-breakers, sneaks, pickpockets, moll-buzzers, burglars, gopher-blowers, tramps, and their ilk.[13]

More sophisticated than the Arlington and Del Coronado were the two world-famous hotels of the eighties in northern California—the Palace in San Francisco and the Del Monte at Monterey. Every traveler of note and tourist of means stopped at those show places, if only for the night.

The seven-story, 800-room Palace at its height was the most modern hotel in the world, and newspapers never tired of listing its innovations, oddities and extravagances. There were 9,000 cuspidors in the five-million-dollar Palace; the staff of three hundred included Negro waiters, porters and chambermaids; rooms were "air conditioned"; the roster of renowned guests ranged from nobility to heavyweight champions; its chefs introduced to the epicurean world the native California oyster, abalone, and various creations built around the canvasback, mallard and teal.

When newspapers tired of receiving promotion handouts they would rewrite items in a ridiculous vein:

> There are thirty-four elevators in all—four for passengers, ten for baggage and twenty for mixed drinks. Each elevator contains a piano and a bowling alley.[14]

The state of California was run from the Palace in the eighties as important hirelings of the Big Four gathered to drink Pisco punches set on the long mahogany bar. There bearded men in Prince Albert coats held preliminary discussions which led to the building of the other great northern hotel that became famed amongst tourists. In his story of the railroad giants, *The Big Four*, Oscar Lewis tells how the Del Monte Hotel came into being:

> In the middle eighties, company officials contemplated their empty trains running over the tracks beyond San Jose and contrived to make a social asset of travel to the south. Southern Pacific capital produced a sprawling resort hotel among the oaks beside Monterey Bay and word passed about that a week-end—or a summer—at Del Monte would be useful to anyone who wished favors of the company.... To be a frequent visitor to Del Monte became an easy but expensive way of attaining social importance.[15]

The Big Four purchased 126 acres for "the largest resort hotel in the world" from David Jacks, and the landscaping included a private racetrack, polo field, several swimming pools and flower gardens that equaled any in Europe. Huge ballrooms with full-length mirrors, and rooms that featured a new invention, the telephone, gave Del Monte first place among modern hotels. Its advertisements stressed economy:

> The extra cost of a trip to California is more than counterbalanced by the difference between rates of various winter resorts and those of the incomparable Hotel Del Monte.[16]

World travelers, along with ambitious dowagers from San Francisco, filled Del Monte, and the activity gave a shake to sleepy

Monterey which had been described as "a town where life is never known to close by any other means than natural causes." The one-time capital, choked by the land-hog Jacks, bypassed as a railroad stop, had even been replaced by Salinas as county seat. Encouraged by the Big Four hostelry, boosters began campaigning for a direct railroad from Monterey to the East.

Promoters without employment after the boom found tourism and boosterism the most promising of activities. They drifted to highway towns that had survived the crash to become active with chambers of commerce or civic organizations. In the scramble for tourists they led Clean Our City drives and arranged for such attractions as circuses, exhibitions, races and county fairs that featured daring balloon ascents.

Smaller cities built sanitariums to compete with the Brewster at San Diego and the Las Casitas at Pasadena; new hotels bid for the overflow from the giant resorts—the $250,000 Vendome at San Jose; the Miramar at Montecito; Anaheim's Del Canto; and in San Buenaventura—shortened by the railroad to Ventura—the Rose.

Advertisers in the *Overland Monthly* bombarded the winter visitors and summer tourists. Needham's Red Clover Blossoms were "the sure cure for cancer, salt rheum, and all diseases arising from an impure state of the blood." [17] Dr. Pierce's Pleasant Pellets attacked the same, and other ailments. The Imperial Hair Regenerator guaranteed instantly to restore gray hair in such a manner that "no one dreams that you colored it." The moustache spoon shield, to prevent soup and coffee discoloration, was called "the greatest novelty of the age." On the scientific side were the American Speaking Telephone Company's rental instruments and Charles Beseler's camera, the "Eclipse" Dissolving Stereopticon.

The idea of relaxation touched the native Californians; "outside resorts" five or six miles on the highway from towns became popular. A reader who signed himself "Old Timer" advised the editor of the Santa Barbara *Press*:

> To the man tired of sameness, the roadside house offers an incentive for a drive and a cigar. The horses can be watered and cooled

off. The drive home becomes more comfortable and refreshing to both man and beast ... the roadside house is a benediction to the town or city it caters to.[18]

THE TOURIST'S TALE

While old residents found the vacationers' search for enjoyment admirable, and profitable, they objected to the change-it-to-our-way propensities of many Midwest and Eastern critics. Books by exuberant travel-wise ladies and puritanical, peevish males found fault with any habits, institutions, foods or amusements that differed from the customs at home. More than that, every travel narrative gave its author's version of California history along with judgments on the Indians, Franciscans, Mexicans, Chinese and "other foreigners."

The "truthful woman," Kate Sanborn, advised her readers that Helen Hunt Jackson had deceived the public in her classic novel *Ramona* and that the Indians she had "depicted so lovingly" were a dishonest fiction.

> The repulsive, stolid creatures I have seen at stations with their sullen stare, long be-vermined locks, and filthy blankets full of fleas, are possibly not a fair representation of the race. They have been unfairly dealt with. I am glad they can be educated and improved. They seem to need it.[19]

Ramona, which author and critic Scott O'Dell felt had "about the same impact as *Uncle Tom's Cabin*," [20] led to the removal of Southern California Indians to a reservation near Palomar Mountain—away from the view of tourists and the clutches of unscrupulous employers. Then was heard the objection recorded by that first-class reporter Clifton Johnson:

> Most of the Indians have drifted off to the reservations to get the benefit of Uncle Sam's coddling. We've managed to pauperize nearly the whole race.[21]

One of those not "pauperized" was the crippled survivor of the Canaleno tribe, Juan de Jesús Justo—Baptismal number 1069.

Juan de Jesús took employment as a street sweeper in Santa Barbara in order to wear a hat and uniform "so people will know I belong to the city."

The Franciscan fathers came under attack from the Reverend Charles Augustus Stoddard of New York, who sat outside Mission Santa Barbara and gave thanks that history had not fastened a Roman Catholic priesthood upon the territory of the United States. The doctor, who observed much evil during his travels, summed up the missionary effort:

> The Indians knew that while the fathers were kind to them, it was that they might use them to enrich their order and enlarge their influence in the land. They gave them service for what they got, but few gave any love; and when the time of persecution came, they fell away from those who had proved themselves only selfish benefactors.[22]

Up at Palo Alto Dr. Stoddard found what he considered true benefaction in the $30-million-endowed Leland Stanford Junior University; but across at San Jose he was disgusted and shocked by the Chinese quarter—the dwelling place of the very people whose exploitation had made possible the university. When carriages of a Chinese funeral passed him, with a gong beating and a sacrificial pig squealing, the righteous traveler declared that it "was a most repulsive spectacle of heathenism in a Christian land, the most public and unpleasant which had then met my eyes."

The railroad view of the Chinese was along more practical business lines as expressed in a Santa Fe publication written by Charles A. Keeler:

> These people have an individuality which impresses itself at once upon all their surroundings.... In the Chinese quarter of Los Angeles are joss houses resplendent with colors and carvings ... restaurants where tea and the daintiest of Chinese viands are served....[23]

Union labor forced the Chinese Exclusion Act after the railroads had imported thousands of the Orientals. When they were of no further use to the Big Four they crowded in Chinatowns—

city slums—or ran laundries and peddled vegetables. Inveterate gamblers and smokers of opium, the Chinese could nonetheless work harder, faster and more skillfully than their Western counterparts. The bad feeling thus engendered was the subject of a poem by Bret Harte about two white card sharps who catch the Chinese gambler Ah Sin trying to beat them at their own game. "The Heathen Chinee" began with the verse:

> Which I wish to remark
> And my language is plain,
> That for ways that are dark
> And for tricks that are vain
> The heathen Chinee is peculiar.
> Which the same I would rise to explain.[24]

Down in the cellar of social standing with the Chinese and Indians were Negroes and Mexicans. Traveling between Tia Juana and San Diego, Clifton Johnson talked with a man from Nebraska who "wouldn't go back to live if you'd give me the state." The man was clearing seven thousand dollars a year on a twenty-acre orchard where he employed from two to six men whom he paid $1.50 for a nine-hour day. He told Johnson:

> I don't hire any Mexicans—I don't like their color; and I don't hire niggers or chinamen.[25]

At best the travelogue historians, and newcomers such as "the prominent businessman" Johnson quoted, regarded the Mexican as a shiftless, immoral peon out of whom the good had died with Montezuma. But ridicule was not confined to the "degraded" races; many an old pioneer was classed as a hobo because he walked in ragged clothes. James W. Marshall had been such a one when he trudged around trying to sell his signature. *"El que cantó Oro!"* the Mexicans would call him—"He who cried out Gold!"

Another vagabond was John A. Swan, the Scotch seaman and innkeeper, who could be seen moving up the road from Monterey toward San Jose with the rolling gait of the foremast hand, to see

a few surviving friends of pre-Gold Rush days, his hatband pro-
claiming him a PIONEER OF '43. Of him Bancroft wrote:

> Down to '85 this kind-hearted old sailor, 73 years old, burdened with
> poverty and deafness, lived in an historic adobe of Monterey.[26]

Warped history, bigoted judgments and other rudenesses of-
fended people of the land—American, European and Latin—less
than attempts to change the very character of the country, as mani-
fested at the settlements of religious zealots. The most prominent
of those blue law towns was on the Monterey peninsula at Pacific
Grove, where liquor, dancing, Sunday games and other fun were
prohibited.

Not only was Pacific Grove the antithesis of California freedom but the land had been provided by the hated Jacks, who was
making heavenly amends in the late eighties; and Southern Pacific
used the site of piety and prohibition to sell thousands of tickets
to schoolteachers, university professors, lecturers, ministers and retired persons interested in culture. Pacific Grove became the headquarters of "The Chautauqua of the West," launched in 1887, to
bring nation-wide sermons, study groups, travel lectures and plays
to California.

If the traditionally hard-drinking, fun-loving, independent people of the West needed anything more than the Jacks' and S.P.
sponsorship to turn it against Pacific Grove, there was the endorse-
ment of Dr. Stoddard:

> Pacific Grove is not a place for Sunday carousals and demoralizing
> sport . . . it is a home for the pious and the cultured, and the gentle
> people who love to meet with the Women's Christian Temperence
> [sic] Union, the Chautaqua [sic] Assembly, the Sunday School
> Convention and similar assemblies.[27]

Cults would always be a part of California and the literature
that noted them in passing seemed never to reach a point of satura-
tion. The ballyhoo of the land boom carried into the 1890s with
emphasis more and more on the attraction and amusement of the

tourist. In the "gay" decade came the Tournament of Roses as an annual New Year's Day pageant, the start of Fiestas, Midwest-type county fairs, rodeos and intersectional football games. The mass of tourists sought bypaths to either side of the Coast Highway, away from the string of shabby railroad stations that were eyesores between San Francisco Bay and the Mexican border.

BYWAYS

Tourists of the nineties who made the Palace Hotel their headquarters rode in carriages from the Palm Court to "see the Elephant," as "doing the town" was called in those expansive years of wasp waists, knickerbockers, the Gibson Girl, the naughty "cancan," and temperance ladies singing "The Brewer's Big Horse Can't Run Over Me." Escorted by guides, the travelers explored the Barbary Coast, Kearney Street, Chinatown, Fisherman's Wharf, Golden Gate Park, the cemeteries, and such famous restaurants as the Poodle Dog, the German Ahlborn House, Tortoni's and the Pup.

The ferry and train carried sightseeing parties up to the wineries around old Sonoma; connections were made with "the crookedest railway in the world" for the tavern on the crest of 2,509-foot Mount Tamalpais; a regular circuit took groups to Sacramento, Yellowstone Park and the ghost towns of the mother lode.

Leaving the shabby, prosperous city by the Golden Gate, which reminded many of an Eastern metropolis, a route ran south to the redwoods of the Santa Cruz Mountains or to San Jose, the "Garden City" of the Santa Clara Valley.

John D. Rockefeller, best fixed in the popular memory by his distribution of dimes, declared that the valley was

> a picture such as I have never seen. Why! it is even worth the expense of a trip across the continent. . . .[28]

The most sweeping view of the Santa Clara farm lands came as tourists rode the Mount Hamilton stage twenty-six miles to wait in line for a two-minute look through the great telescope at Lick Observatory. Twelve special stages, and low-hung tally-ho coaches, plied up the scenic road, driven by whips who wore corduroy suits and broadbrimmed sombreros. A bugler rode in advance to announce special sights and the approach of stops at Hall's Valley for a change of horses, and at Smith's Creek, where Mrs. Hattie Garnosset supervised meals served in Snell's Hotel. Up to that point the $85,000 road ascended only seven feet per hundred; thereafter ears popped on a winding steep ascent of nine miles.

Northwest of San Jose tourists always "did" the Stanford campus and the adjoining stock farm where racehorses trained on two tracks and in a trotting park. At that center of horsebreeding in the West a noted photographer of the seventies, Edward Muybridge, took pictures of horses running past twenty-four cameras. These he mounted on a wheel—the "Zoopraxiscope"—which sightseers were told was the very first motion-picture projector.

Buggies traveled over to Searsville where an artificial lake covered what was once a mill town, visited the historic country store of Gold Rush days at Woodside, and drove south to the famous Los Gatos Hotel, run by John W. Lyndon of Vermont. Close by in the Santa Cruz redwoods was the resort spa of Congress Springs.

The first Easterners who visited the Santa Clara Valley looked with amazement at peas ready for market in February, strawberries and asparagus a month earlier, and lettuce all year round. Many returned home only to sell their farms or small businesses so they could "locate" in the land of such plenty. By the early nineties orchards and farms were being profitably run even by folks who had never before been outside the city limits of Boston, New York or Chicago. The laborers they hired for twenty-five dollars a month lived in white tents the year round; household help was paid only fifteen dollars.

With eggs twenty cents a dozen and no need for coal, snow shovels, heavy clothing or preserving, the new fruit ranchers were the envy of each succeeding tourist wave, half of whose people came back to set up a congenial society that was proud of its culture—

personified by Indian relics, South Sea Island curios, rare china with a history, pianos and books; to join the ordinary people came ladies who were Wellesley graduates and others who had studied at the Boston Conservatory of Music.

Every highway town seemed to profit by the tourist invasion: Gilroy revived with its Hot Springs to wax even more prosperous than in stagecoach days; Paso Robles likewise capitalized on its springs, where Spanish soldiers had watched the grizzly bears nurse sore legs; Santa Maria's inn became a favorite and tourists went to see the town's first house, a twelve-by-fourteen structure erected in '79 by the German emigrant John G. Preel, who had paid for the privilege of walking beside a wagon, across the continent.

Vacationers at Santa Barbara rode north past Elwood Cooper's rows of tall eucalyptus trees, and a few went beyond Gaviota Pass to see the beautiful Santa Ynez mountains. Nestled there at Lompoc was a temperance colony with six churches and constant fights when saloons attempted to open, or druggists sold too much tonic.

Until the coming of a through railroad from the north many rode the stage over San Marcos Pass to visit Santa Ynez Valley towns and look over range land. Farther south, on the road from Ventura to Los Angeles, Montalvo was laid out to honor the medieval Spanish author who had first used the name California in a novel. In the area was the town of Nordhoff, not yet changed to Ojai.

At Los Angeles and neighboring cities people from the East were going into a wide variety of small business ventures—canning tuna, raising ostriches, manufacturing "authentic" Mission furniture, making artificial stone for sidewalks, buying orchards and opening restaurants. Sightseers voyaged to Catalina Island where Captain William Banning took them from Avalon hotels, cottages and shops on a wild stage ride over to the town of Cabrillo.

At San Diego a favorite jaunt was out to the large hilly park where Kate Sessions, a former schoolteacher, was planting trees from all over the world. One day the beauty spot would be known as Balboa Park. Few bothered going down to National City—noted mostly as the site of West Coast Match Company's plant where "dainty parlor matches" were produced to replace the sulphurous, Chinese-made "California Stinkers." The border town of Tia Juana was likewise unpopular—a place of open vice, bullfights, doubtful curios, unsegregated poverty and unsanitary tamales.

Most of the one million people who remained in California after the railroad-inspired migration settled along the Coast Highway and its bypaths. For all the carping and righteous bleating of their most articulate spokesmen those newcomers of the eighties and nineties were en masse a rugged people; the Midwest and Atlantic Coast farmers and small businessmen matched in their way predecessors who were described by David Starr Jordan, president of Stanford University:

> The "Argonauts" of '49 were a strong, self-reliant generous body of men.[29]

Settlers in that flower-garnished land of milk and honey needed the greatest fortitude to withstand the travails of the nineties: the nationwide financial crash of 1893 brought thousands of failures; into California poured bums and bindlestiffs—"snow birds"—come to escape a depression winter; units of Coxey's Army—the unemployed en route to Washington—ravaged the countryside in the tradition of the Micheltorena and Frémont battalions; during that same year of '94 a railroad strike saw travel halted and thousands of tons of coast citrus spoiled; and on everything pressed the heavy heel of Southern Pacific.

As though to temper adversity the heralds of progress sounded through the last five years of the century: the graphophone, telephone, camera and networks of electric trolley cars. And with tourism came the bicycle, father of the horseless carriage and precipitator of the hard-surfaced road.

THE WHEELMEN

In his 1895 guide for the "traveler, invalid, pleasurist and home seeker," G. Wharton James advised:

To the enthusiastic cycler who peruses this book before starting for California we say, by all means bring your wheel with you, and to him who is not the fortunate possessor of a silent steed, we say go and purchase one as soon as you arrive in Los Angeles, for you will need it for the proper appreciation of our beautiful country.[30]

More than a quarter of a century earlier, cycling had made a start in America, and at Los Angeles in 1869 the Gold Rush blacksmith John Goller had built a velocipede. By the seventies the dangerous "high wheelers" were a familiar sight on the toll road from San Francisco out to the Cliff House, and along Los Angeles' Ventura Boulevard. When the "safety bicycle" came into general use toward the end of the eighties hundreds of California wheelmen read the articles of Colonel Albert A. Pope, pioneer manufacturer of bicycles, and owned his book, *The American Bicycler*; wheelmen argued the relative merits of the Columbia and the Fowler, or, a few years later, discussed the new air-tired product of Ignaz Schwinn.

Schwinn bicycles led the pack in the race to attain great speeds, building "quintets" on which five pedalers paced racers who trained to beat the record of Charlie "Mile-a-Minute" Murphy. In California during the fall of 1894 wheelmen set new marks with the famous Rambler bicycle.

The reckles speedsters frightened horses, pedestrians and the ladies and gentlemen who rode tandem bicycles out into the country for Sunday picnics. Two newspapermen, Reginald Cleveland and Sam Williamson, wrote of the law at work against those menaces to safety:

So many wheelmen raced through big city streets that police bicycle squads were formed, and a helmeted bluecoat pedaling furiously after a "scorcher," his handle-bar mustache stiff in the breeze, was a thrilling sight.[31]

In the late eighties a dragnet of pedaling cops failed to run down San Francisco's "Bicycle Bandit" who left the clue of tire treads at the scene of his crimes. The swift and silent terror reigned only for a brief period but added to the highway's unsolved murders when he killed Cornelius Stagg, owner of the Ingleside Inn, and made off with the contents of the roadhouse safe.

A sports and pleasure vehicle, with little commercial use at the time, the bicycle did perfect many things that would go into the "horseless carriage"—the wire wheel, inflated rubber tires, knee action, shaft drive, steel tubing. And The League of American Wheelmen began tho fight for bettei highways that led to Congress' appropriating ten thousand dollars in 1893 for a United States Office of Road Inquiry. When members of the League stormed Sacramento they brought the first road map of El Camino Real which had appeared in *The American Bicycler*.

R. C. Irvine, who became one of the first men identified with California highways, declared that "the influence of the bicycle upon this agitation for improved highways cannot be overestimated." He further pointed out that:

> Any machine which permits a man to travel for pleasure, without discomfort and practically without expense, forty miles a day, is evidently one which has come to stay and the number of wheelmen will surely reach extraordinary proportions in the years to come.[32]

A FACE FOR THE ROAD

To the voice of the wheelmen was added the noisy evidence of the gasoline-powered horseless carriage which had shown tremendous improvement since the first demonstration of J. Frank Duryea in 1893; the vehicles two years later had maintained speeds of five miles per hour at the Chicago *Times-Herald* races.

On March 27, 1895, Governor James H. Budd signed a legislative act creating the Bureau of Highways and appointed Irvine and two other commissioners—Marsden Manson and J. L. Maude. During the next year Maude and Irvine, "accompanied by a Gordon setter, Maje, who had a bone buried in every county," [33] made a thorough survey of California roads.

The Los Angeles *Times* stated editorially that "If the state were to build a few hundred miles of first class highways ... the people would cheerfully furnish the money necessary to continue the work ..." [34] The San Francisco *Chronicle* believed it "obvious that good roads would help production and trade as well as facilitate the pleasure of bicycling." [35]

The San Francisco *Call* hailed the findings of the surveyors:

> There is something fascinating in the declaration ... that it is the intention of the Bureau to see that a finely macadamized highway is built from one end of the state to the other.[36]

In 1896 the commissioners had recommended establishment of twenty-eight state routes, most of them to extend or connect with the Coast Highway. Even at that early date the Bureau received complaints: Why was the main road to go round the hill and bypass historic, commercially important San Juan Bautista? Were the commissioners so ignorant that they did not realize hard surfacing rendered a road useless since it forced *teams* to use shallow side ditches?

The cry of the diehard rose from stables, carriage companies and teamsters. One of the few who resigned himself to the inevitable was the mule-skinner Con Tieck, then pulling freight between San Pedro and Los Angeles. He scratched out a letter to another gray-beard, Pete Barrett, who had deserted the California wagon outfits and was trying to cure his gout in the backwater country of Florida:

> ... you was maybe wise to hang up yr. bells. The Jerk Line Team is done.... Soon folk won't know a _____ black snake from the gee string ... [37]

The gravel-voiced Tieck, with more foresight than many an affluential buggy maker, packed his Swiss hame bells (tuned in thirds to sound a musical chime) and stowed away with eastbound express baggage to join his friend Barrett.

In 1900 twenty million horses and half that number of bicycles were about to be driven into eclipse.

Ten   Gasoline Alley West

"HOLD YOUR HORSES!"

The twentieth century opened with only a scattering of the nation's ten thousand horseless carriages on the streets and highways of California. Those few expensive contraptions had arrived in crates to be assembled by machinists and bicycle mechanics for such well-to-do men as J. M. Wilkins, proprietor of San Francisco's Cliff House, or Dr. F. A. Conant, the Santa Barbara oculist. But the number of owners was no measure of the enthusiasm—and resentment—created by the new gasoline, steam and electric vehicles. Once the Spanish-American War had run its course newspapers gave wide coverage to races, production and personalities connected with the new *automobile*.

The French-coined word automobile finally replaced motor wagon, buggyaut, petrocar, quadricycle, gasoline-steam-electric carriage, and other labels that sought to improve on the U.S. Patent Office designation, "gasoline road locomotive." At Coast cities a new-born "automobile craze" came under attack by conservatives whose faith—and investments—remained in horses, trolley cars, bicycles, ferries and the railroad.

As more of the "infernal machines" entered the state, the old order began its anti-automobile campaign. The Santa Barbara *Press* reflected the attitude of smaller cities:

> Now Santa Barbara is distinctly a horse town. This unpleasant morning, when just enough wind is stirring to get on the nerves and make half-broken ranch horses remember their bronco ancestors, suppose an automobile driven by someone who ought to know better turns off the highway onto State Street at say an eight mile gait. What are the chances? It is not only the team that runs away that suffers ... but the helpless horse tied before the shop must take what comes his way.[1]

A remarkable compassion for the horse was suddenly evidenced by those who raced him to uselessness, lashed him to death in front of drays, or were responsible for his slaughter at railroad crossings. Marin citizens tried to have automobiles completely barred because they lived in an "essentially horse-keeping and horse-loving county" while the livery stable owners of San Francisco warned of "dangers to the life and limb of those who drive horses, if these gasoline-burning machines are permitted on the park drives and city boulevards." [2]

The chauffeur, or chauffeuse, who left the automobile stable (people would not yet go so far as to accept the French word "garage") faced a variety of restrictions: no driving was permitted between sunset and sunrise; speeds in excess of what some police officer thought was eight miles an hour might result in a fine or an order to cease operating the vehicle; ferries required that automobiles empty gas tanks before they could be carried; instead of being able to pass wagons—while teamsters "held their horses"—the auto driver was obliged to pull over and wait.

The noisy one-cylinder cars that trailed noxious blue gasoline fumes, dripped oil and clattered to unexpected stops as bolts gave way, became the targets of ridicule, scorn and legal trickery. Automobilists in long dusters, goggled masks and gauntlets were taunted with the challenge, "Get a horse!" and every one of them was regarded as a "rich playboy" because autos cost from $650 to $5,000. Cops went so far as to hide behind bushes and throw dummies in front of inexperienced drivers who were whistled down if they could not stop before hitting what might have been a living thing.

Automobile enthusiasts soon rebelled by forming clubs, the earliest in California meeting in 1900 at San Francisco and Los Angeles. Those social groups, and others throughout the country, soon became public-service organizations that pushed for legislation, better highways, and protection for the motorist.

In an attempt at promoting good will the California State Automobile Club at San Francisco in 1901 sent a circular to livery stables suggesting a "horse-education" plan to cut down accidents:

> ... previous experience with bicycles and electric cars has demonstrated the fact that horses will become accustomed to any strange object, whether stationary or moving, after they have seen it a few times; and to hasten such familiarity with automobiles, the Club will, as often as it appears necessary, station one or more automobiles at some convenient place in the city; and the owners of timid horses can bring or send them to be trained ...[3]

The Club received a letter from one horse owner, who failed to show up for an appointment.

THE AUTOMOBILISTS

California automobile clubs were looked upon with suspicion in the early nineties when any organization of prominent men was taken for granted to have legalized larceny as its main aim, thanks to the reputation maintained by Southern Pacific and various so-called public utilities. The automobile was the toy of the rich and membership in the Club included the very wealthy. But there were also members, from San Francisco to San Diego, who had an eye on the automobile for its commercial possibilities—oil men, realtors, coal dealers, auto agents and civic boosters. Stablemen, teamsters, hackmen and housemovers who had been organized in the big union movement of 1901, resented both the idle rich and employers seeking to replace the horse.

A Riverside clergyman expressed the view that automobilism was traveling on the highway to perdition:

> In Los Angeles a club composed of wealthy, intelligent and prominent citizens goes out for an auto run on Sunday and by doing this they say as forcibly as they can that the next generation shall have no Sabbath.[4]

But the automobile soon transcended group prejudices and made most people forget any consequences it might eventually bring.

The feeling of power and the attainment of speed made driving an automobile something unique in man's experience. If most people could not own a car they hoped for a ride in one, and even to watch the "bubbles" was to partly share a thrill. The Southern California Auto Club catered to the speed demons, both racers and spectators, and in May of 1901 held the Pacific Coast's first race meet at Agricultural Park in Los Angeles.

Obstacle races tested the maneuverability of the Olds, Haynes-Apperson, Winton, Peerless and a number of steam and electric cars. Mile time runs saw a new steam carriage speed faster than thirty-seven miles an hour! The gasoline automobiles performed with greater consistency but the steamer, when pressure remained up, was then the champion. It had one speed, used kerosene, and had no exhaust; it required ten minutes for the coils to heat.

W. S. Redington purchased one of the steamers in 1902 and drove it from Los Angeles to Santa Barbara where it created a sensation. Its reception by the *Press* showed that paper's change of attitude toward automobiles:

> The machine is a White Steam Carriage and is the only one of that well-known make in town. Of course, hay-seed horse will look at them askance for a while but there is no reason to suppose they will not get used to them.[5]

Proper Santa Barbara during the fall of that year was more sympathetic toward the electric car than either the steamer or the gasoline automobile. In October, Brentner & Company announced it had arranged "to start an automobile stable in this city" to introduce the Waverly Electric Machine.

To the automobile enthusiast M. M. Musselman the electric car that "rolled along the avenue as smug and silent as a fat cat stalking a birdbath" was doomed by its femininity. Its maximum speed was twenty miles an hour; instead of rattling, fuming and banging the little electrics purred in a way to match their dainty interiors: ruffled silk curtains on curved plate-glass windows; fawn-colored upholstery; vanity compartments and bud vases. Musselman put his finger on the "red-blooded" objection of the time:

> Soon the average man would rather have walked down the street without his pants than to drive an electric coupé.[6]

The gasoline-powered car was a "he-man" machine. Boys wanted to be like the ex–"hell-for-leather" bicycle racer Barney Oldfield who in 1903 pushed Henry Ford's "999" to a dramatic victory at Grosse Pointe; or like the two daredevils who had crossed the continent that year. Men took new Fords, Packards and Oldses on reliability drives around San Francisco Bay; endurance runs were staged on rough highways out of San Diego and Los Angeles.

By 1905 Coast Highway towns had started the change to an automotive way of life. Bicycle men, blacksmiths and stable owners began tinkering with engines; most general stores sold gasoline at twelve cents a gallon; farmers and delivery people talked about new "trucks" in use back East and old-timers declared, "You can't teach a milk route to a motor truck!"

Californians were singing Gus Edwards' popular song, "In My Merry Oldsmobile"; women with long veils secured under their chins protested against the charge that they were too nervous to operate a gasoline car at twenty-five miles an hour and resented the *Outing* magazine barb implying they would get around inherent lack of skill the way ladies "always manage to get around the male sex." [7]

In 1905 more than fifty companies had manufactured and put

on the market 25,000 automobiles, featuring such innovations as windshields, tilted steering posts, roadster and touring bodies, and the Gabriel tubular horn. Dealers returned from New York and Chicago auto shows to report future innovations: front bumpers, speedometers, left-handed steering and baked enamel finishing. They told of wild times at the plush Everleigh brothel where they had been entertained at the expense of Midwest manufacturers.

Speed records were being established and broken every month. Oldsmobile made the transcontinental run in forty-four days; Robert Gano drove from Los Angeles to Santa Barbara behind the wheel of a four-cylinder Packard in thirteen hours, including stops to let wagons pass. The "devil wagon" man Barney Oldfield came to the coast to race and also drove a car into the lobby of San Francisco's Continental Hotel.

The cops cracked down on speeders by shooting tires and laying speed traps. The Southern California Auto Club presented the Los Angeles police with two patrol cars, chauffeurs and speedometers to protect its members from unfair arrest. The Club was less effective in curbing the first cases of reckless driving.

In 1905 a girl was killed in Los Angeles and newspapers campaigned against "carelessness, incompetency, recklessness and inebriety." Under attack came the roadhouses where:

> foolish young men with too much money are enticed to ruin, and young girls are debauched.[8]

Automobilists were urged to observe the "Don'ts" listed in the *Automobile Handbook*—such sensible admonitions as:

> Don't keep on running when an unusual noise is heard about the car. Stop and find out what it is.
> Don't start or stop too suddenly. Something may break.
> Don't use a lighted match to see if the gasoline tank is empty. Something unexpected may happen.[9]

To their pleas for sensible driving motor clubs added a campaign for better paved roads. They sent representatives to Sacramento with suggestions based on information members had gathered when placing automobile direction signs on numerous routes.

The state of the Coast Road along its northern sections came into dramatic focus early in 1906 just as the automobilists believed they were making progress in road building; on the morning of April 18th the ancient San Andreas fault began to slip along the line that ran from ninety miles north of San Francisco, down into the southwestern desert.

THE CRACKED ROAD

In its history coastal California had felt greater quakes than the one in 1906 but that upheaval was the most devastating within the memory of man. At crowded San Francisco the counted dead numbered 452, and fires that raged in the wake of the shock destroyed 28,199 buildings. With the water supply cut off, flames swept across four square miles; the damage in terms of money was estimated at half a million dollars.

Great twenty-foot splits opened the highway from Mission San Rafael down to San Juan Bautista; passes were closed; embankments slid. So mighty was the blow from underground that at Lick Observatory the needle flew from the recording disk of the seismograph. On the Stanford Campus the stone vaulted ceiling of the memorial chapel fell, along with the great arch and the library building. In the cemetery of Mission San José marble shafts were broken squarely in two; for miles north and south the highway showed cracks, peculiar twists and great humps. Thousands of accounts, in the days and years following the quake, listed remarkable contortions to the road and houses along its sides.

Alan Maxwell described "waves" three feet high that coursed from east to west over San Mateo farm land. He was standing about one hundred feet from a tank and told an earthquake investigator

> A 30-foot tank tilted so I could see the water inside; then it swayed right back in place.[10]

Dan Pickering described the same terrestrial seaway about one mile south of Santa Clara and said it "sounded like a stampede of cattle," while H. R. Johnson at a roadhouse near Schutzen Park, below San Jose, claimed that building had "shimmied like a flivver." Two men lost their lives at Del Monte when twenty-five chimneys toppled. Five-foot-thick redwoods snapped in the Santa Cruz mountains, bridges warped across the Parajo and Salinas rivers, earth-lurches caused walls to crack at Mission San Juan Bautista.

The flows and slumps scarred the land south and east of El Camino Real; back waves stopped clocks at Paso Robles, Pismo Beach and Lompoc. Along the coast below Point Concepción people were shaken awake and there were reports of windows rattling as far south as Anaheim.

The Los Angeles *Times* "re-created" the scene at San Francisco:

> Rapine and vice, assault, robbery, and desecration of the dead were included in unspeakable horrors. There was short shrift for at least a score of these bestial wretches . . .[11]

Southern California papers heard "from unimpeachable sources" that the Pacific had enveloped the Bay Area, drowning tens of thousands while submerging cities south of the Golden Gate. When William Randolph Hearst's *Examiner* consoled the homeless of San Francisco with "news" that a great tidal wave had buried most of Southern California, the *Times* called its northern rival "the longest leased liar in the world."

Among the casualties of the San Francisco quake and fire was the pickled head of Joaquin Murieta, finally cremated after half a century on morbid display. Military officiousness caused a far more serious loss when two uniformed guards barred old William Heath Davis—of the Boston hide ships—from entering his home to rescue two thick manuscript volumes he had written on the history of California. Fire never reached the house but the books were stolen; Davis laboriously rewrote a shortened version from memory.

The catastrophe which sent desperate people fleeing the city was unforgettable: on the highway wagons, carts, wheelbarrows and baby carriages joined automobiles, piled high with salvaged possessions; people fought for places on southbound refugee trains and many who headed for Los Angeles never returned to the ruined city.

With the world spotlight on California, public figures stepped onto the stage of misery, spouting brave predictions, lauding the indomitable spirit that would rebuild San Francisco. The railroad harped on its contribution to the stricken area; working stiffs were pictured as heroes when they converged on the ruins, attracted by high wages; the mealy-mouthed gave thanks that no subway, such as New York's, had been built.

FOUR-CYLINDER PIONEERS

The exodus of the destitute and the inflow to San Francisco of laborers, material and food called attention to the sorry condition of the Coast Highway and the dependence of the state on its monster of a railroad. Since the passing of the stagecoach the turnpike had steadily deteriorated. Around cities and towns automobilists held "road-building days" when members manned shovels, gravel carts, "stone boats" and split-log drags. In the opinion of the California State Automobile Association

> Automobiling was only slightly less rugged than trail-breaking, and a drive off a city thoroughfare was an adventure into the unknown.[12]

The San Francisco and Los Angeles auto clubs, now rival organizations that began to envelop smaller clubs in their areas, posted signs to mark the highway but more often than not markers merely told the motorist the location of his distress. The adventurer on wheels was frequently seen changing a blown-out fabric tire, or trying to patch it if he had neglected to bring along spares.

In winter the turnpike was as impassable as of old and motorists in hipboots were seen struggling with planks or lengths of line used around tires to give traction. Between Salinas, San Luis

Obispo, Santa Maria and Santa Barbara rustics were known to set up obstacles in order to exact towage tribute from "them rich city automobilists." The Northern California Club commented:

> These experiences led to stories of ranchers who hauled motorists out of mud holes in the daytime and who spent their nights re-filling the holes with water.[13]

Excerpts from the journal of C. D. Cox on a motoring expedition from Nordhoff to San Luis Obispo illustrated the hazards of 1906:

> *April 14*—Nordhoff to Santa Barbara: crossed nine fords on the creek road and three streams in Ventura River. Stuck in third. Young man with team pulled us out. Left the road and ran through fields down a very steep hill back onto main road. Oiled road horribly rough.
>
> *April 24*—Waited at Santa Barbara eight days for new tires from Denver. Put on new tires and went for ride. Water pump gave out. Battery repair was also necessary.
>
> *April 25*—Santa Barbara to Los Olivos: Had to stop at creek and fill radiator. Pipe working loose on top of cylinders. Road from here to Gaviota horrible. Crossed 45 creeks and canyons up one steep hill after another. Most discouraging. At Las Cruces passed automobile with broken spring. After passing Santa Ynez Mission engine missing. Took out battery and put in dry cells. Filled radiator with tumbler from horse draught.
>
> *April 26*—Los Olivos to San Luis Obispo: High wind blowing. Stopped every few minutes to tighten up water pipe, or fuss with wiring. Sand deep. More battery trouble. Broke front spring clear in two.
>
> *April 27*—San Luis Obispo: I decided to abandon car here.[14]

The actual condition of the road in no way dampened the spirit of planners. The Mission Bell Association started erecting 450 signposts—one every mile—along the ancient path of El Camino Real; cast bronze bells hung from iron standards that resembled Franciscan walking staffs. The early work of Tessa Kelso, Anna Picher, and Mrs. A. S. C. Forbes was carried on by historical-minded members of the Mission Bell, Landmark and other associations. By the time the State Legislature offered an 18-million-dollar bond issue surveyors would at least know where to begin on "The Birth of the Amazing Era of Modern Highways in California."

On that unpaved road of signs hardy automobilists found personalized directions, auto club markers, dedications to "The Los Angeles Produce Exchange," and many repetitions of "Jesus Saves" or "Prepare to meet thy God!"

The Santa Barbara *Press* lashed out editorially against the religious enthusiasts, and others whose messages cluttered the highways:

> As yet the county is free from hideous billboards that have appeared in other sections. At the Supervisor's next meeting steps will probably be taken to prohibit painting of signs along public roads.[15]

The many announcements, resolutions, and the cheery slush of "live wire" civic leaders still described nothing more than a dream road. Whenever funds became available they seemed to disappear into pork-barrel projects. Automobiling remained a pioneer endeavor through almost two decades and led to such stories as the Los Angeles *Times* ran about the ingenuity of Dick Whittemore, who was able to proceed after a blowout

> ... by pumping the punctured tire of his Overland full of ingredients left over from a camping trip. This included 10 lbs. of flour and several bottles of beer.[16]

This was at about the time when someone suggested that roads be constructed of rubber and tires made out of iron. Reversal in a way became the earliest solution to travel by car along the state's principal north-south artery: off the Ford Motor Company's assembly line came a road-defying marvel, the Model T.

THE "TIN LIZZIE"

The to-be-famous four-cylinder Model T touring car was advertised in the October 3, 1908, issue of the *Saturday Evening Post* at the low price of $850. That brewster green, five-passenger car, was guaranteed to make twenty miles on one gallon of gas, speed forty miles per hour, and "to work on hills, on sand and mud roads, in good and bad weather."

Californians were at first skeptical. Henry Ford had produced a number of experimental cars—including his six-cylinder job that required an underbody pan to catch the dropping nuts and bolts. Too, it was a time of many ideas—flying machines; Ralph Starr's perpetual-motion tide engine at San Francisco; moving pictures at Los Angeles and Santa Barbara; a gold-from-seawater dredge of the San Luis Obispo gas engineer E. S. Hoyt; and Martin Seely's scheme at Santa Clara to use monkeys as fruit pickers. But the Model T soon established itself as the most popular and practical car ever built.

The year the Tin Lizzie was announced 65,000 cars and other vehicles were manufactured by 175 auto firms. Five years later production had soared to an annual half a million and out of Ford's assembly plants came one thousand cars a day. "The Universal Car"—new, light, fast, agile—could, and did, go everywhere. Whatever superlatives Ford's salesmen did not think of were supplied by satisfied customers at all levels. Santa Clara and San Diego County farmers scrimped to buy a Model T. It became more of a necessity than a bathtub (people said, "You can't ride into town in a bathtub"), for the flivver served as pleasure car, tractor, truck, and could go places inaccessible to a horse. To the man in the Ford the condition of the road was almost immaterial.

So great did the demand become for the Model T that after 1914 it was available only in black, although advertised with a choice of such popular colors as carmine red, touring blue and brewster green, with black trim and red striping. Busy Henry Ford announced that his customers "can have any color they want, provided it is black!"

The Model T, spreading the idea of individual motorized transportation, shook off the grip of the Southern Pacific more effectively than any other single agent. One of the many offshoots of its influence was described by the authors of *Oxcart to Airplane:*

In 1913 there sprang up in Los Angeles and other centers a "jitney" service, which with amazing rapidity employed thousands of individually owned second-hand automobiles. These machines—Fords strongly predominating—were made to carry unbelievable loads of human freight, and at the rush hours they almost choked the city streets for numbers.[17]

The jitney spread in a few years to run between San Francisco and San Jose and out of Los Angeles to San Diego and Santa Barbara. This was the start of busses which called themselves "stages." The railroad interests cracked the whip and saw to it that jitneys and motor busses came under the California Railroad Commission. But the average man had tasted some freedom from arrogant public transportation which in time would lead to a largely automotive state.

The Model T craze did not end until the mid-twenties when there were *fifteen million* of them on the roads; at the height of popularity every other car in California was a Ford. One of the Model T's numerous historians, Philip Van Doren Stern, wrote:

> ... it was, as no car before or since has been, truly the people's car. It became part of the fabric of American life, celebrated in song and legend and folklore.[18]

CALIFORNIA MOTORLAND

The last of the Coast Highway towns to admit that the automobile had definitely ended the livery stable era was Santa Barbara whose city council finally authorized the purchase of a Model T in 1912 for $685. But the following year the mayor vetoed a muffler ordinance and expounded on the importance of warning the horse.

While Harry Wood and other progressive stable owners shifted operations to get the patronage of the automobilist, many continued their boarding and livery stables, harness shops, saddleries and feed barns. People still liked to ride into the Santa Ynez mountains where even a Model T could not venture; and seventy-five horses remained in the corral of the Flying A Movie Studio. There were also some independent souls who held onto the reliable horse:

Edward Kleet, the mail carrier, did not give up until the twenties, driving his famous "Chicken Coop" on the fifteen-mile route to Montecito. Ed's gray mares for thirty years were a mother, daughter and granddaughter.

If there were no other signs, ignorance of horses that had set in before the First World War would have shown the future course. Fred Longawa, interviewed in his old age by the enthusiastic historical writer Walker A. Tompkins, told of the sad pass things had come to in his final days of renting saddle horses:

> Sailors off visiting ships used to have races on rented horses up and down State Street. I remember one sailor renting a horse from me, and when I asked him how long he wanted it—meaning the number of hours, of course—he replied "Long enough for three sailors to get aboard at once." He wasn't joking either.[19]

Horses went to the movie studios at San Diego, Los Angeles, Santa Monica and Santa Barbara; or on the rodeo circuit up to Salinas. The Ed Kleets and small truck farmers used them; in cities they came to proclaim the poverty of their driver. Only on the racetracks was the horse revered.

A new language emanated from the Coast Highway "gasoline alleys," where mechanics talked of "classy outfits," "easy riders," "speedsters" and "super-sixes." Mechanics knew the prices of parts by heart: a Ford fender cost $2.50, a carburetor $6 and a new radiator $15. Instantly they could reel off the record runs—in 1909 René Brassy drove a Thomas Flyer from Los Angeles to San Francisco in 16 hours, 45 minutes, including time wasted when he was given a speeding ticket in Santa Barbara; the Los Angeles to San Diego record mark, set the same year by a Rambler, was 10 hours and 32 minutes.

Men who worked in the new automobile stations cared less about the European War of 1914 than they did about mechanical innovations and oddities: electric starters that banished the arm-breaking crank; Pierce-Arrow headlights in fenders; the sixty-horse-power Locomobile with rear-wheel drums, three hundred feet of line, anchor, crowbars and other gear for hauling cars out of mud, holes or fords. The story was told of visitors to a lunatic asylum who were calling to see a demented mechanic and were told to look under the bed: "He works there all day on the slats."

By 1914 more than two million cars operated on American roads, and car thievery became a profession. In Los Angeles the "Pico Gang," the "New Year's Eve Gang" and the "Broadway Gang" snatched automobiles off the city streets or out at the beaches for sale to "fences"; stolen cars driven across the border came back as "jalopies," a word taken from the name of a Mexican town where second-hand machines found a market; some thieves dismantled cars and sold parts to crooked second-hand dealers.

Auto clubs, new car insurance detectives, and the industry, waged war against car "clouters" who faced stiff prison sentences and heavy fines. Automobile dealers had reached the point where they spoke gravely of reputation, integrity and service. *Service*—to replace *caveat emptor*—was suggested as the watchword in the highly competitive auto sales field.

Until America entered the World War, tourist and industrial automobiling boomed along the rutted highway and its washboard by-paths. Whenever a heat wave hit the San Joaquin Valley well-to-do families headed for the Coast to fill boarding houses and small seaside hotels. Easterners rented machines for $5 a day while they stayed at Del Monte, Del Coronado or the million-and-a-half dollar Potter Hotel at Santa Barbara.

To lure California and out-of-state vacationists new resort cities were promoted at Pismo Beach, Oceanside and Venice. That "Italy in America," west of Los Angeles, featured lagoons, a Grand Canal and Venetian gondolas, and had been launched with a performance by the great Sarah Bernhardt who was familiar to theatergoers at every town along El Camino Real.

The automobile would never break down the political and business barrier between Northern and Southern California, but it did open the eyes of even long-time residents as to who lived in the Golden State. Travelers visited the artist colonies at Laguna Beach, between San Diego and Los Angeles, and up on the shores of Carmel Bay; from Marin County down to Point Loma, facing San Diego Bay, they saw Portuguese farmers and fishermen from the Cape Verde and Azore Islands, Swiss dairy farmers, and scattered Mexican ranches. Around Morro Bay, in Cambria, and across the southern Santa Lucias to San Luis Obispo, Japanese abalone fishermen, Welsh and French farmers, and Chinese truck gardeners lived in some harmony. Up in the redwood forests above Santa Cruz the Scotch had founded the town of Ben Lomond and gave Old World names to their country houses—Bonnie Doon and Bracken Brae.

Tourists flocked north of the redwood area, to the annoyance of the writer J. Smeaton Chase, who made a coast trek on horseback to get away from the automobile crowd. He shunned Boulder Creek, "chiefly remarkable for supporting an equipment of twenty-one saloons," and found the quiet he sought in the tall timber of the Big Basin, where "the shade was almost unbroken and the trail carpeted deeply with fallen leaves of madrone and tanbark oak." But at Pescadero, where Portolá had almost died of scurvy, Chase met a large party of automobile picnickers.

> When I learned that the noisiest, thirstiest, and most obscene of the group was a banker of San Francisco I congratulated myself that no funds of mine were in his keeping.[20]

While Americans from the boom of the 1880s predominated in the cities, and at rich farm areas like Downey, south of Los Angeles, numerous little foreign settlements had formed in what were isolated spots until the coming of the automobile. In the Santa Ynez Valley, on the deserted stage road, Midwest Danish church leaders brought their people to found Solvang, adjoining the old mission. Far to the south, in Baja California's mountain town of Guadalupe, the Russians established a religious settlement. This was the Malakan sect, whose members wore long beards, shunned tobacco and took steam baths.

Where they still held forth at old missions padres of the Franciscan order wore brown robes, the gray habit having been cast off in 1898. The Indians living at those first civilized homes of their ancestors were as scarce as the little sea otter, brought close to extinction by greedy fishermen.

Italians, West Indians, Basques, Africans and men who retained the garb of Eastern deserts gave a cosmopolitan shading to the state even if their young people quickly drifted to coast towns, drawn by the automobile, motion pictures and the new airplane. In February of 1915 thousands of them were on the road, headed for San Francisco's $50 million Panama-Pacific Exposition where people from all over America, and the world, came to celebrate the recovery of the devastated city and the opening of the Panama Canal.

BLUEPRINT HIGHWAYS

Three years before the "Rainbow City" exposition plans were announced for the building of an ocean-to-ocean turnpike and the revival of El Camino Real as a concrete thoroughfare.

In the summer of 1912 the first shovelful of earth was turned over in San Mateo County. Statewide enthusiasm would tolerate no obstacles and even the Southern Pacific, then beginning to weaken, was forced to cut in half its rates for hauling pavement material. All along the old Royal Highway women's clubs, chambers of commerce, auto clubs and the California Mission Trail and Landmark organizations campaigned. At Santa Barbara's Rincón Point—where stagecoaches had been able to splash through the surf—a viaduct of eucalyptus logs was built for automobiles. But inadequate funds retarded the much publicized road and two years after the groundbreaking travel writer Thomas D. Murphy described the route northward from Palo Alto:

> ...in sad disrepair, unmercifully rough and full of chuck-holes. It was being rebuilt in places, compelling us to take a roundabout route, which, with much tire trouble, delayed our arrival in San Francisco until late in the afternoon.[21]

The much more ballyhooed and heavily financed transcontinental turnpike showed even less progress than the Pacific Coast artery. Conceived by Carl Fisher, that vigorous creator of Presto-Lite, the Indianapolis Speedway and Miami Beach, the concrete descendant of the covered wagon trails west had become the national rage by 1913 under the sponsorship of the Lincoln Highway Association. A motorcade whose autos dipped rear wheels in the Atlantic surf lumbered over a proposed route and seventy days later wet front tires in the Pacific; automobile manufacturers and philanthropists subscribed money, the press gave the project space, and the Portland Cement Association built complimentary "seedling miles" in states along the path the Lincoln Highway was to follow.

What caused the Lincoln Highway to bog down was a long battle that commenced over which way it was to cross the continent. Politicians, civic organizations and a variety of chiselers stormed the Association with demands. Ohio's most distinguished citizen, Senator Warren G. Harding, disapproved of the proposed route through his state; Mormons raised obstacles because of the name Lincoln; even President Woodrow Wilson wanted the highway to swing through Washington; and the Automobile Club of Southern California put up a bitter fight to have the terminus at Los Angeles rather than San Francisco.

The Lincoln Highway was supposed, among other things, to stimulate a "good roads program" in every state, but the bickering that attended its direction dragged the building out over fourteen years. By the time an actual through road was laid out the federal government had replaced the name with numerals.

Among other obstacles that confronted the Lincoln Highway, as well as El Camino Real and all new state roads, was America's entrance into the Great War.

GASLESS SUNDAYS

After the United States declared war on Germany in April of 1917 the new garages soon found themselves short of spare parts and filling stations hung out "closed" signs for a week at a time. The new model cars with their slanted windshields, disk clutches and pressure lubrication became scarce, and most of the traffic along El Camino Real was created by a newly designed motor vehicle that hauled cotton, foodstuffs and young men in uniform.

Factories sprang up at bursting Los Angeles and the city filled with laborers from below the border, come as replacements for men gone to war; they would give L.A. the largest Mexican population in the world outside of Mexico City. Up at San Francisco the military hand choked off the infamous Barbary Coast to end temporarily an era of sanctioned sin.

In 1918 California newspapers wrote the obituary of its most colorful crusader against vice when old Major Horace Bell, scourge of highwaymen, went to his reward. The major had left the Rangers to practice law and journalism; at the warrior's passing the press quoted his victory chant:

> I have hung the gory scalps of the last mother's son of them on the ridge-pole of my tent.[22]

The European War brought memories from even farther back than post–Gold Rush desperado days: a few very old men and women shrugged wearily at another speculation on a possible coastal foray, this time by Count Felix von Luckner, the German sea raider then scouring the Pacific. And echoes came from beyond a century of time when the Mexican revolt from Spain had cut off California and missions were its mainstay; by 1919 Coast industry and agriculture had turned to support 3,500,000 persons. The automobile had brought a migration that dwarfed all others and caused the first big change in population density since the influx of forty-niners.

The 1920 census showed peninsular San Francisco, city of union labor, graft and nature's perils, to have 506,000 people, while Los Angeles, sprawling metropolis on wheels, counted 576,000. And "The City of Destiny" was only at its start in a suburb-swallowing rise toward becoming the earth's most populous city.

The automobile industry was likewise ready for a dramatic spurt that would make its post-war annual production of two million vehicles seem almost tiny. From the era of gas-tank dip sticks, kicking cranks, isinglass side-curtains, hand-operated windshield-wipers and klaxons the car was to move into a wondrous age that started with four-wheel brakes, balloon tires, closed cars and other innovations to make the automobile good-looking as well as functional—what Charles E. Wilson of General Motors typed as "a blond who can cook!"

Eleven U.S. 101

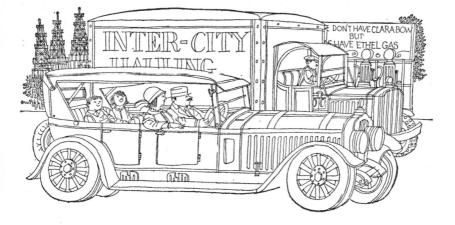

FIGHT FOR A HIGHWAY

Most of California's one million automobiles and trucks operated on city streets in 1921 with only work vehicles and adventurers using the Coast and other rough highways. As thousands of new cars wheeled into the state every month, automotive interests pushed for good roads, showering every town with literature, lecturers and free Charlie Chaplin movies—shown after highway speeches. Women's clubs entered the campaign to canvass by telephone for easier, safer access to schools, churches, markets and vacation spots; war veterans, many of whom had invested their five-hundred-dollar bonus in service stations or garages, joined the fight.

In that automobile age there were few enemies of the "good roads" campaign—the shell of the railroad monopoly; farmers located close to the tracks; minority groups like the Amish sect from Pennsylvania, Ohio and Indiana whose creed outlawed motor vehicles. But if few spoke against road building there were many who protested long and loudly when asked to sanction further spending.

During ten years $73 million had "gone down the rat hole"— in the minds of the citizens—to line the pockets of politicians, contractors and suppliers. The road mileage along the Coast in no way justified the money being spent, and activity seemed confined to sweeping up debris, cleaning sand drifts and patching broken pavement. A federal survey stated bluntly:

> California has the narrowest, thinnest and leanest concrete roads in the United States.[1]

It was the government that broke the barrier of resistance with the passage of Federal Road Acts in 1916 and again in 1921, the latter bringing money and capable, trustworthy men to back the Bureau of Public Roads' statistical messages which assured increased property values, low building costs and direct benefits for everyone.

People wanted to believe J. E. Pennybaker, Chief of Road Economics, when he declared after a survey trip that California could have "the most notable system of highways in America, if not in the world." [2] The men employed by the Bureau as supervisors were of a caliber to inspire confidence and give some weight to Pennybaker's pronouncement. Ben Blow of the California State Automobile Association described that civil servant of the 1920s:

> In the first place he is a road-builder engineer whose competency is guaranteed. In the second place the honesty of his purpose and his personal integrity are above suspicion. He has no personal axe to grind; is not personally interested in this material or that material; has no local interests.[3]

Blow spoke for the CSAA which was then at odds with the California Highway Commission over road building and implied that the federal engineers were the only honest men breathing highway dust. But with them was an army of honorable and able men, freed of log-rolling and chiseling orders, who had served through undramatized years under the distinguished Austin Bradstreet Fletcher.

Fletcher had been State Highway Engineer for a dozen years

after coming to San Diego from the Massachusetts Highway Commission in 1910. He was a strict but kindly man and during his tenure along the Coast organized a personnel which could have built highways to pace the Eastern states had money and honest orders been forthcoming. The few spots where they did work in early days resulted in roads good enough to elicit such praise as this San Mateo County press report:

> ...young folk of the peninsula towns have taken up the fad of utilizing the new State Highway for roller recreation.... Moonlight skating parties are quite a common thing on the new, smooth surface of El Camino Real.[4]

When Fletcher was called back to the Bureau in Washington in 1923 he remained a staunch champion of the Coast Highway he had hoped to complete; like José de Gálvez, that absentee patron of 150 years before, Fletcher kept an interested eye on El Camino Real.

THE CONCRETE FACE

After the government pledged $200 million to aid state roads the California legislature met in a special 1923 session to approve a two-cent tax on gasoline. Onto the patched Coast Highway moved $3 million worth of World War surplus graders, road drags, iron mules and cases of blasting powder, along with new caterpillar tractors, steam rollers, stripping machines and scarifiers. From Sonoma plaza down to the Mexican border contracts were let for stretches of the old Spanish trail most urgently in need of repair. Engineers and surveyors sketched plans to widen and improve the grades at Torrey Pines, Casitas, Cuesta and other difficult passes. State and federal highway experts studied the problems of construction along the sheer face of the Santa Lucias, around Rincón Point where the sea was battering the old eucalyptus viaduct, and on the coast above San Diego.

Thomas H. MacDonald, the United States Commissioner of Roads, warned of difficulties and admitted that

We are but laying the groundwork which is not much further advanced than the modern science of surgery and medicine fifty years ago.[5]

There could be no standard procedure on that 500-mile way for either material or equipment in the 1920s. Up in Marin County, where oil-macadam roads had been wrinkled "by heavy hind wheels," a smooth, durable turnpike was imperative for trucks hauling loads of 64,000 eggs. Highway Engineer W. H. Lynch suggested "a width of roadway of at least twenty-four feet . . . with concrete five inches thick." South of San Francisco three main roads through San Mateo County were each in a sense the Camino Real for their hard surfaces covered trails favored by Portolá, Rivera and Anza; and going on to Monterey or the Salinas valleys dual highways followed paths worn by Serra and Fages.

The road-builders of the 1920s set a modern pattern for establishing the general trace of what had been in Spanish times the King's Highway, and in the distant past Indian trails selected from man's best way along the pre-historic corridor. Future historians would engage themselves in the interesting pastime of fixing old locations along the concrete way: and it might very well be true that at the spot where an old Japanese woman smoked her porcelain pipe in front of a beach shack at Hueneme, Indians had dragged Miguel Costansó into the surf to explain that a Spanish ship had been sighted off their shore.

Construction men dumped rock and poured concrete over yellowed bones at forgotten Indian cemeteries near San Luis Obispo, Ventura and Oceanside; aged adobe buildings, in ruins or being used for Chinese laundries, became foundation material together with abalone shell, bones of drought-stricken cattle, and weathered fence posts. History was literally in and under the new road.

Groups dedicated to preserving California's past, and her natural beauty, pressured the Highway Commission and the State Legislature. Work had already been started on restoration of old missions by energetic priests and members of the Native Sons and

Daughters of the Golden West, and the Landmark Association. Archaeologists and museum people watched at excavation sites to save treasures of the past; warnings were issued against any action that might mar the beauty of the land. On May 24, 1924, the Los Angeles *Times* reported that "heavy fines are being assessed for plucking blooming yuccas...." [6]

Also seeking to influence the direction and character of the Coast Highway were the two automobile clubs, each striving to get more mileage and appropriations for the north or south sections, with San Luis Obispo the highway point on their "Mason-Dixon Line." Those "non-commercial, non-profit-making organizations with the sole objective of service" battled at the automobile tourist level for the most part and were constantly advocating extra routes to popular vacation spots in their respective areas.

The Automobile Club of Southern California pressed for half a dozen good roads out of Los Angeles, a coast and inland route down to San Diego, and rebuilding of the old San Marcos Pass stage road to relieve traffic through Gaviota Pass. The southern laterals were to serve the "homey" Midwestern farm people who had faith in advertisements. The "jays" from Nebraska to Ohio had millions to spend and wanted to locate away from the jazzy world of shingled flappers, sugar daddies, gin cocktails, the Charleston, and open talk of birth control.

In the north the policy of the CSAA was affected by the sophistication of metropolitan San Francisco where bootleggers had started to shunt traffic to roadhouses. Demands were made for the improvement of the Skyline, Ocean and other boulevards leading out to the oasis inns; men in myrtle green chamois topcoats, with matching suede hats, swigged from flasks as they drove erratically in Daimlers, Napiers and Rolls Royces with uninhibited butterfly girls.

To accommodate more solid citizens there came agitation for a new turnpike through the redwoods to Santa Cruz and beyond, where visitors toured the historic buildings of Monterey.

From the old capital sightseers motored along Seventeen Mile

Drive to Pebble Beach and then through the toll gate kept by Sam Powers, an aged stage driver, on into the famous artists' colony at Carmel. Tourists of the twenties always stopped to take pictures of the mission chapel whose altar rose above the graves of the Franciscans, Junípero Serra, Juan Crespí and Fermin Lasuén.

Taxpayers in other parts of the state sulked over spending at Monterey, but they were outspokenly critical of a project that extended from the tourist spa southward along the rugged coast to Morro Bay—the Carmel–to–San Simeon scenic highway. Why should money be poured into a road that served so few? Living in the Monterey Forest, around Big Sur, were a dozen or so homesteaders—the John Pfeiffers, William Posts, Sam Trotters, and such non-conformists as Jaime de Angulo and Kenneth E. McConnell. Were state and federal funds by chance being funneled into a private ninety-seven-mile boulevard for the lavish castle at San Simeon where the wealthy newspaper publisher William Randolph Hearst was storing European art treasures?

The Highway Commission, with federal backing, had announced that the road started in 1921 along the face of the Sierra de Santa Lucia was "intended to supply a link in that all-coast highway which will some time undoubtedly stretch from the Oregon line to Mexico." [7] The "wonderful scenic route" eventually cost $9 million and took sixteen years to build with its thirty-two bridges, one of them at Bixby Creek 342 feet, the longest reinforced concrete arch in the West.

The Carmel–to–San Simeon road encouraged hamlets and resorts on every lateral of the main artery to demand a concrete cover. But those were minor difficulties compared to natural catastrophes that held up completion of a through road: the 1925 earthquake that wrecked the city of Santa Barbara and wrenched land along the channel coast; the huge bore of water that rushed down Ventura's Santa Clara Valley to the sea in 1928 when the St. Francis Dam collapsed to flood 8,000 acres; the sludge of oil that gushed from thousands of new wells south of Santa Barbara and Los Angeles as the petroleum industry went into high gear.

THE OIL SLICK

Through the twenties California's oil production climbed toward a record annual 300 million barrels boosted by auto consumption. The new oil fever led to wildcat speculation that dwarfed the craze of the 1900s when the world read with awe of the 135 derricks that pumped four barrels of heavy oil from the ocean offshore at the former spiritualist colony of Summerland, south of Santa Barbara.

From Monterey County to San Diego travelers along 101 came to accept the wayside derricks, around which cattle grazed, just as a later generation would scarcely notice TV aerials. But the discoveries of the big oil companies—Shell, Union and Standard—around Los Angeles set off a frenzied era of land gambling that did not end until the Wall Street crash. Signal Hill, Santa Fe Springs and Huntington Beach strikes created a mechanical forest along the Los Angeles Basin path of the Coast Highway.

The solid economy that spread from the petroleum industry was buried for the average man and woman under the exciting promise of easy wealth. The average person's symbol of flamboyance in that era was Chauncey C. Julian, the Texas oil-rigger who became "gusher king of ballyhoo," and bilked thousands with his get-rich-quick oil promotions. W. W. Robinson, the California historian, listed a few of the prodigalities of "C.C."

> ...as when he tipped a cab-driver $1500, when he fought with Charlie Chaplin in a Hollywood night club, when he spent $25,000 on one spree, and when he bought a gold-lined bathtub.[8]

Such blatant opulence proved a sure lure for "suckers."

The derrick-fringed city of Los Angeles became a menace to through—and all other—traffic by the mid-twenties when the oil boom brought another great wave of people from the East. In 1924 voters approved a plan which would provide speedways with synchronized traffic lights. Those quickly built boulevards were as

221

quickly choked by new cars which came into the city at the rate of five thousand a month. When Sunday drivers headed for the beach, or out-of-town drives, the north-south highway became a bottleneck.

Before an adequate highway pierced Los Angeles the Southern California Auto Club had launched still another publicity campaign to lure small town motorists to the "City of Destiny." Also in the booster act was the All-Year Club of Southern California which raised a "war chest" among businessmen and civic organizations "for the purpose of advertising this area's charms among outlanders in remote regions." [9] The population of L.A. had already passed the one million mark and the voice of progress shouted down the plea for a moratorium on migration while the city built adequate streets, sewers and houses.

With the apostles of growth came personalities whose actions would echo longer than the ring of the cash register: the tree-planting endeavors of John McLaren, Superintendent of Golden Gate Park set an example for road beautification south of San Francisco as did Kate Session's shrubbery for the new road out of San Diego's Balboa Park; James Irvine, owner of a 108,000-acre Spanish grant in Orange County, deeded a right of way without cost; at Santa Barbara the newspaper editor, Thomas M. Storke, convinced such wealthy oilmen as Sam Mosher and Reese Taylor that they should keep dirty drilling operations three miles off shore; and in the channel city that dynamic lady Pearl Chase fought industrial plants, railroad junk heaps, billboards and ugly commercial buildings with her battle cry: "We must protect and beautify our Boulevard!" [10]

As the concrete carpet rolled out one cent was added to the gas tax and the Department of Public Works returned to embrace, temporarily, the Division of Highways. Roads were reclassified and additional districts created; signposts on the Coast Highway came down and in their stead were erected shields that gave a numbered designation to El Camino Real.

ONE HUNDRED AND ONE

Increased road building had created so much confusion by 1925 that the Secretary of Agriculture called a meeting of state and federal officials to work out a plan that would clarify the designation of routes. On March 2nd the joint board adopted a nation-wide system whereby federal intra-state roads each received a number carried on a shield marker.

Principal east-west turnpikes were given even numbers, starting at the Canadian border; north-south arteries bore odd numbers, the count being from the Atlantic seaboard. It was planned to have main thoroughfares numbered under 100—in order that three-digit roads might indicate from which stem they fed—but so numerous were the meridianal roads that the Coast Highway lay west of 99, and so drew 101.

It was the summer of 1928 before the two California auto clubs began erecting shields bearing the unique 101. Since oddities were frowned upon by sound businessmen unless they had some commercial value, the drab name 101 was not popular. Tub-thumpers could find no inspiration in the numeral and managed to sub-head it with the romantic embellishments Mission Trail, Royal Highway or El Camino Real.

To the men and women who were making California's modern road maps the simple 101 seemed a blessing. And for the motorist traveling any distance it was a relief to sight the familiar shield on reaches of coastal highway that often changed name when politicians acted for nagging constituents to pass resolutions naming a segment of road for some president, national hero of the moment, historical figure or town benefactor.

Since the turn of the century, when bicyclists plotted the first maps, the charting of highways and byways had developed into a mechanical art. By the late twenties people joked about signs that were common fifteen years earlier when they were directed to follow a mountain range to some fork, then "take the rut that leads off to the right." The medieval directions had given way to thousands of road, historical, and advertisement markers so numerous that there were only a few sections of highway where summer-idle young fellows could have the fun of directing a "tin can tourist" down a country road into a cleverly disguised mud hole.

Oil companies, auto associations and the Highway Division sent men up and down 101 to measure, check and map every mile of highway. Photographs were taken from elevations, off shore, and out of airplanes. Interviews with old-timers—Juan Dana, Sam Hunter and Joseph G. Foxen—attempted to get names correctly spelled. Surveyors flew over Santa Barbara County in the plane of Simon Shepard who pointed out wagon roads of the 1880s which he knew as well as his strawberry patches.

The free road map—which would eventually reach the astonishing figure of 168 million a year in the United States—was the tourist's bible. The give-away maps not only showed mileage between towns but had marked on them the locations of historic spots, missions, universities, emergency telephones and campsites. Supplementary literature gave average driving time between towns, recommended hotels, and offered bits of lore about the country through which the tourist passed. The auto clubs brought road information to the point where motorists felt that it rivaled their first-class emergency road patrol.

The making of maps, like their distribution, was to attain a remarkable peak in the future when the science of photogrammetry was applied to picturing the highway. But in the twenties the road map was mostly an interesting and informative picture story of the road. For many persons it was an education in state history; it showed graphically the language imprint of four ruling nations as well as the cultural trace of immigrants. A statistical summary in the *California Historical Society Quarterly* reported:

Of the 3,600 geographic names in use within the state . . . 31% are Spanish, 56% English, 9.5% California Indian. The remaining names are French, Italian, German, Russian, and of other linguistic sources while .6% are synthetic—Anaheim, Buena Park, Early-mart...[11]

Along 101 there remained a stronger predominance of Spanish than in other parts of the state for it was here that navigators, soldiers and priests of Spain remained isolated for half a century. To early Americans the commonplace Castilian words—*Baja, Angeles, Soledad* and the saints' names *Diego, Barbara, Maria* and *Francisco* —carried a romantic softness.

To the pretty-sounding names along the highway were added the personal monument labels—Fullerton, Oxnard, Daly, Tustin, Downey, Buellton, King, Tanforan and Morgan Hill. The railroad honored executives or sought to butter statesmen with Fillmore, Colfax and Delano and showed a turn of wit in the coinage Coalinga which many averred to be of old Indian extraction; actually it was a contraction of Coaling Station A.

Homesick Easterners christened towns Manhattan, Beverly, Norwalk or Saratoga and the coast town of Newport Beach came from the steam schooner *Newport*. Real estate promotors, inspired by the lure of gain, founded towns described by sun, sea, beach, heights, orange and other words of paradise.

Map makers were approached by clubs, societies and old families to have figures of the past remembered on signs above the concrete. Should not Gervaccio Ayala be honored for having clung to the antlers of an elk on a wild ride from the Santa Ynez to El Rincón? His wife Rafaela had sworn that Ayala made the ride, after failing to kill the beast he pinned to a tree with a large nail fired from his muzzle-loader.

Sometimes a promoter could make people disregard an honor conferred in the past, for whim or business reasons. A cut-glass manufacturer from Ohio bought land, built a hotel, and donated a park to Nordhoff whereupon that town's name reverted to Ojai.

By the time 101 had been surfaced, posted and traced on maps most of the Mile Houses, Crossings, Forks and Corners were already hopeful little towns whose clusters of service stations, hot dog stands and auto camps proclaimed the "snappy" service of the twenties: Elite, De Luxe, Square Deal and Ready-Go.

WAYSIDE STOPS

The super service stations of the big oil companies dominated the through highway, successors to the twenty-one missions and the later stages where coaches had hitched fresh teams. From Charles Hervey's Maryland Hotel in San Diego up to the new Sonoma Mission Inn billboards and signs told the motorist he was approaching a gasoline pump: "We Don't Have Clara Bow But Do Have Ethel Gas!"

In the late twenties more than 150,000 automobiles a year came onto 101 and no matter where else they drove every one of them at some time headed for the fabulous movie capital of Hollywood to see palatial homes, visit studios and if very lucky catch a look at some of the stars whose depravities had become legend. John Walton Caughey in his historical volume, *California*, wrote of the lavish dissipation:

> Through gossip-mongering reporters these details are broadcast to the world at large with nothing lost in the telling, but there is a special impingement upon the Los Angeles area.[12]

After driving on the wide, clean boulevards of the southland's metropolis—struck by the whiteness of houses and the brilliant, colored flowers—Easterners in automobiles went up the coast to Santa Barbara and lodged in the blue-roofed cottages of the Miramar, at Frederick Clift's El Mirasol, or the new Biltmore that faced seaward above Castle Rock. Traveling salesmen checked in at the Carrillo, the California or the Faulding.

The dedicated tourist drove on through town to one of the first highway auto camps, established by Charles W. Kirk, secretary of the Santa Barbara Chamber of Commerce. There for fifty cents per car per day—no matter how many in the party—tourists had the use of a spacious building which featured stoves, hot water, showers, towels, and electricity. On the grounds were swings and sand boxes as well as a wash stand for cars, a grease pit, gas pumps and an attendant.

After the earthquake of 1925 Santa Barbara became the most beautiful of cities, for planners had seen to it that a Spanish adobe motif replaced the ugly frame buildings of pre-quake days. Most of State Street and even highway gas stations recalled Castile; a crowning achievement for Pearl Chase and her fellow workers was Southern Pacific's cooperation in building their locomotive round-house to resemble a Madrid bullring.

A favorite stop heading north on 101 through Gaviota Pass was a new town at old Mission Crossroads named after the local rancher Rufus T. Buell who had come from Vermont via a cattle ranch on Point Reyes. The dean of Santa Barbara historians, Owen H. O'Neill, wrote that "The town of Buellton is the child of U.S. Highway 101." [13]

The feature attraction at Buellton was the special pea soup served at Anderson's Electrical Café by the Danish restaurateur Anton Anderson and his French wife Juliette. Before the end of the twenties "Pea Soup" Anderson was serving 100,000 plates a year, each season importing the entire 25-ton split-pea crop of Joe Zebb from Moscow, Idaho.

Readers of Arthur Brisbane and O. O. McIntyre knew that those columnists always scheduled themselves to arrive for Anderson's soup while en route from Los Angeles to Hearst's castle at San Simeon. So prosperous did Anderson become that he bought a hotel which his wife christened the Buelltmore.

Another stopping place at the old Mission Crossroads was Knud Knudsen's hotel which the Nebraskan Dane had started as the Buellton Café. Before continuing north tourists made the journey over the state road a few miles to visit Mission Santa Ynez, sometimes pausing at the old Los Olivos stagecoach tavern, still run by the Matteis, and the Danish town of Solvang. Going on the north fork from Buellton a sightseer could reach the Mission La Purísima Concepción over a mountain road, and go down to Lompoc. That dry town, smug over Prohibition, was the home of the remarkable Chinese "weather wizard," Gin Chow, who predicted the Santa Barbara quake. He also predicted World War II and a short time later was run over and killed by a truck—whose driver was Japanese.

Santa Maria, forty miles up the new highway from Buellton, advertised the ten-unit autocourt of Mrs. Sadie West which that lady sold to Paul Markling, the former Associated Oil Company truck driver, who expanded to cover a part of the valley where Captain Anza's settlers had camped. Nearby was the famous café of Anna Holmes and the "high-class pool room and cigar store" of Charles Bassi, son of a Swiss dairy farmer. And Frank J. McCoy had started his famous Santa Maria Inn.

The next stop on 101 was San Luis Obispo which gained renown in January of 1925 when Arthur S. Heineman opened the first motel in the world. That was his claim for the Milestone Mo-Tel when he registered the name of the then huge 70-unit haven, built in Spanish-type architecture. Heineman had hoped the Milestone would be the first of a chain but did not live to carry on what would later develop into a tremendous type of accommodation.

Twenty miles north of the Mo-Tel another man with expansive ideas projected the "Dream City" of Atascadero, the name meaning "deep mire" in Spanish. E. G. Lewis, "King of the Promoters," bought 23,000 acres and from subscriptions, stock and land sales was able in ten years to build an ornate civic center and administration building, complete with statuary, as well as a hospital. The planned community was to be supported by a dehydration plant, toy factory and a mill that would turn out pumpkin flour. In 1924 the card castle collapsed; 11,000 creditors lost their savings from "too great trust in a fellow man."

Among other enticements, Atascadero had offered its mid-way position on 101 between Los Angeles and San Francisco. That overnight travel business—since the journey took two full days—went to Paso Robles where the inn was the fashionable place to "put up" through the twenties. Motion-picture companies, traveling north, or on location to shoot western scenes, stopped at the inn. The better-known stars usually went out to the Anderson Ranch.

For the most fashionable resort living in the north Del Monte and the Del Monte Lodge still ruled. Many preferred the Lodge, which Samuel F. B. Morse had built at Pebble Beach out on the Seventeen Mile Drive, because it adjoined the famous golf course.

California's continuing nationwide publicity urged the drivers of twenty million automobiles to come West and "vacation along the trail of the Padres." Travel bureaus compiled lists of "first-rate" auto courts, resorts and camp grounds that had everything: sunshine, flowers, beaches, band shells and museums. Persons with an eye to locating in the Golden State were assured that business-men expended a minimum of time and effort in work with ample leisure for golf, "talking pictures" and mah jong. And it was whispered by traveling salesmen that the Coast was "wide open."

The continuing influx that saw 3,000 cars an hour pass single intersections in Los Angeles, brought still another change in transportation to the north-south highway as motor busses began to compete successfully with the Southern Pacific.

THE MOTOR STAGES

From the start the railroad had waged a losing battle against the automobile. The successors to the Big Four had been able legally to outlaw jitneys, hold back road construction and delay the arrival in California of the large passenger-carrying vehicles that had become popular in the East. But by 1928 there were six hundred bus companies in the state and all the railroad could do was to buy into the principal bus lines.

The history of the bus, long called the stage, followed much the same pattern as the six-horse coach. At the start small operators converted Model T's and other cars to run between highway towns. A typical service was one started in 1915 by Mr. and Mrs. Henry Sprietz to connect Santa Barbara and Carpinteria. The couple used makeshift automobiles for three years, then bought five regular busses and when they received a city franchise added eleven more. In time the Sprietz Transportation Company employed twenty-six men and women while their busses each year covered 720,000 miles.

In San Diego J. T. Hayes used a jalopy to pull up at trolley stops on rainy days and offer waiting commuters a ride for a "jitney"—a nickel. He expanded to half a dozen converted Model T's and broadened his route until he had a bus service running to El Centro—the route of the old "Jackass Mail." Because he used the curb in front of Pickwick Theater in San Diego as his depot, the Hayes fleet became known as the Pickwick Stage Company and in the late twenties called itself "The modern seven-league giant of transportation." A contemporary account described the daily Pickwick busses on 101:

> The "Franciscan" and the "Comet," running between San Francisco and Los Angeles, and the "Jesuit" and the "Angelus," between Los Angeles and San Diego, are provided with every needed comfort and refinement, including cushioned reclining chairs, adjustable heaters, hot and cold lunch, radio and upper deck for observation. With the introduction in 1928 of the "Nite Coach" of the Pickwick system, providing comfortable accommodations for sleeping as well as the luxuries of day travel, it has been claimed that "a new planet has appeared in the transportation sky." [14]

Like the old-time stages the coast line followed the transcontinental operation, Pickwick having first extended his El Centro service over the Butterfield Ox-bow trail to St. Louis and then to Chicago. And another northern line joined Chicago with San Francisco via Salt Lake City.

From every crossroad a motor stage soon connected with 101 and before the end of the decade 33 million people were traveling by bus. Pickwick came under the wing of the giant national combine of sixty bus lines known first as Motor Transport and later as Greyhound. It was then that Southern Pacific, unable to compete as it cost $50,000 per mile to build new trackage, bought into the bus company.

The railroad was also forced to take cooperative steps by another highway behemoth in the twenties when the trucking business began to grab freight that had always gone by train.

THE LONG-HAUL TRUCKS

The First World War developed the truck and gave soldier drivers the know-how that would start another giant American industry after the coming of good highways and the pneumatic tire. Between the time Henry Ford launched the Model T, and the start of federal aid to 101, the number of trucks in the nation mounted from 50,000 to more than one million.

Progress in trucking was as spectacular as its numerical rise and the simplicity of the start is caught by Samuel W. Taylor in his book, *Linehaul:*

> In the 1920's, any man with a couple of hundred dollars and the spirit of adventure could go into the trucking business. That was enough for a second-hand Model T or a down payment on something bigger, with enough left over for a tankful of gas. That's all you needed.[15]

Jim Coughlin was one of those who started out as a solo truckman on the San Francisco waterfront when Captain William Matson was running his first ships to the Hawaiian Islands. The two men became friends and Coughlin built the Red Line Transfer Company out of baggage-hauling from piers to the railroad depot.

When artichoke shippers wanted loads hauled to Los Angeles without having to pay railroad rates, J. J. Coughlin organized the California Motor Express—called Cal Motor—and after a few trips his "bobtail" gas-burning trucks were returning up 101 with back loads. Other outfits went on the road, some getting themselves certified as common carriers, others obtaining permits. With them were the "gypsies"—Sam Taylor's man with a couple of hundred dollars.

Since a dependable night run was considered impossible the railroads and coastwise "butter-and-egg" ships were not harmed by trucks that stopped overnight and in addition suffered frequent breakdowns. Good drivers were hard to get, for by the late twenties hijackers lay in wait for any big truck that might be carrying liquor.

But Cal Motor pioneered the night run from San Francisco to Los Angeles and set up a terminal organization. Main-haul drivers from north or south would swing down from their cabs at San Luis Obispo for a twenty-four-hour rest while a relief pushed on. The big company, along with Pacific Intermountain Express—P.I.E.—and a few others, built feeder services along 101. Dependable, reasonable and courteous service eventually forced the railroad to sidle into the trucking business.

The big trucks were popular with the shippers but not with automobile drivers who were shoved off the road, cursed at by rough truckers, and forced to breathe gas when unable to pass on some long, winding hill like the section of Torrey Pines known as the Biological Grade—the old road down to the Scripps Institute of Oceanography at La Jolla.

Truck companies were always delighted to read—outside of their house organs—such cheery contemporary history as was set down by the authors of *Oxcart to Airplane*:

> There is something thrilling, something romantic, about the night travel of the auto truck in California, making its way hither and yon, the willing slave of a dynamic people.[16]

BOOTLEGGERS AND HIJACKERS

Violent death from a new breed of highway killers was the extreme and anything but romantic thrill that shadowed trucking through the twenties when the Eighteenth Amendment to the Constitution forbade the sale of liquor and brought gangster war between rival contraband operators.

To evade the unpopular legislation bootleggers began smuggling foreign liquor across the Mexican border, using pack mules, open cars whose cases were covered with oranges, "candy wagons" (a form of panel) and big trucks.

When a bootlegger was held up between Tia Juana and Ensenada by Mexican police who took his cash on a fake rape charge, California bootleggers bought 110-foot war surplus submarine chasers to run between Ensenada and Pismo Beach or Halfmoon Bay. Fitted with Liberty engines, the sub chasers made forty-five knots which was ample speed to outrun any Navy or Coast Guard patrol. Those "rum-runners" landed 18,000-gallon cargoes—worth up to $250,000—which were stowed away in hillside caches, then loaded in big trucks that met candy wagons along 101. Deliveries were made to the speakeasies, private homes and "clubs" along the Coast.

One of those numerous clubs was the Paradise on Turk Street in San Francisco's tenderloin. It was owned by the much-publicized Vince "Pegleg" Lucich, a tough but pleasant-mannered bootlegger, hijacker and convicted—but pardoned—murderer who in 1960 recalled a violent era in which he was as formidable a figure as any of California's notorious desperados.

Vince was known as a "natural shot"—the gun was scarcely clear of his belt when he fired, his eyes having sighted on the target. "But you couldn't depend on bullets alone," he said, "which is why most guys carried a razor in their upper left-hand coat pocket. A hijacker with a slit throat didn't talk while he was dying—and he died."

As proof Vince winked and tapped the artificial limb that got him his nickname, Pegleg. Traveling alone from Half Moon Bay to San Francisco, he had been stopped by a roadblock. Two hijackers hauled him from the truck, shot him in the groin and shoved him into a ditch. Before driving off with the liquor one of the men shot him again in the thigh. But Vince's guard, trailing him as was the way to avoid a "bootlegging rap" if caught, rushed him to the hospital where one leg was amputated.

Pegleg got personal revenge but he also got nineteen years in San Quentin and Folsom. "The prosecution attorney was out to stretch my neck so maybe I was lucky to draw life. And I came out with all my marbles—many don't."

In a career that covered the Prohibition era Pegleg was mixed up with every form of violence and law evasion known to the racket. "The men in it were like soldiers of fortune fighting in a foreign war," as far as Lucich was concerned. "They knew they would probably get it eventually but there was money—and people wanted the stuff. In the late twenties I collected a dollar a case on everything landed north of Paso Robles."

Sometimes the guile of the good businessman had to be substituted for such violence as killing, breaking arms and beatings. In the early days Pegleg had been cheated at Ensenada when Mexicans switched 1,600 cases of "real stuff" and left him holding undrinkable molasses alcohol. There was no comeback so Vince flew up to Portland where he heard that a speakeasy serving "Pink Ladies" and other fancy drinks was short of supplies. "My liquor would be okay in a drink that had a lot of lemon and sugar and grenadine. We made a deal."

Pegleg's gang "borrowed" a big oil truck for a week-end, "steamed it out pretty good," and two boys were hired for twenty dollars each to drive the 16,000 gallons north.[17]

On the Pacific Coast, as elsewhere, the business of smuggling, hijacking and distilling was based on connections that went to state capitals and Washington, D.C. The Feds—Prohibition agents, or "prohi's" as they were known—waged a war that often conflicted with local police, sheriffs, and the military; and there were countless stories of pay-offs, kick-backs and lay-off orders from higher-up. With the gangsters and life-long criminals Prohibition attracted not only adventurers like Pegleg but anyone hungry for money, including women—both tramps and "high-class" ladies.

Women were used as decoys by bootleg gangs and were preyed upon by hijackers who committed mass rapings and disfigurations. Retribution ignored the law and the guilty—or suspected—ones were beaten and tortured to death then put in cider barrels into which were poured cement, and thrown offshore.

The hijacking of liquor shipments spread to holdups of every kind of truck that might be loaded with valuable merchandise, but the big profit was in booze—at first the imported liquor, then the poisonous cut hooch.

Turkey legs and freshly killed snakes were stewed in alcohol to make "rice wine" and gin was concocted in bathtubs. Antidotes went into poor grade embalming fluid and home brew whiskey was made from peaches, corn meal, prunes and dried apples. Along the skid rows of San Diego, Los Angeles and San Francisco bums drank shellac or, if they could get it, bay rum hair tonic.

One hundred of California's established wineries kept cultivating grapes to supply medicinal, sacramental and cooking wine and each family was permitted to make two hundred gallons of wine a year. From that license sprang the stills that were found on farms, where drunk cattle and chickens led to their discovery, and even in churches.

Most protests were so tinged with hypocrisy that California could not be aroused. With little result the newspapers campaigned for decency as did the clergy in condemning the licentiousness of the times: people going blind and insane from rot-gut liquor; adolescents necking and petting in rumble seats as they swigged from pints of applejack; women so degraded by the grog that they now openly smoked cigarettes and showed too much knee and bosom.

THE CRASH

In September of 1929 stocks wavered on the Wall Street exchange. But people were assured the market could go only one way in the "foreseeable future" and that was up. Henry Ford had declared that ninety per cent of the people were in good shape and the folksy Western philosopher Will Rogers sharpened the quote by saying that ninety per cent of the people just didn't give a damn.

For another month the parade of trucks, busses, tankers and automobiles sped along 101 with people who were making money or who didn't need it; hilarious kids hung on the running boards of crowded Tin Lizzies whose sides were painted with the humor of the dying twenties: "Leaping Lena," "Standing Room Only" and "The Mayflower—Many a Puritan has come across in it!" Youthful slang proclaimed the spirit of the wild decade: "Banana Oil!," "Is Zat So?," and "So's your Old Man!"

In October of '29 the Wall Street crash began America's most terrible depression.

Twelve *Dead End*

THE HOMELESS SWARM

Business failures and bank closings were followed by suicides, public demonstrations and finally bread lines at San Francisco and Los Angeles as California joined the nation to sail into the bewildering, tragic thirties. Along 101 the through busses ran light while jalopies chugged under heavy loads with displaced persons until gas tanks were empty. Repossessed cars filled the second-hand lots and loan sharks foreclosed mortgages. For the first time in more than ten years people were forced to walk instead of ride. At every Coast city and town employers posted NO HELP WANTED signs; open hot dog stands, new motor courts, filling stations and restaurants were "For Sale—Cheap."

At the helm of the foundering Golden State "Sunny Jim" Rolph "spent big" and beamed as he shook hands, kissed babies or led parades, the while creating jobs for his friends. To further harass small investors who had lost millions of dollars, the spendthrift governor signed a general tax bill unmindful of the angry jibe, "pennies for Sunny Jim."

Appeals to Sacramento were as futile as requests for loans from those firms and individuals lucky or astute enough to weather the storm. Disenchanted people viewed with disgust what Robert Glass Cleland, the historian, termed their "stuffed-shirt leadership in the economic and business world, as well as in the field of politics." [1]

Back in the cold, soot-begrimed tenements of the East millions of unemployed viewed the antics of Sunny Jim as they did the wholesale fleecing of investors by the crooked oil promotor C. C. Julian: there was money in California. From refuse cans bums recovered and read the booster literature turned out by California civic organizations. A ragged, hungry army was soon converging on the freight yards of New York, Philadelphia, Chicago and St. Louis. Defying the railroad "bulls" by their numbers, the "bindlestiffs" clung to flat and box cars, in their minds the warm, soft pictures of some Chamber of Commerce artist—palm trees, glistening houses with red-tile roofs, oranges, azure water and beaches of white and perfect sand. Another migration to California was under way.

Like a swarm of locusts the "undesirables" descended on the Coast to swell bread lines, crowd jails and strip orchards. Hungry amateur "moochers" were driven off the streets to vacant lots outside of town—"jungles"—where they cadged coffee and mulligan from resentful old hoboes.

As conditions grew worse in the East through the opening years of the thirties, desert roads to California streamed with men, and later women, who felt there *must be something* for them in the Land of Promise. Throughout the terrible year 1931 the California Newspaper Publishers Association and the State Chamber of Commerce sponsored a plan of continuous fiestas as a prelude to the Olympic Games at Los Angeles the following year. *Touring Topics*, in an editorial captioned "Spirit of California," told the world—

> ...a year of fiesta will tend to increase the number of visitors and also induce them to prolong their stay and it is a well known fact

that the annual army of tourists is an asset of major importance to this State and its inhabitants.[2]

Before long newspapers were urging that visitors be screened to keep out the "vicious and dangerous hoboes." The Los Angeles *Times* recommended a ban on the detrimental invasion that was adding to the state's 1,500,000 idle poor.

Florida and Washington are both stopping indigents at their borders. California should do the same. . . .

From the days of Rome in its decline to Paris just before the revolution, the problem of civilization has been to compel the unemployed and unemployables to stay in one place.[3]

YOUTH ON THE ROAD

The "big trouble," as the hoboes called the depression, made conditions in American homes so desperate that hungry boys and girls still in their mid teens went "on the rods" or hitchhiked West. Kids who had run away swung off the S.P. freights at San Luis Obispo, Santa Barbara and other towns where a fiesta or rodeo gave promise of handouts. Fifteen-year-old girls went "on the street" as prostitutes at the seaports of San Diego and San Francisco; boys tried to get jobs "pearl diving" (washing dishes) for a meal; gangs learned to roll drunks, snatch purses and set up roadblocks to rob tourists.

To find out at first hand what was going on among the quarter of a million drifting youngsters, Thomas Minehan, a University of Minnesota sociologist, spent the summers of 1932 and 1933 on the road. He collected life histories of boys and girls he met on the bum and recorded their conversations, habits and view of America at the time.

In his book *Boy and Girl Tramps of America*, Professor Minehan told of the life being led along the roadsides of the nation:

The most common place for stealing clothes is off a clothesline in a back yard; the best time immediately after dark. . . . Open garages, too, at this time furnish clothes. . . .

A quarter of a mile down the railroad tracks thirty-four boys and girls are waking in another jungle.... In the center of this clearing a huge smudge has smoked all night long, watched carefully by pairs of boys serving turns.

Begging is the first thing they learn. But a few years ago it was almost a profession. Good panhandlers in 1929 made $4 or $5 a day in any city. Today, the best seldom make forty cents.

Of late there has been an increasing number of maverick girl tramps. They follow the boys, living in the jungles and box cars, serving as mistresses and maids.... The girls are available to any and all boys in the camp including adults and late arrivals.[4]

On the trip out to California young girls teamed with boys or older men, wearing dungarees, jackets and peaked railroad hats to hide their sex from the "harness bulls." Hitchhiking girls traveled in pairs and were given rides by truck drivers and traveling salesmen; some were lured down to the Mexican border by promises of work, then snatched by white-slavers or the "Coyotees" who smuggled "wet-backs" across the Rio Grande and Colorado to further glut the labor marts.

The automotive industry participated in the disgraceful exploitation of wandering youth by offering boys the chance to drive new cars to California—expenses paid—with ample opportunity at Los Angeles and San Francisco to earn transportation home or settle on the Coast. Caravans from Detroit, guided by a manufacturer's representative, arrived in some California town at night; boys returning in the morning might find the representative gone or non-cooperative. But in every case they were stranded.

Good people along 101, in desperate circumstances themselves, were forced to hang out signs that read "DOGS AND VAGRANTS NOT ALLOWED!" while hungry kids and adults were told by cops to "Keep moving!" Civic organizations, reformers and mission workers pleaded for relief which finally came through the alphabetical bureaus of President Franklin D. Roosevelt's New Deal.

THE TRANSIENT CAMPS

Secretary of the Interior, Harold L. Ickes, who was both praised and damned for his administration of the government's emergency rescue efforts, recorded the prelude to federal relief:

> With the deepening of the depression and with the development of more terrible and frequent symptoms of unemployment—the apple salesman, the breadliners, the beggars, the half-starved wandering children, the emaciated hitch-hikers, the tragic and futile riots—more apparent each day, the chorus of voices favoring public works grew in volume.[5]

To the underprivileged of the time the programs that were launched in the lee of the Blue Eagle after 1932 spelled hope. One and a half million California families went on relief and their sons became eligible to enter the CCC—the Civilian Conservation Corps. The PWA poured money into road building that saw the hopelessly unemployed put to work repairing the damage caused to 101 by heavy trucks, busses and trailers. And along the trace of the old Mission Trail camps were set up where vagrants could bathe, rest, eat and if they wished regain some measure of self-respect by doing odd jobs to earn their keep.

Homeless travelers whose suspicions were overcome by hunger or illness shuffled into buildings at San Jose, San Luis Obispo, San Diego and half a dozen camps around Los Angeles or several near San Francisco. They were given a physical examination, had their clothing fumigated, and after a hot bath and all they could eat, found a sheltered, clean place to sleep.

Into the transient camps came agitators—Communists who passed out copies of the *Western Worker* and tried to enlist recruits to fight the lettuce growers at Salinas and waterfront employers at San Francisco where a big maritime strike was shaping up in 1934; a variety of "parlor pinks" from the universities; and professional bums who had attended the Hobo College in New York City and could show cards issued to them by the Hobo President certifying that they had earned the title "Jack the Drinker" or "Bill the Sailor."

Career tramps—men like Jeff Davis, self-styled "King of the Hoboes"—shunned the charitable "swill" of government havens, preferring to mooch along the stem for dimes that would buy them "day olds" at a bakery, or a ten-cent breakfast of hotcakes, eggs and coffee at shacks doing business by the tracks outside of San Jose, Paso Robles, or close to a hundred make-up yards and water tanks.

And there were people of a generation that could not tolerate charity who founded their own camps and by a community effort managed to survive. One of those settlements of about three hundred war pensioners lived in shacks amid the sand dunes below Pismo Beach. With monthly checks only enough to buy an occasional bottle of wine, some tobacco and at intervals new shoes, the veterans lived mostly on produce snitched from Japanese truck farms and clams poached at a nearby government preserve.

To pass time the retired soldiers reconnoitered two neighboring nudist colonies or went into the little town of Oceano to sit in a row along the main street where the townspeople made them welcome. Motorists driving through Oceano were often startled by the long row of what appeared to be legless men as the veterans rested their feet on the bottom of a drainage ditch.

Roadside colonies, jungles and transient camps began to thin slightly in the mid-thirties as vast government spending relieved the dire want of the first depression years. On July 31, 1935, a composite report from carriers and resorts stated:

> A total of 107,345 out-of-state summer tourists arrived in California last month to register an increase of 36.8% over June of 1934. The influx of indigents into the state decreased 30% in the last three months.[6]

Since the spring was not the indigent "season" the report was just another manifestation of the "positive"—or hopeful—thinking that had started to come into vogue with recovery-conscious businessmen.

Even in 1936 the depression still held California in its grip and the transient camps during their last days saw another perplexed and broke class of Americans who foundered on the highways, in status somewhere between solvency and destitution. George E. Outland of Santa Barbara State College wrote from his experience with the Transient Service that the group was

> ...well educated, well dressed and above the level of even the usually high quality of men found on the road during the period 1932–1936. They ranged in age from 17 to 25.[7]

THE OKIES

In the westward migration an extreme of family destitution showed among miserable people of the Oklahoma–Arkansas–Texas Dust Bowl.

Following a cycle of droughts which gave the area its name, their small holdings were grabbed by banks and syndicates who sent in caterpillar tractors—"cats"—to plow under vast acreages.

Poor families salvaged what they could, purchased jalopies from chiseling second-hand-car salesmen, and headed for the much publicized California. Not only did they carry the by then universally spread booster image of a Golden State, but they *knew* there was work: the agents of California farmers, making sure of a too great labor supply to keep down wages, had passed the word at filling stations and in juke joints of the Dust Bowl; many of the migrants carried broadsides that told them how much they might earn picking cotton, fruit and lettuce.

Awaiting the "Okies" and the "Arkies," as these successors to the "Pikes" were called, was a rude reception. There were already more migrant workers and hungry vagrants than could possibly find employment and, in the words of Robert Glass Cleland, "the unprecedented influx of this moneyless, unskilled horde came at the worst possible time for California. Agriculture, of all kinds and in every section, was nearly prostrate." [8]

243

Fortune quoted one of the Okies who stood helpless with his hungry family of six:

> I don't know what to do. There's nothing back in Oklahoma for us to go to now and there's nothing here. Somehow somethin' don't seem right—I want to work and I can't . . .[9]

Wretches from the Dust Bowl found themselves not only hungry and unwanted but with other migrants became the butt of the contention between Communist organizers and the Associated Farmers as attempts were made along the Coast to settle the matter of wages and living conditions. Reporting on that California labor war, *Fortune* told its readers that "Vigilante activity against strikers and organizers since 1932 has been bloody and direct." Writing about the part played by the Associated Farmers in 1938, the article stated:

> A.F. members were in the thick of the worst recent strikes. In the particularly bloody Salinas lettuce strike, the county head of the A.F. himself convoyed the lettuce trucks against the strikers . . .[10]

The whole country was stirred by the plight of the Okies and their brothers in misfortune with the 1939 publication of John Steinbeck's *Grapes of Wrath* which, like *Uncle Tom's Cabin* and *Ramona*, dramatized how shabbily one group of human beings could treat another.

THE BRIDGE

Throughout their depression pilgrimage to nowhere vagrants were shunted between San Francisco and Los Angeles. At the northern city even good union members were out of work; college graduates were thankful to get low-paying, ten-hour-a-day jobs jerking sodas; a man with a jacket, shirt and necktie tried to eke out a living as a brush or hosiery salesman; panhandlers were chased off Market Street to the flophouses and missions of Howard Street's skid row where they might pick up precarious part-time employment as strike-breakers. In Los Angeles it was even tougher to survive for that city continuously reaffirmed its policy of keeping out indigents and went to the extreme of a border patrol to "discourage undesirables."

The open road of 101 was the only choice left to the drifters who hitchhiked or walked from one construction project to another. The WPA workers were the fortunate few. Thousands of bums crowded the freights while hundreds could be seen sleeping or loitering in junk yards, under signs advertising "Good Eats," and along the summer-dried banks of the Parajo, Salinas, and Santa Ana rivers.

With repeal late in 1933, many of the hirelings in bootlegging were thrown out of work. The higher-ups retained their "guns" and went into the rackets. Two-dollar prostitutes flourished in every town of any size, and syndicates circulated them back and forth on 101, using tourist cabins and cheap hotels. Narcotics came across the docks at San Francisco and up from Tia Juana. Wealthy Los Angeles businessmen and Hollywood celebrities became the targets of extortion or blackmail. Pacific Coast gangsters who had grown wealthy in the tradition of Arnold Rothstein and Al Capone explained their lavish spending at parties and the racetracks of Tanforan and Santa Anita behind such fronts as promoters of prize fights and owners of night clubs.

Between the foreign-flavored extremes of wealth and want an effort at recovery was being made in California during the mid-thirties. Many towns would follow the example set by the Farmer's Market which opened in 1934 at "Gilmore Island," the large open field in Los Angeles that was owned by the oilman Earl B. Gilmore.

The Farmer's Market was the idea of Roger Dahlhjelm, a four-dollar-a-week bookkeeper in a Los Angeles bakery-tearoom. Roger noticed that farmers along 101 were operating roadside stalls but doing very little business because traffic was so light. He figured if they were all in one centrally located spot people would come to them for fresh vegetables, eggs and fruit. Roger sold the idea to Gilmore and opened with eighteen stalls; word of mouth publicity brought crowds and the idea spread.

On Gilmore Island—where wells had started the big Gilmore Oil Company, known all over the state for its red lion sign—amusements and restaurants became a part of the Farmer's Market that would expand to 150 stalls and shops, visited by 40,000 people every day.

The same year the Farmer's Market opened, Gilmore Stadium was erected. The big wooden bowl seated 18,000 sports fans and because of its popular prices was known as the "workingman's stadium." There midget auto racing started and almost any kind of new entertainment had the chance of being promoted.

At the helm of the Gilmore interests was the beloved Gene Doyle, a Boston newspaperman who came out to the Pacific Coast in 1908. Through the years he dreamed up promotions and publicity ideas whose fun and freshness were happy antidotes to the many crooked deals for which Southern California was so well known.

To raise money for soldiers' athletic equipment in World War I Gene master-minded a baseball game between a team captained by movie actor Douglas Fairbanks, Sr., then king of the movie stars, and another under the great evangelist, Billy Sunday, who had once played with the Chicago Cubs. And Doyle, friend of a thousand sports celebrities, brought Babe Ruth out to the Coast for exhibition games.

If the prosperity Herbert Hoover promised was "just around the corner" had not yet made the turn, there were signs that it lurked somewhere ahead. The Roosevelt Administration, after a resounding victory in '36, was being pelted the following year for its "socialistic" actions. The "coddling" of labor, pump priming and the swashing away of taxpayers' money were among the many charges. But to the millions who had been saved, Roosevelt was still a great man. And along 101 the enduring signs of recovery were being completed—new stretches of highway, new PWA buildings and new jobs in a growing bureaucracy.

The crowning achievement of the decade—and a landmark in the history of El Camino Real—came on May 27, 1937, with the opening of the Golden Gate Bridge, a final link in the road between San Diego and Northern California.

The five-foot-tall giant among bridge builders, Joseph B. Strauss, had realized the ambition that first seized him when he looked across the Golden Gate in 1917. The great bridge had been started in 1933 and on completion was the longest in the world, its span between towers measuring 4,200 feet. Newspapers printed statistics, from the diameter of individual bridge wires in inches— .195—to the cost—$35 million. At the opening ceremonics Strauss summed up his twenty years of planning, convincing and building: "The struggles of peace are sometimes as bitter as the conflicts of war." [11]

Harold Gilliam, the author, caught the spirit of what the bridge meant to the 200,000 who hiked over it on opening day:

> The first man across had to be content with a small share of the glory. Dozens of less speedy pedestrians contrived to be first in one way or another. Among those claiming titles were the first person to cross on stilts; the first twins; the first mother pushing a baby carriage; the first person to cross walking backwards; the first dog ...and the first person to cross with her tongue hanging out.[12]

In less than twenty-five years the Golden Gate Bridge would be used by more than 300 million vehicles and produce a revenue of close to 90 millions. But during the depression years while it was being built—to a large extent by imported specialists—there were many who thought that so expensive a project might well wait until care had been taken of the needy.

HAM AND EGGS

Out of the depression in California there did come schemes to ease the lot of impoverished people—for all time. The first voice to be heard was that of the famous author, socialist and reformer, Upton Sinclair of Pasadena, who in 1934 almost won the governorship of the state with his EPIC (End Poverty In California) plan. The combined forces of the "haves" used every scurrilous propaganda trick known to politicians in the battle against the Utopian candidate.

In addition to slandering Sinclair as a free-lover, anti-Christ, Communist and telepathist, motion-picture "newsreels" were distributed free to theaters and voters saw a horde of hoboes poised on the California border ready to rush in and take over the state once Sinclair was elected. In his history of Hollywood Leo Rosten told the "newsreel" story:

> The pictures were taken on the streets of Los Angeles with cameras from a major studio; the anarchists were actors on studio payrolls, dressed in false whiskers and dirty clothes, and wearing sinister expressions . . .[13]

While the EPIC supporters awaited the decision of the voters a retired physician named Dr. Francis E. Townsend of Long Beach launched his Old Age Pension Plan that guaranteed national prosperity and the then outlandish provision for pensions to all citizens sixty years of age. Two hundred dollars a month was the proposed stipend.

Before it sank the Townsend Plan gave birth to other pension projects the most publicized of which started out as the "Thirty-Dollars-Every-Thursday Plan." High-pressure Los Angeles promoters fastened onto the idea and launched a gigantic campaign under the slogan "Ham and Eggs" which was publicized up and down the Coast with mass meetings, parades, barbecues and a traveling circus. Ballyhoo brought in more than a million votes for Ham and Eggs as an initiative measure in the election of 1938 and new exploitation began.

During 1939 thousands of senior citizens headed for California to be on hand when the pension plan became a reality. More than 100,000 volunteer workers traveled between coordinating headquarters at Los Angeles and San Francisco in the shrewd collecting of dollars from pitiable old folks who saw fulfillment and ease for the twilight of their lives.

Typical of the method used to ensnare voters was a honky-tonk picnic held at Selig Zoo Park in Los Angeles on July 4, 1939, and heralded by advanced radio enthusiasm that promised the folks

> As you enter the main gate, you will go up Ham and Eggs Boulevard; wander down Retirement Warrants Lane; turn out Thirty Thursday Street, and find yourself entering Security Highway.[14]

The big wheels of business rolled over Ham and Eggs and after a few months of futile bleating, gullible aged sought solace elsewhere. Waiting for them was a virtual smorgasbord of cults that promised wealth, wisdom, health and salvation.

In the Santa Susannah Mountains where 101 twined between the San Fernando Valley and the sea, two ladies claimed to be the witnesses mentioned in the Book of Revelations and guaranteed soon to have word from the Angel Gabriel on lost measurements to pin-point all the gold and oil in California. Arthur Bell of Mankind United gathered 14,000 followers with his tale of little brass-headed men from inside the earth who would make possible the four-hour, four-day week, to be enjoyed in $25,000, swimming pool–equipped homes. The secrets of Lemuria were offered in competition with those of the Psychosomatic Institute and the Ancient Mystical Order of Melchizedek. Doubtful people consulted highway gypsies to ask who was right: Aimee Semple McPherson, Nothing Impossible or The Rosicrucian Order?

Those who scoffed at the mystics—the jitterbugs, candid camera fans, sitdown strikers, soapbox orators, Bund members and would-be "big wheels" in "zoot suits"—along with the rest of California's 7 million people, were about to witness a practical miracle as the "terrible thirties" closed. Almost overnight unemployment ended and even a renewed migration could not satisfy the demand for help.

SOMETHING FOR NOTHING

Business had started to pick up along 101 even before September of 1939 when the German Wehrmacht rolled into Poland to start

World War II. Trucks had been hauling scrap from automobile junk yards to the docks of San Francisco for shipment to Japan; oil was being hauled down to San Pedro, bound for the same destination. Payrolls had increased in aircraft factories around the pioneer plant of Donald W. Douglas at Santa Monica, and in the San Diego area where Charles A. Lindbergh had tinkered with his *Spirit of St. Louis* in 1927.

The political campaign promise of 1940 by Franklin Roosevelt—"No American boy shall die on foreign shores"—saw Army trucks crowding the highway out of induction centers as young men went into uniform to get over with their peacetime service. The additional promise that America would be merely "the arsenal of democracy" helped elect Roosevelt to an unprecedented third term as President of the United States.

By Christmas of 1940 farms and factories were advertising for men and women. The derelicts of the depression could pick and choose, and pleas for more workers that went East offered high wages and safety from any possible German air attack. The quarter of a million new migrants who came in the winter of 1940–41 ignored the San Joaquin Valley and headed down 101 to San Diego, defense center of the Pacific Coast where more than half that number found work. Around San Francisco the shipyards needed 20,000 workers—men or women—and 2,000 house trailers converged on the airport installation at Paso Robles. Camp Roberts near King City, Camp Nacimiento at San Miguel and other cantonments were erected to billet the peacetime draftees. Travelers on 101 stopped to pick up the new American soldier—GI Joe—where a few years earlier they had avoided the doughfoot in an ill-fitting uniform of hairy material who could barely afford to buy 3.2 beer.

In May of 1941 a National Emergency was declared and people wanted to believe that the big-money honeymoon would go on forever. Warnings by such Americans as Lindbergh that we were standing into danger were shouted down by interventionists. Manufacturers and shippers knew that vastly greater profits would follow an outright involvement in the war.

Tremendous congestion at San Diego, Los Angeles and San Francisco developed in that first year of defense work and the Highway Commission drew up plans for a system of freeways together with a long range program to widen 101 for its entire span. State and federal engineers huddled with military men to work out a system of rerouting civilian traffic in the remote event of attack.

At highway restaurants and bars juke boxes played a succession of new war songs—"Don't Sit under the Apple Tree" and others which never caught on like the tunes of the First World War; paunchy, apologetic men bought drinks for GI's and told the monotonous story of being on the dock at Hoboken, ready to sail for France, when the Armistice whistles of 1918 robbed them of glory.

DIM-OUT

On Sunday, December 7, 1941, shocked Californians listened to news broadcasts that each hour added a few details to the astonishing report of a Japanese air and submarine attack on Pearl Harbor. By night it was known that the United States Pacific Fleet had been all but wiped out; rumors spread about the imminence of a Coast bombardment and invasion.

At San Francisco the next day radio bulletins told of enemy planes sighted southwest of Daly City; that night civilians near Monterey, Santa Barbara and Long Beach called local newspapers to report "signal" lights seen offshore. A rising tension gripped the coastal towns as black-outs and dim-outs were ordered; all non-military traffic was screened at points where 101 skirted the shore; a horse patrol went into operation on beaches and soldiers wearing World War I helmets strung barbed wire.

People were ready to believe anything possible after the extent of the Pearl Harbor damage became known—the 100 Japanese carrier-based planes, together with midget submarines, had sunk or seriously damaged 18 ships and destroyed 177 planes; more than

3,000 Americans lay dead. And the Japanese were bombarding Manila.

The shooting war reached the Pacific Coast December 20 when a Japanese sub made an unsuccessful attack on the tanker *Agwiworld* south of the Golden Gate; and that same day the San Francisco garbage scow *Tahoe* claimed to have rammed and sunk a Japanese sub near the Farallons. Four vessels were chased off San Pedro, one going down after an hour of shellfire, and the *Absaroka* making San Pedro breakwater to show a huge gap in one side. Numerous reports were received of Japanese subs that surfaced off the coast, calling attention to America's unpreparedness: the out-turn of airplane factories and shipyards was being delivered to our allies or sent into the Pacific.

A smoldering resentment against Pacific Coast Japanese threatened to flare up when news was received of mysterious signals seen flashing from the hills above Morro Bay. On February 12, 1942, the President ordered all Japanese evacuated from strategic locations; the same day the FBI uncovered 60,000 rounds of ammunition cached at Monterey together with rifles, shotguns and maps.

Since 1900 when they first began to arrive in California the Japanese had unobtrusively increased their number from 10,000 to 115,000. The Army found they had deployed mostly along the coast and when evacuation started it was learned that the little farmers had been selective in picking out acreage: Santa Maria County air fields, utilities and power lines were surrounded; from Gaviota south along 101 the Japanese chose only land near El Capitan, Ellwood and Summerland oil fields; fishermen berthed as close as possible to port installations and garages run by Japanese were near cantonments.

After February 23, when a Japanese sub shelled Goleta and destroyed oil tanks, the Army rushed enemy nationals away from their homes and farms under a heavy guard. People shook fists and cursed at convoys of displaced Japanese that ran along the highway to assembly centers set up at Salinas and at the Tanforan and Santa Anita racetracks. From these temporary quarters the Japanese were transferred to inland camps. Even in those hard days American critics complained because there was no furniture at the assembly centers and evacuees had to sleep for a short time in horse stalls. But the Army was not sensitive; its own men were on the Death March from Bataan, or were being tortured and starved to death in Japanese prison camps.

THE WAR EFFORT

Almost immediately after the declaration of war the sale of tires and tubes was frozen, followed by a ban on the sale of new cars to civilians. One year later nationwide gasoline rationing went into effect over the protest of Southern California where public transportation was almost non-existent. Permanent dim-out warning signs appeared along 101 and beach areas were closed.

Onto the homefront battlefield came the racketeers: the operators of black markets in gas, oil, tires and meat stamps; garage mechanics, 4-F salesmen and landlords who cheated the wives of soldiers and sailors overseas; bartenders and panderers who preyed on furloughed service men; draft dodgers and profiteers.

Traffic jammed the highway every hour of the day and night as swing shift workers poured in and out of plants or shipyards. Hitchhikers crowded the roadside at the Marine Corps 125,000-acre Camp Pendleton north of Oceanside and Fort Ord, the Army's giant training center near Monterey. Women carrying infants waited in line to get aboard crowded busses while relatively unimportant military officers were given siren-screaming police escorts. Southern Pacific's luxury night train, the *Lark*, carrying influential civilians between Los Angeles and San Francisco, forced vintage wooden coaches filled with troops onto sidings.

As the tide of victory turned, the military arm reached out to take over such establishments as the famous old Del Monte Hotel and to create new embarkation ports—Hueneme and others—where long convoys came with fresh troops for Pacific island invasions.

Henry Kaiser, an ex-photographer and salesman who helped

build the San Francisco–Oakland Bay Bridge and Boulder Dam, set a pattern of record-breaking, assembly-line ship construction by turning out Liberty freighters in less than one month. Henry J. was said to sleep only four hours a night and to spend $200,000 a year on phone calls.

The hauling of parts for ships, bombers and tanks brought the heavy truck into prominence and 101 began to crack; Army convoys and the stream of defense worker's "pool" cars continued the damage. With maintenance at a minimum the Coast Highway took on a shopworn look. And no new mileage was built during the war except access roads into military bases.

A great splurge of production preceded the Normandy Invasion and did not let up even after the defeat of Germany; new calls for help went out as shipyards and aircraft factories were given higher quotas for an expected invasion of the Japanese home islands.

Good pay and plenty of overtime swelled the migration of Negroes on the old Spanish Trail used by their ancestors, who in early times had made up nearly half the population of Los Angeles. By the end of the war a quarter of a million of them would be living in the city where the former slave Biddy Mason, a pioneer real estate operator, had been one of the pueblo's largest landowners. About 150,000 Negroes traveled up 101 to settle at San Francisco and Oakland; another 20,000 went to work in San Diego plants.

Before two atomic bombs completed the defeat of Japan the payroll to individuals in California had passed $12 billion and the population of the state had leaped during war years to almost 9 million. In addition there were hundreds of thousands of service men arriving and sailing.

On V-J Day the destitute people of the thirties were on the average far better off than at any time in their lives. Women and older children had been working; almost everyone owned war bonds; many found their cheap houses worth four times the purchase price. With luxury items scarce, savings accounts mounted. For the California civilian World War II was a financial success.

THE HIGHWAY EMERGENCY

The most popular way of celebrating the World War II victory was to buy a full tank of gasoline and head for the open road. Gas rationing ended in August, 1945 to give many their first unworried —or unguilty—long drive in four years.

The week-end traffic that jammed 101 lifted a wail of protest, especially from Los Angeles which had pushed its over-crowded war-born population north and south. On Sunday nights cars full of tired people crept, bumper to bumper, toward home. Even the big Arroyo Seco parkway that joined Pasadena with Los Angeles, and the wide mile-long stretch of boulevard through Cahuenga Pass, could not handle the first rush of post-war traffic.

Legislators huddled with the California Highway Commission to see what could be done to get an adequate program underway before conditions became altogether impossible. People had to travel, some of them long distances, on account of the housing shortage in cities. The condition was bad enough with most people unable to buy new cars. But once Detroit went into production 101 would become a series of dead-ends.

Thirteen Freeway

"GOLD-PLATED HIGHWAYS"

Throughout the global war U.S. 101 developed on state and federal drafting boards, contour maps and scale models. That engineer's embryo grew and took refined shape as the experience of World War II constructors improved road materials, equipment and know-how. Surveys and projections of future traffic caused the planners to regard as obsolete the old "ribbon road" that at every Coast city interrupted the flow of vehicles with its speed laws, cross streets, railroad tracks and lights. By V-J Day the vision of highway experts went even beyond the radical "freeway" system first proposed for Los Angeles.

The future Freeway 101 was to be a six-lane, divided turnpike that would permit a motorist to travel from San Diego to San Francisco without encountering a single toll station, stop light, sharp curve or left turn. The public authorities would designate separation points with access ramps channeling traffic off and on the freeway by over or under passes leading to interchanges. Wide medians

—dividing strips—were to provide for expansion; shrubbery on them was designed to shield headlight glare.

The freeway concept abolished the custom of routing travelers past city business establishments to encourage spending stops. Service stations, motels, restaurants and former roadside tourist attractions would be set back outside a wire mesh fence on "frontage roads."

Because 101 was a federal highway work started on sections of freeway as soon as war-time restrictions were lifted. But more than twenty years passed before there was a continuous ultra-modern artery since maintenance, work allocations and coordination with other freeways and secondary roads came under the jurisdiction of the California Division of Highways. Until the 1960s 101 would be part freeway, part expressway and part main street.

When a state-wide network of freeways was first proposed in 1945—to cost a minimum of $2.4 billion over a ten-year period—the battle that ensued would long be remembered as the most stubborn in California legislative history. The massive-headed, popular Senator Randolph Collier, who presided over the Fact-finding Committee charged with making recommendations, fixed the then seemingly exorbitant cost. And Collier stung a number of interests with his suggestions as to how freeway money should be raised.

A proposal to make heavy vehicles pay for the damage they did to highways brought the powerful trucking lobby down on the Collier Committee; oil companies protested a raise in gas and diesel fuel taxes; farmers said metropolitan freeways should be toll-supported; city residents feared rural log-rolling; and tax weary citizens howled against an increase in license and registration fees. For two years the cause of the freeway program seemed doomed.

But Collier was a fighter—and a good practical politician—who watered down his demands and with the support of a Los Angeles legislator (whom he helped push through a horsemeat labeling bill) got the Collier-Burns Highway Act on the statute books. From that beginning there developed the largest freeway program ever undertaken by any state—what was praised by the

Bureau of Public Roads in Washington as "the finest job of planning a highway network in history." [1]

The principal criticism of freeways in the 1940s was their cost. "Gold-plated highways" they were called by the economy minded. Los Angeles City Engineer Lloyd Aldridge, known as the "Father of the Freeway" because of his pioneer work as early as 1933, had an answer for the critics. His views were set down by Sam Taylor, author of *Linehaul* and himself something of an authority on highways:

> Aldrich has pointed out that the freeways carry three times the traffic of a similar surface street, twice as fast and five times as safely.... He estimated that a motorist saved 2 cents a mile by driving on a freeway. There is also the value of time directly measurable in the wages of truck and bus drivers. Such savings could repay the original cost of the "gold-plated highways" within ten years. Also the initial costs, while high, is the last cost. Freeways are a permanent investment.[2]

RIGHTS-OF-WAY

After the idea and expense of freeways had been accepted by the public and grudgingly approved by oil, truck and utility interests, the constructors faced the headache of acquiring rights-of-way without depleting their budgets. In the case of 101 the greatest difficulty was experienced at such crowded bottlenecks as the outskirts of Los Angeles and San Francisco.

Coming from the San Fernando Valley, the Hollywood Freeway into the center of Los Angeles could not be laid until 1,728 buildings were moved and 90 others destroyed; the cost per mile just for right-of-way amounted to more than $2½ million. Around the crowded San Francisco peninsula, down to San Jose, the bill was also huge. The Santa Ana Freeway, along which 101 headed south, ran through a heavy defense plant area but there the Highway Department had secured title in advance of industrial development which set a precedent for future building.

Soon after the freeway began to take shape speculators bought in the path of where they thought the bulldozers would come, made "improvements," and waited to hold up the right-of-way negotiators. To avert stampedes and assure that 101 could follow the practical route of the old Coast Highway without detouring to avoid a cluster of factories, the Legislature in 1952 and 1953 appropriated $30 million for a revolving fund out of which advanced purchases of land could be made. In two years the saving by this method throughout the state amounted to $95 million.

At the start the individual suffered. A service station shoved onto a frontage road along a few miles of freeway faced ruin, for the motorist could find a handier gas up the road where the old-fashioned highway resumed. Freeway appraisers had to be as calculating as bankers in fixing the value of a little house that might have an intangible sentimental value; all the owner could hope to gain would be the amount of a sales commission and a few extra real estate titles. There was no recourse against the inconvenience of construction in the neighborhood—and the work gangs were loud and sloppy—nor was there any protection against noise and fumes if a person lived just off the completed freeway.

The Division of Highways attempted to soothe the irate taxpayer with brochures. One of these showed Mr. Average Man leaning back in a chair, wearing an ego-inflated smile, under the caption, "More than 14 million people want my property." [3] The brochure pointed out the responsibilities of the citizen under a democracy and listed eight departments from governor down who should be blamed—instead of some local employee of the Highway Department. Finally, the brochure with its illustration of clean-cut, happy, average people, belied nasty rumors that political skullduggery ever tarnished the escutcheon of the freeway.

To the majority of motorists the samples of new 101 were a boon. When the Hollywood Freeway opened April 15, 1954 it became the most heavily traveled road in the world, with the *daily* count of speeding vehicles clocked at 168,000. Through fifteen postwar years the concrete carpet rolled out while new equipment and more money made it and satellite freeways wider, longer and faster for 13, then 15, on past 17 million people. The common reaction to freeways became the complaint: "As long as they were doing it they should have made it bigger!"

BEYOND FRONTAGE ROAD

The millions of GI's who came back to California after World War II and the Korean War formed a migration that would be unique even in the varied westward procession since the invasion of Athabascans 500 years before Christ. Young couples arrived from every state in search of full living—good wages and climate; unlimited opportunity; and most of all orderliness. For participants in two disillusioning wars—overseas and at home—the underlying ingredient of order transcended the noisy rush of traffic, the hammering hard-sell voices of TV and radio hucksters, the stench of smog and gas fumes, and all the combined blares of business. Along Freeway 101 cities dominated by a mass search for neat existence clung to the white lifeline with access ramp arms.

Cities spread beyond the frontage roads and by the mid-1950s population "explosions" brought thousands of real estate developments whose quickly-built homes masked the rolling hills along old El Camino Real where Franciscans had sown the yellow mustard seed. The Carolands Company sold $17,000 lots at Paradise Cay off San Quentin Prison and in a few years the property went up to $25,000. On the San Francisco Peninsula Coast west of San Mateo, Fredric Lane, author turned investment broker, wrote:

> This particular area from Montara to Half Moon Bay is due to explode just as soon as the highway comes through the mountain from Linda Mar, and a lot of fortunes will be made here.[4]

At San Mateo, where 101 was a dual highway—the Bayshore Freeway flanked by industry and El Camino Real running past suburban shopping centers—newcomers had built a community with an assessed valuation of $100 million—ten times what it had been before the war.

The explosion in the north was dwarfed by the inflow to freeway cities south of Los Angeles, risen amid sprawling assembly, distribution and manufacturing plants. Once-sleepy little Downey, where farmers raised 200-pound pumpkins and the corn grew twelve feet high, was an almost deserted railroad flag stop until the coming of war and then the freeway; but before the end of the 1950s the population neared 80,000! Another little railroad stop was Norwalk, home of E. C. Cawson's African ostrich farm and one of the victim communities in the 1933 earthquake that rocked Southern California; the Norwalk Chamber of Commerce changed the population sign every six months up to 90,000 and that marked no end to growth. The mother city of L.A. was near three million, topped in the United States only by New York and Chicago.

From Ventura, where 101 became two separate highways for its passage through crowded L.A., on down to the Mexican border, active chambers of commerce proudly pushed their towns and sought to lure the endless wave of twentieth-century pioneers. Buena Park in Orange County had the famous tourist attraction, Knott's Berry Farm and Ghost Town, along with the 90-acre plant of Kraft Foods, Sears, Roebuck's largest Pacific Coast store, and luxury homes selling for $150,000. Pretty little Carlsbad, near Mission San Luis Rey, proclaimed itself at "the center of the magic weather circle" and folders said Chula Vista on the freeway outskirts of San Diego "Tops the World for Sunshine and Sociability."

People lured to the West could usually choose where they wanted to live and work. Aircraft factories opened special parking lots for job applicants and the average weekly wage of factory workers was $100, while the unemployed could draw $160 a month for twenty-six weeks. On Sundays the Los Angeles *Times* ran sixteen pages of male help-wanted ads. Along the old Coast Road there was almost every kind of employment except the shoveling of snow. Many wives worked; families sought the proverbial nest egg and when taxes ate up earnings, salaried people speculated in property.

Houses in subdivisions near larger freeway cities sold for "as little as" $15,000 and at the plush residential areas of Beverly Hills

261

and Hillsborough building sites could fetch $100,000. Families in that whirlpool of good living put 10 per cent down on a $20,000 house, paid $140 a month, then sold in a few years at a profit of several thousand dollars. The gain went into a more expensive "home"—a custom built place—and so on to greater social approval. As overbuilding threatened drainage, and the state's water table reached a dangerous low, backyard swimming pools, flagstone patios and bomb shelters were built with careless abandon. The valleys, hills and shoreline began to take on the glutted look of those Eastern suburbs the newly-arrived had abandoned.

The British magazine *Economist* surveyed the Golden State where it concluded there was too much of everything, including people:

> ... in the main it is with the pressures of prosperity that Californians have to struggle. In doing so they are showing the rest of the United States what the future has in store for it. ...
>
> Can it now go farther and meet the latest challenge ... opened up by the question: After prosperity—what? [5]

FREEWAY FEVER

To Californians the prosperity of the early 1960s was the milestone in the advance of mankind which would mark an end to economic slumps: steadily increasing prosperity—with a possible lull to convince an unenlightened enemy—foretold the obsolescence of the very word. The pressures of speed, noise and tension were the comparatively easy lot of modern men.

In *McCall's* magazine Samuel Grafton compared the sunshine states of Florida and California. He reported that the once easy-going Westerner had become brisk and metropolitan as he hurried everywhere in a dark Ivy League suit, talking of money and progress, interested in urbanity rather than orange groves, cattle ranges, fresh air and a siesta. Grafton found that:

> Along El Camino today the Californian lives a sophisticated life. He has, within freeway distance, nightclubs, concerts, opera on oc-

casion, a bewildering array of foreign restaurants, major sports events, the beer and coffee joints of the intelligentsia, off-beat foreign movie houses, art galleries, and book stores.[6]

A rigadoon of high-speed cars sent people dashing home from work to flick on TV sets still warm from afternoon soap operas. A fifty-mile drive to a cocktail party was a mere jaunt on the freeway and couples would travel that distance without thought to see a movie at some drive-in theater; new automobiles hummed along at eighty miles an hour to the 101 sports events, themselves dedicated to speed—the racing of horses, dogs, boats, aeroplanes and autos.

In the fuming parade moved a polyglot of vehicles: the beaten-up bargains of Mad-Man Muntz, a garish used car dealer; the elongated teardrop designs that were Detroit's version of "jet-age refinement"; custom-made $2,500 hot rods with raked windshields, chrome-plated under the hood; Frank Rose's 1927 Model T converted into a rod; the sports cars—MGs, Mercedes, Jags and Corvettes—headed for their rallies, Gymkhanas and concours d'élégance; Max Balchowaky's Old Yeller II from Hollywood and the dragster Green Monster, powered by a 3,000-horsepower P-38 engine—both prizes trailered.

Crowding the freeway in the 1960s were the little cars of foreign make—said to have become popularized by efforts of a California educator's co-op—and the American "compact-compacts." Dwarfing them came monstrous vehicles of the Highway Department—bulldozers, mixers and 38,000-pound slipform pavers, along with giant house trailers.

The bane of drivers in the days of a narrow 101, the homes on wheels that moved between highway trailer areas began to grow with the freeway. The Santa Barbara engineer L. E. Dresback converted a bus into a house trailer, but that was a dwarf compared with the Roadcraft Imperial, introduced at San Francisco in 1959; seventy feet long, ten feet wide with living room, dining room, bedroom, all-electric kitchen and bath.

Another freeway crowd hauled half a million boats, some of

them small ocean-going yachts, all of them given the tender care lavished on racehorses pulled in wheeled stalls between Tanforan and Del Mar. Near Anaheim cattle used a special underpass.

Into the feverish procession entered such occasional off-beat machines as Wally Will's motor scooter, *The Pregnant Grasshopper*, bound up to San Francisco from Los Angeles after crossing Death Valley in the summer heat of 1959. And 101 was traveled by *La Tortuga*, the amphibious jeep of Frank and Helen Schreider on its 20,000-mile trip from the Arctic Circle to Tierra del Fuego.

The magic freeway attracted deer around Gaviota Pass and bears wandered down to stand behind the mesh fence and watch the speeding humans. One of them—dubbed "Salinas Sam"—was put in jail by the police of that city, then shot full of tranquilizers and loaded in a small truck bound toward Fleishhacker Zoo in San Francisco. But Sam died en route.

Other non-motorists lured by the white artery were the pranksters. In Los Angeles two "boys" over twenty years of age were fined $50 apiece and given 180-day suspended sentences for tossing golf balls from a ramp into the path of traffic.

More unique, and more of a hazard, was a 35-year-old blond who created a traffic jam on the Bayshore section of the freeway late in 1959 as she promenaded naked. The San Francisco police officers who picked her up were treated for bites, sustained as they struggled to get the lady into coveralls.

To overlay that high-temperature freeway, to some extent on the Bayshore approach to South San Francisco but mostly at Los Angeles, there descended a blight called smog. The still, sun-heated airs of the southern metropolis thickened with the multi-million dollar exhaust fumes of automobiles, diesel vehicles, factories and aircraft to produce the noxious phenomena. While scientists tested for a cure, the daily weather reports forecast the probable density of the smog and the amount of eye irritation it would cause. Visiting historians seldom failed to recall that in 1602 Captain-General Sebastian Vizcaíno observed the even early presence of smog and named the offshore waters *Bahía de los Fumos*.

Smog, like the sonic boom of a jet breaking the sound barrier, or the chilling wail of police, ambulance and fire engine sirens, was accepted in the name of progress. A truck driver making $1,000 a month, and a man who could afford to drive a new push-button, air conditioned convertible, complained a bit while he sighted ahead. But 7 million California freeway users sped without too much concern about any single problem, unless it was the universal lookout kept in rear-view mirrors for the cruising guardians of the road.

CALIFORNIA HIGHWAY PATROL

To protect and regulate humanity that hurtled along the potentially dangerous freeway required law enforcement as efficiently streamlined as the road itself. The California Highway Patrol, with about 3,000 men and half that number of vehicles, had been geared in ten years to operate along 80,000 miles of road with military precision. By the 1960s the organization under Bradford M. Crittenden was responsible for traffic that registered 70 million miles a year—the heaviest of any state in the nation. And of California highways and freeways 101 was the most traveled.

The story of the modern highway patrol—whose predecessors were Spanish soldiers, Mexican *juezes de país* and American Rangers—began in 1929 with 280 officers. This was the State Legislature's response to the bootleggers and hijackers war along the Coast; 80 roadsters and 225 motorcycles began their war against gangsters. At its head was Eugene Biscailuz, who was later well-known as sheriff of Los Angeles County.

In 1935 the patrol went under the Department of Motor Vehicles, replacing the emphasis on bullet-proof vests, folding armor plate body shields and Thompson submachine guns with a campaign to rid California roads of their share in mass death and injury from accidents. That was about the time one million injuries and 36,000 fatalities on American highways inspired J. C. Furnas to write his classic horror report "... And Sudden Death":

. . . a pair of youths were thrown out of an open roadster this spring —thrown clear—but each broke a windshield post with his head in passing and the whole top of each skull, down to the eyebrows, was missing.[7]

Two years after the end of World War II the guardians of the road became the Department of California Highway Patrol. The operation was divided into three state geographic zones under supervising inspectors; the zones were split into districts headed by supervisors, and those each had captains or lieutenants in charge of areas. The protection of the motorist from accidents, criminal action, nature's perils—and himself—was the mission of the Highway Patrol.

Along 101 the CHP operated chiefly over unincorporated areas but officers could make an arrest on any city street. Freeway gaps at San Diego, Santa Monica, Santa Barbara and on up to San Jose, together with through-city links, built a liaison between the Highway Patrol and City Police with Clifford E. Peterson, former Chief of Police of San Diego, as commissioner. This was further strengthened in March of 1953 when L.A.'s most famous cop, Bernard R. Caldwell, became commissioner of the CHP.

A red-headed hillbilly from Calico Rock, Arkansas, Caldwell was twenty-one years old when he arrived in Los Angeles in 1925 and landed a job as a street car motorman. Three years later he began a career with the police force, persistently climbing the hill of slow promotion, studying nights to supplement his country high school education. Caldwell had made captain by 1941 when the Los Angeles traffic situation was being used throughout the world as an example of the ultimate in automotive confusion.

Captain Caldwell accepted the frustrating job of untangling the knots. He had only a small force to start with—fifty motorcycle cops and a hundred men for downtown traffic control—but he had a free hand.

Captain Caldwell launched his program at Los Angeles by picking men for the force who were enthusiastic about police work.

Then he instituted a policy that gave those officers some authority and dignity. All violators began to receive tickets, and when motion-picture celebrities and honorable deputy sheriffs came in to get theirs squelched they advanced no farther than any little man. If a VIP demanded the firing of a cop Caldwell was never on the side of influence. Special training, advancement for new ideas, radio educational programs, accident-prevention films and public speaking engagements became part of Los Angeles police work. In ten years the city was the safest and most efficiently patrolled in the country.

Caldwell gave hot rod drivers a break when they had become a nuisance by drag racing through city streets; he organized them under the Southern California Timing Association. He was also behind the move that sent uniformed traffic cops into schools to demonstrate safe bicycle operation and to answer the questions of kids taking driver education courses. When Captain Caldwell moved to Sacramento as head of the Highway Patrol in 1953 he tackled problems on a state-wide scale, using the L.A. formula of placing morale high on the list of things that made a good force.

By 1960 the CHP was using more than a hundred FM stations and ten AM stations to operate an independent network that directed radio-equipped patrol cars, panel trucks and motorcycles. High caliber men were selected from civil service lists and took competitive examinations to qualify for rigid training at the Police Academy. Officers making a career in the Highway Patrol were as smart-looking and as devoted to duty as any patrol in the country and shared a common reluctance to being singled out for publicity. "Why don't you write something about George Kallemeyn, or George Mitchell?" they asked in the summer of 1959.

On July 25 more than 250 law enforcement officers from the San Francisco Bay Area were in a two-and-a-half mile motorcade that followed a hearse carrying the body of Patrolman George E. Kallemeyn, the twenty-nine-year-old father of four small children.

Kallemeyn had died after lying twenty hours under his heavy

motorcycle which overturned while he was chasing a gang of hot rod motorcyclists; the punks roared off into the night when they might have saved the man.

One week after the Kallemeyn funeral the San Francisco *Chronicle* carried a story from Santa Cruz:

> Police officers in four counties tonight were trying to track down five hoodlums who brutally beat up a State highway patrolman after he stopped them. . . .
>
> The victim, George Mitchell, 37, was in serious condition in Santa Cruz Hospital with skull fracture, deep cuts and bruises.[8]

Mitchell, who was a decorated Marine and the father of two children, had been assaulted by the delinquents when he sireneddown their heap. After being beaten to unconsciousness Mitchell was tied and thrown over a 40-foot cliff.

Every surly-faced kid in a low-slung rod was not an assailant, and the usually peculiar-looking adolescents in orbit on noisy motorcycles and motor scooters had not been medically certified idiots. As a result the lone law-enforcement officer must approach the possible maniac as he would any errant citizen. On reflection that short walk became an act of great bravery, repeated countless times.

By the law of averages, and from the extent and speed of freeway traffic, the apprehension of criminals did not figure on the books as a major part of the CHP operation. Neither did the accidents along 101—compared with casualties on any ordinary road —but when there was a smash-up it often turned out to be spectacular. Drunks, "road snails," people short on sleep, chattering drivers, the slow-reacting aged and speed demons who plowed into another car were sure to cause an accident involving a dozen or more oncoming vehicles. With no room to stop, expensive, cheaply-made cars folded like accordians.

Every holiday week end law-enforcers issued warnings in the form of projected statistics to show how many would die on the California highways. News stories urged caution and columnists tried to impress their readers. Typical of the unhappy expectancy were the figures given by Vincent X. Flaherty in his Los Angeles *Examiner* column on the eve of the 1960 Memorial Day week end:

> After digging into the World Almanac I find a half a million people have been killed in needless traffic accidents in the United States during the past ten years—almost twice as many Americans as were killed during World War II.[9]

TRAFFIC JAM

Fifteen years after the start of California's freeway program it required no long week end to jam traffic. In the spring of 1960 a Wednesday check showed more than 40,000 vehicles an hour pouring in and out of downtown Los Angeles. At peak hours the loudspeakers of helicopter patrolmen directed motorists to leave the burdened lanes of Hollywood and Santa Anna freeways for surfaced routes.

Six bridges that led 101 traffic across San Francisco Bay handled half a million cars, trucks and busses every twenty-four hours and the once open highway showed a steady stream even between small towns. Californians who went away and returned at intervals found the character and topography of the country altered beyond recognition.

One of the most striking changes was a broad swath cut by the freeway as it bypassed the old stagecoach town of San Juan Bautista. Lewis A. Lapham, who wrote a column for the *Examiner* before he went East to become a shipping executive, then a banker, recalled the San Juan grade he had driven over so many times traveling between San Francisco and Monterey. He was arrested starting up the grade; fifteen minutes later, on the way down, he was stopped again.

> The second cop saw the first traffic ticket as I produced my license and he and I repaired at once to the Salinas Traffic Court. Ten dollars for the first offense, twenty for the second, and ten for the indecently brief interval between pinches.[10]

The by-pass for the distance that separated the Lapham citations can be traveled today in a few minutes for the gradation is less than ten per cent. But the fines have become steeper.

The rerouting of the freeway, that made ghost towns out of such famous stops as San Juan, became a necessity and the people of little cities built around frontage road businesses grew nervous whenever the Highway Commission announced hearings.

At Buellton in 1960 District Highway Engineer A. M. Nash listened to citizens in a typical session to determine the best route through or around the old Mission Crossroads hamlet. A two-mile link was being forged in the 101 freeway chain at an estimated cost of about $3 million.

The Buellton Businessmen's Association urged that the historic adobe of *Rancho de la Vega* be left undisturbed; an elderly lady wanted to know if the state would move her house instead of buying and destroying it; a young man with an oil company agreement wondered what would happen to his newly remodeled service station.

In every county 6,000 state employees began car counts that summer at 4,150 crossings and the total for sixteen hours showed 75 million vehicles. More freeways seemed to be the only answer— through Los Angeles, in Orange County, and a "salamander" to squirm past expanded San Diego. Up at San Francisco Dick Chase of the *News-Call Bulletin* wrote the running story of the city's fight against any more freeway approaches to the Golden Gate Bridge; the compromise was a 125-million-dollar twin-bore tunnel.

The California Highway Commission set 1980 as completion date for an overall Freeway-Expressway System to cover 12,414 miles and cost $10½ billion. That network would accommodate 17 million vehicles in a land occupied by 31 million persons.

EN ROUTE TO AUTOMATION

The expansion of today's freeways is not the picture seen in the crystal ball of scientific seers. Researchers and inventors predict that a new type highway will begin to evolve before twenty years have elapsed.

The 101 of some day after tomorrow will first be equipped to carry automatically driven cars, moving through a magnetic field that will make collision impossible. Trucks will run under the freeway along an air conditioned subterranean road. Arches above 101 will support a 500-mile monorail.

In the scientist's vision the tri-level 101 must change before 2000 A.D. into a wide landing strip and continuous control route for the helicars that will develop from the Curtis-Wright "air car," the wheelless vehicle that moves on a cushion of compressed air.

Columnist Jim Bishop researched plans for the future helicar and reported:

> When they near their destination, the approaches will be clearly marked by rows of colored lights, low-flying traffic will follow a pattern, and the helicars will land, fold their rotors, and start into town as automobiles.[11]

The cities of San Diego, Los Angeles, San Jose and San Francisco had already started an upward expansion in the 1960s, defiant of an earthquake history: twelve-story ramped motels; downtown skyscrapers with heliports; the first geodesic homes of transparent plastic on the sides and crests of lofty hills.

Sound-proofing, air conditioning and piped music sought to banish noise; anti-smog devices became mandatory for the exhaust pipes of automobiles; intercoms, escalators, moving sidewalks and electric eyes reduced the need for physical effort. Experimentation concentrated on making life clean, easy, enjoyable and largely automatic.

The prediction for the appearance of the lateral connecting cities and suburbs along 101 was a solid strip of dwellings, factories, laboratories and landing fields. In the distance the rolling hills that suggested feminine voluptuousness to trudging Spanish soldiers of the eighteenth century would underlie a mask of concrete, glass, aluminum and plastic. The terrible waste of annual forest fires would then be of the past when only formal parks and strips of greenery cut precise patterns across the synthetic earth skin.

All grazing land might go the way of the 65,000 acres taken over by Vandenberg Air Force Base near Point Concepción for America's "Man in Space" program. In his *News-Press* column Thor M. Smith, a U.S. Air Force officer during World War II, speculated that from Vandenberg

> Santa Barbara County might become the Number One jump-off point for interplanetary exploration.[12]

LIVING AGAIN

Santa Barbara, historic hub of the coastal thoroughfare, represented the extremes of time in the 1960s. While space experiments probed toward the distant constellations, archeologists of the city's museum and the University of California, along with oceanographers from Scripps Institute, sent more expeditions out to Santa Rosa Island in search of prehistoric man's remains.

The lure of a less remote past focused attention on the early trail that brought California into being. In 1948 twelve coastal counties had joined forces under the sponsorship of the California Mission Trails Association for a dramatic reenactment of Governor Gaspar de Portolá's trek. Interest in the old trace mounted and Santa Barbara's state senator, J. J. "Jack" Hollister of the renowned family, put through a resolution for the official remarking of Freeway 101 which in the 1960s again became El Camino Real.

Fourteen   The Royal Road

THE MISSION TRAIL REBORN

On Point Loma stands the National Monument that honors the Portuguese navigator Juan Rodríguez Cabrillo, first European to pass the headland and anchor in San Diego Bay. Beyond the statue lies the residential section of people descended from the Portuguese of Azore and Cape Verde Islands. One of them is Anthony Mascarenhas, former merchant mariner, naval officer and commercial tuna fisherman, turned to the insurance business that daily brings him to the city risen over the beach where his countryman stepped ashore 360 years ago.

Above a concrete expressway island in the downtown San Diego district a plaque marks the ancient Spanish beach encampment and burial place; from that point a newly posted El Camino Real winds northwest and northward to the town plaza of Sonoma, site of General Vallejo's presidio and the Franciscan's twenty-first mission.

On road maps and signs the big freeway is still 101 but along its length are other signs, and mission bells that hang from replicas of the Franciscan walking staff, to proclaim the way as El Camino Real.

Speeding down and up the freeway, tops weighted by baggage, are more in-state sightseers than ever before—new residents on two-week vacations, as eager to view California as any Easterner. Between Disneyland, Forest Lawn Cemetery of Los Angeles, Hearst Castle and the Golden Gate Bridge the tourists check a mass of literature that gives the dates of flower, wine and fruit festivals, frontier breakfasts, roundups and "days" dedicated to Indians, Old Spanish, Mexicans, pioneers and forty-niners.

The yearly Salinas Rodeo is one of America's "Big Four" roundups and every summer 100,000 persons stop at Santa Barbara to watch *El Desfile Historico*—the parade of horses, *carretas*, stage-coaches and floats on which *caballeros* and señoritas dance again the fandango. Spanish soldiers, Chinese highbinders, road agents, Rangers, bluejackets of '46, Indian fighters, Argonauts, Barbary Coast belles, temperance ladies, and pioneer women mingle in the gay fiestas.

Loud-speakers tell people in the "rubber neck" busses that the Los Angeles *Times* building rises over the site of the Overland Mail stage depot; that at San Juan Capistrano every year the swallows leave on St. John's Day, October 13, to return St. Joseph's Day, March 19; and that the buildings of UPI president Frank Bartholomew's Buena Vista Winery in Sonoma were once part of the old mission.

Civic groups and women's clubs join the Redwood Empire, Mission Trails and Landmark associations to preserve and promote every possible tie with the past. New towns—Encinitas, Cardiff and Leucadia in the San Diego area, and dozens of others—unearth the names of forgotten rancheros to blend history with progress.

Disneyland, off the freeway near Anaheim, brings to life every era of the procession and the millions who visit that wondrous creation of Walt Disney feel the thrill of recognition on viewing scenes of the West that match the authentic backgrounds of television. Here is the frontier road of desperados and lawmen, and the duplicated world made familiar by the actor sons of California: Leo Carrillo, descendent of the famous family, and Richard Boone of Los Angeles, seventh generation nephew of Daniel.

TV westerns give the travel agents the easily sold interest in history to more than replace hot springs, scenery and resort living. School kids are eager to visit national and state monuments; in 1960 crowds responded to a brief notice that paintings of the 1791 Malaspina Expedition would be shown along El Camino Real. These rare works of art were brought from the Spanish Naval Museum by Lieutenant Julio Guillén, son of the famous admiral whose name he carries on.

Wells Fargo is again a favorite of the people and headquarters is its History Room, located in the bank in downtown San Francisco. There a real stagecoach is surrounded by mementos of the past; Irene Simpson and her staff bring back the vigor of the old proclamation: "By God and by Wells Fargo!"

The rechristened road is showered by a new outpour of historical writing at every level from advertising superlatives to the erudite research of such Western scholars as Arthur Woodward. Strangers learn of the dying condor, the reviving sea otter, Vancouver's music box and the story that the Indians around Monterey thought all Spaniards were the sons of she-asses—because they had with them no women.

There is an argument now among the historical writers about the trace of the original El Camino Real used by Portolá, and later Father Serra. Descendents of old families carp at slight divergences. Critics of the historical resurrection—which they claim is a business racket—charge that the direction taken by the modern "path of the padres" is along the line of the most cash registers. And cynics tell that actually there never was a Royal Road. The scoffers are rebuked by Father Maynard Geiger who stands today in the place once occupied by Father Francisco Palou:

Though this King's Highway was often no more than a trail, it was a definite road, and padres and soldiers almost always used the exact route. At any given point parties traveling it in opposite directions would always meet.[1]

THE CONCRETE CENTIPEDE

Approaching its 200th anniversary El Camino Real is more than a freeway connecting the sleepy head of Sonoma to bustling San Diego, with a dusty tail dragging down Baja California to the other lethargic terminal at Loreto. Like all roads—which the British essayist Hilaire Belloc regards "as much the creation of man as the city and the laws" [2]—El Camino Real has its multiple appendages: the access ways to the cities and missions that brought it into being.

Excepting the twenty-five cents it costs to cross the Golden Gate Bridge there are no tolls on the freeway—which is the reason behind the name—and the motorist can make the run from Sonoma to San Diego in a single day. But if a couple travels leisurely, turning off 101 to visit missions, historical landmarks and tourist attractions they will spend $50 a day for motel, meals, tips and admission tickets.

The tourist visits the old mission at Sonoma, looks at plaques that mark the house of Vallejo and the Blue Wing Inn, then heads through open country that gradually thickens with housing developments as the freeway swings ironically close to grim San Quentin. A frequent traveler in—and out—of "Esque" is the former fighter and pharmacist, Frank Carter, now a restaurateur and boxing referee who brings athletics and hope to prisoners.

Coming off the big red bridge, heading toward downtown, traffic passes a row of ornate motels, grown to three and four stories, the new caravanserai of this "Bagdad on the Bay" as San Francisco has been christened by her tireless troubadour, columnist Herb Caen.

On the Monterey peninsula the wise traveler avoids the five o'clock rush of workers, service men and business people whose horns do not let him drive slowly enough to read the markers on a dozen buildings of the old capitol. The destination for almost everyone coming into the area is Carmel-by-the-Sea, that last California stronghold against progress as embodied in no parking meters, service stations, neon lights, street numbers or the removal of trees.

Carmel, once the home of artists and writers, now a pretty place of expensive little shops, captures the hearts of people caught in the modern mesh of speed and noise and dirt. A measure of the quiet power exerted by peaceful Carmel is that it can generate intrastate treason. Stan Windhorn, columnist for Florida's Sarasota *Herald Tribune*, found that the town

> breeds strong discontent for living anywhere upon this earth except in Carmel. A dedicated sense of responsibility, family ties, friendships and a team of wild horses will not be sufficient to drag us from this loveliest of cities. If Florida wants us back they'll have to extradite.[3]

The fight to bar developments, department stores, and supermarkets—the gold mines of the 1960s—continues outside Carmel at only one other city, Santa Barbara. But the tide of channel progress washes away the imprint of old-timers Pearl Chase and Tom Storke: the tax-burdened owners of $300-an-acre farm land sell it for $7,000; real estate tracts push south from the Arroyo Burro, hideaway of the Jack Powers gang and fugitive Ned McGowan.

Heavy rigs thunder down once quiet De La Vina Street; hot rods and "Karts" shatter the quiet of Hope Ranch and Montecito. Southern Pacific has added to its nuisance of noise by starting trackside fires as speeding engines spill fire round the curves; offshore oil platforms loom like mechanical monsters out of science fiction.

The sword of enterprise has slashed and scarred the pretty land along El Camino Real from the grave of Junípero Serra in the Carmel vale to the hilltop museum that honors his name at San Diego. And at his missions no flocks of *neophytes* gather when the Angelus bells peal out the call to vespers. Military establishments, so badly needed in another time, now surround the churches. The wayfarers of the day are tourists who leave offerings; cattle—

the California banknotes on the hoof—graze on inland acreage where they are rounded up by mechanized *vaqueros*—the jeep cowboys.

At the border city of Tia Juana in the third quarter of the twentieth century the remnants of old Spain are the language and bullrings, along with the *mañana* promise of great things for Baja California. The southbound tourist quickly senses a truth expressed by the author-newspaperman team of Stanton Delaplane and Robert de Roos:

The United States is rich enough to hide its poor. Mexico is not.[4]

PADRE KINO

Tourists fly south to fish off La Paz where Visitador-General José de Gálvez first outlined his plans for the march of Portolá. At Cabo de San Lucas, landing place of the *conquistadores* and of Sebastian Vizcaíno, natives tell their hopes to the Los Angeles *Times* reporter Charles Hillinger: "With a road everything will come. Without it there can be nothing." [5]

To the devout there is a sign that the ancient trail of Jesuit priests, pushed northward from Loreto, will one day soon commence to grow into a great Camino Real. This is the new farming community some 150 miles south of the American border which takes its name from the pioneer of the "Devil's Road" who first prophesied a highway to Monterey—Padre Kino.

ACKNOWLEDGMENT

The acknowledgment to a work that has occupied its author for three years, and draws on an additional thirty years of personal experience and observation, must commence with the familiar apology for omission—offered here with great regret. To keep this acknowledgment within reasonable boundaries I have left out of the list below most of the names which appear in the text, bibliography or quoted sources.

Among the societies, organizations and individuals concerned with California history I wish to thank: the Royal Academy of History, Madrid, and its director, Vice-Admiral Julio F. Guillén; the Academy of American Franciscan History and Father Kiernan R. McCarty, OFM; the Book Club of California and Mrs. Elizabeth Downs; the California Historical Society and members of the staff; Father Maynard Geiger, OFM; the Historical Society of Southern California; the Junípero Serra Museum and G. F. "Jerry" MacMullen, director; the San Luís Obispo Museum and Mrs. Louisana Dart; the San Luis Rey Historical Society; the Santa Barbara Historic Society and W. Edwin Gledhill; the Santa Barbara Museum Library and Cliff Smith; the Society of California Pioneers and Mrs. Hester Robinson and Mrs. Helen S. Giffens; and Irene Simpson, director of Wells Fargo's History Room in San Francisco. To the foregoing, I would add a special word of thanks to numerous persons at the twenty-one missions, the state landmark sites, and the county historical societies along the route of my story.

Among the individuals who kindly supplied me with material or advice I am in the debt of: Karl A. Bickel, Joseph L. Cauthorn, Pearl Chase, Rosario Curletti, Gene Doyle, George Fields, Lewis A. Lapham, Vincent Lucich, John A. Lucian, the Fred Matteis, Fayetta Philip, Suzanne Pochelon, Mary Rice, Lester Roberts, Carroll DeWilton Scott and William P. Wreden. Whitney T. Genns, the Santa Barbara bookman, is especially remembered for his generosity over a period of several months.

Other persons who advised me on a variety of points include: Elizabeth Chapman, Robert Condon, Rear Admiral Ernest M. Eller, USN (Ret.), Director of Naval History, U.S. Navy, David Magee, Charlotte Newbegin, Frank O'Mea, Hank Peters, Marjorie Phleger, James Quint, Constantine Raises, Colonel Raymond Stone, USA (Ret.), Pidge Temple and Harlan Trott.

To the considerable California State family I must offer blanket thanks with a separate nod in the direction of Lester S. Koritz, public information officer in the Division of Highways; Richard Malone of San Lúis Obispo, operating out of District V under A. M. Nash; and Homer C. Hixson of Buellton, maintenance superintendent. In the California Highway Patrol much information was supplied by Russell R. McComb and his assistant John R. Ryan at Sacramento headquarters and by numerous officers including Clay Hess of San Francisco and John D. Lowe at Santa Barbara. An overall picture of the U.S. Forestry Service was supplied by Earl E. Bachman at San Francisco.

Library research brought me to the stacks of more than one hundred collections. My thanks to Carma R. Zimmerman, head of the California State Library; Allan R. Ottley at Sacramento; Richard H. Dillon, Sutro Librarian at San Francisco; Dolores Cadell, head of the Reference Division of the San Francisco Public Library; John E. Smith and his able staff at the Santa Barbara Public Library, especially Elizabeth Howell and Mrs. Howard Lewis; Marco G. Thorne, assistant to Claire E. Breed, at the San Diego Public Library; Patricia J. Clark, San Lúis Obispo Public Library; Lindsey Bliss and the Huntington Library; the Pasadena and Los Angeles Public Libraries; Ethel M. Solliday of the Monterey City Library; Ellen Shaffer of the Rare Book Room in the Free Library of Philadelphia and Mrs. Ruth Galvin Thormberg of the Harrison Memorial Library at Carmel.

A sizable directory would be required to note by name all the individuals who have contributed to *Golden Road* and the following few are those on whom I have imposed most heavily: the Atascadero Chamber of Commerce and L. C. Gibaut; from the several motorist clubs, William H. Newbro, Jr. and his secretary, Phyllis Maresh, of the Automobile Club of Southern California, and William Ellis of the California State Automobile Club; Myrtle Broam of the Carlsbad Chamber of Commerce; Mrs. Doris H. Husted of the Carpinteria Valley Chamber of Commerce; Richard W. Cochrane of the Montecito Inn; Russ Good of the La Jolla Cab Company; J. J. Rose, supervisor of Western Greyhound Lines at Santa Barbara; Richard P. Irwin, manager of the Valencia Hotel, La Jolla; Robert M. Seavers, the Santa Maria Chamber of Commerce; Abbott Thomas of the Valencia Hotel; Donald E. Brown of the Tustin Chamber of Commerce; and the Wine Institute, Philip Hiaring, public relations diretcor and Dora Coleman, librarian.

In the difficult task of obtaining illustrations for the line drawings of this book, I have been given immeasurable help by: the Bancroft Library staff of John Barr Tompkins, notably his second in command,

J. S. Holliday, and staff members Richard Bernard and Elizabeth Hamilton; at the California Historical Society photos were selected by Robin Blasek, assistant to Librarian James de T. Abajian; Ralph Buffon and his staff of California Mission Trails Association; John J. Cuddy of Californians, Inc.; Eric W. Coster of California Rodeo; Glen Dawson, the Los Angeles bookman and publisher; Disneyland, Inc. through Jim Nugent, Editor of Vacationland; H. H. Evans of the Porpoise Book Store; Warren Howell of John Howell Books who has also advised me on other matters concerning the work; Nathanial Hurwitz, the Pacific Coast publisher; Charles Hillinger of the Los Angeles *Times*; James Reynolds, the Van Nuys bookman; the Redwood Empire Association and Joel Y. Rickman; author W. W. Robinson; the Santa Barbara *News-Press*; John Swingle of Berkeley; Charles E. Fulkerson of the Title Insurance and Trust Company of Los Angeles.

Dictaphone transcriptions amounting to a quarter of a million words were done by my daughter, Joan Barrett, who also typed the preliminary and final drafts of the manuscript. On a number of points Joan had the advice of her husband, Hoyt B. Barrett, Jr., working for his doctorate in Psychology at Purdue University. My son, Felix III, accompanied me during some of the travel incidental to the book, as did Stan Windhorn, the newspaper columnist and writer. Much of the research in California county histories was done by my wife, Priscilla, who supervised the setting up of the bibliography. Final corrections were done by my secretary, Nancy Weber. I thank them all.

NOTES

CHAPTER 1

1. *No Stone Unturned, An Almanac of American Prehistory*, by Louis A. Brennan, New York, 1959.

2. *Memoirs of the Society for American Archaeology*, No. IX, by Gordon Ekholm, Salt Lake City, 1953.

3. *Chu-fan-chi, Chinese and Arab Trade in the 12th and 13th Centuries*, by Chau Ju-Kua, translation by Friedrich Hirth and W. W. Rockhill, St. Petersburg, 1911.

4. *A Spanish Voyage to Vancouver and the North-West Coast of America*, by José Espinosa y Tello, Cecil Jones edition, London, 1930.

5. *Noticia de la California, etc.* by Miguel Venegas, Madrid, 1775.

6. *Juan Rodríguez Cabrillo, Discoverer of the Coast of California*, by Henry R. Wagner, San Francisco, 1941.

7. *Divers Voyages Touching the Discovery of America*, by Richard Hakluyt, London, 1850.

8. *The World Encompassed by Sir Francis Drake*, by Francis Drake, London, 1854.

9. "Voyage of Pedro de Unamuno to California in 1587," translated by Irene A. Wright, *California Historical Society Quarterly*, July, 1923.

10. *Voyage to California of Sebastián Rodríguez Cermeñon in 1595*, by Henry R. Wagner, *California Historical Society Quarterly*, April, 1924.

11. *Spanish Explorations in the Southwest*, by Herbert E. Bolton, New York, 1925.

12. *Diario*, Sebastián Vizcaíno, Mexico City.

13. *Derrotero*, Fr. Antonio de la Ascension.

CHAPTER 2

1. *Las Sergas de Esplandián*, by García Ordónez de Montalvo.

2. *Kino's Historical Memoir of Pimería Alta*, edited by H. E. Bolton, 2 vols., Cleveland, 1919.

3. *Correspondence of José de Gálvez*, 1768.

4. *Diary of Junípero Serra*, 1769.

5. Correspondence of Gálvez, 1768–70.

6. *Diary of Miguel Costansó*, 1770.

7. *Diary of Pedro Fages*, 1769–70.

8. *Diary of Juan Crespí*, 1769–1770.

9. *Ibid.*

10. *Diary of Vizcaíno's Voyage*, various translations.
11. *Report of Gaspar de Portolá, 1769.*
12. *Crespí's Diary.*
13. *Pedro Fages Report to Viceroy of New Spain, 1775.*
14. *Diary of Pedro Font, 1776.*
15. *Ibid.*
16. *Outpost of Empire*, by H. E. Bolton, N.Y., 1931.
17. *Diary of Pedro Font.*

CHAPTER 3

1. *La Vida, etc., Junípero Serra*, by Francisco Palou, Mexico, 1787.
2. *Representación 21 Mayo 1773*, by Junípero Serra.
3. Palou, *op. cit.*
4. *Noticias de la California*, by Francisco Palou, 4 vols., San Francisco, 1874.
5. *Ibid.*
6. *Los Tres Siglos de Mexico*, by C. M. Bustamente, Jalapa, 1870.
7. *History of California* vol. II, by Hubert Howe Bancroft, San Francisco, 1885.
8. *Voyage Round the World*, by J. F. G. de la Pérouse, Boston, 1801.
9. *Ibid.*
10. *Voyage of Discovery to the Pacific Ocean*, by George Vancouver, London, 1798.
11. *History of California*, vol II.
12. Governor of California to the Viceroy, 1798.
13. Horra's report to the Viceroy on Missions, 1798.
14. *Amador's Memoirs of the History of California*, 1855.
15. *Fabricas*, by Elisabeth L. Egenhoff, 1952.
16. Rezánof-Zapiski Letters, 1806.
17. *Ibid.*
18. Correspondence of José Antonio Guerra, 1818.
19. Correspondence of Pablo Vincente Sola re Insurgents, 1818.
20. *Narrative of a Voyage to the Pacific, etc.*, by F. W. Beechey, London, 1831.
21. *Voyage Around the World*, by August Duhaut-Cilly, 1835.

CHAPTER 4

1. *Two Years Before The Mast*, by Richard Henry Dana.
2. *Life in California*, by Alfred Robinson.
3. *Seventy-Five Years in California*, by William Heath Davis.
4. *History of California*, vol. IV, by H. H. Bancroft.
5. Mission Regulations, Governor of California, 1840.

6. *Indians of California*, pamphlet quoting Dr. A. L. Kroeber.
7. *Indians of North America*, by John Collier.
8. *Seventy-Five Years in California*, by William Heath Davis.
9. *Diary, 1838–48* of John A. Sutter.
10. *Seventy-Five Years in California*, by William Heath Davis.
11. *History of California*, vol. IV by H. H. Bancroft.
12. *Life, Adventures and Travel in California*, by T. J. Farnham.

CHAPTER 5

1. *History of California*, vol. V by H. H. Bancroft.
2. *Digest of Correspondence-1843* by Manuel Micheltorena.
3. *Ibid.*
4. *Diary 1839–48*, by John A. Sutter.
5. Correspondence of Micheltorena.
6. *Journal of Lt. Tunis A. M. Craven, USN, 1846–49*, edited by John Haskell Kemble.
7. *California Correspondence and Reports of Mexican Government, 1843–44*.
8. *Official Correspondence of U.S. Consul and Navy Agent 1844–49*, by Thomas O. Larkin.
9. Proclamation of José Castro, March 13, 1846, Bancroft Library.
10. U.S. Government Document #4, 29th Congress.
11. *History of California*, vol. V by H. H. Bancroft.
12. *Four Years in the Pacific, 1844–48*, by Frederick Walpole.
13. *Californian*, October 3, 1845.
14. *Sketch of the Life of R. F. Stockton*.
15. *The Cruise of the Portsmouth*, by Joseph T. Downey.
16. *Ibid.*
17. *Ibid.*

CHAPTER 6

1. *Diary of a Mormon*, by Henry W. Bigler.
2. *Early Recollections of the Mines*, by James H. Carson.
3. *Californian*, May 29, 1848.
4. Miscellaneous Correspondence, 1849, of Commodore Jones.
5. U.S. Government Executive Document No. 37, James K. Polk to 30th Congress.
6. Houston *Democrat Telegraph*, January, 1850.
7. *Arkansas State Democrat*, December, 1849.
8. *El Dorado*, by Bayard Taylor.

9. *A Dangerous Journey*, by J. Ross Browne.

10. *The Land of Gold*, by Hinton R. Helper.

11. *History of California*, vol. VI, by H. H. Bancroft.

12. *Reminiscences of a Ranger*, by Horace Bell.

13. *History and Proposed Settlements, Claims of California Indians:* Attorney General of California, 1944.

14. *Transactions, Commonwealth Club of California*, 1926.

15. *A Frenchman in the Gold Rush*—the Journal of Ernest de Massey, translated by Marguerite Eyer Wilbur, in *California Historical Society Quarterly*, September, 1926.

16. *History of California*, vol. VI, by H. H. Bancroft.

CHAPTER 7

1. *Alta California*, July 2, 1851.

2. Santa Barbara *Gazette*, May 2, 1855.

3. *Reminiscences of a Ranger*, by Major Horace Bell.

4. San Franciso *Alta*, August 23, 1853.

5. *Bad Company*, by Joseph Henry Jackson.

6. *History of California*, vol. III, by Theodore H. Hittle.

7. *The Life and Adventures of Joaquin Murieta, etc.*, by John Rollin Ridge.

8. *Westways*, September, 1952.

9. *McGowan vs California Vigilantes*, Biobooks edition.

10. Sacramento *Union*, June 2, 1857.

11. *Reminiscences of a Ranger*, by Bell.

12. *Memoirs, etc.*, by Harry N. Morse.

CHAPTER 8

1. Sacramento *Union*, September 3, 1857.

2. New York *Herald*, September 26–November 19, 1858.

3. San Jose *Telegraph*, October 16, 1858.

4. San Francisco *Bulletin*, October 16, 17, 1858.

5. New York *Herald*.

6. *The Butterfield Overland Mail*, frontispiece.

7. San Francisco *Bulletin*, May 12, 1859.

8. *Six Horses*, by Capt. William and George Hugh Banning.

9. San Francisco *Argonaut*, September 29, 1890.

10. California *Chronicle*, May 4, 1854.

11. *U.S. West-The Saga of Wells Fargo*, by Lucius Beebe and Charles Clegg.

12. *Two Years Before the Mast*, by Richard Henry Dana.

13. *Alta California*, February 24, 1866.

14. *Sixty-four Years in California*, by Harriss Newmark.

15. Los Angeles *Semi-Weekly News*, April, 1864.

16. *History of California*, vol. VI by H. H. Bancroft.

17. *Ibid.*

18. *A County Judge in Arcady*, by Cameron Rogers.

19. *This is Monterey* (magazine), May, 1960.

20. *Ibid.*

21. *History of California*, vol. IV by Zoeth Skinner Eldredge.

22. *Six Horses.*

23. *Occidental Sketches*, by Major Benjamin C. Truman.

24. San Juan Bautista Historical Monument, No. 180.

25. *The Story of Ventura County*, by W. W. Robinson.

26. Santa Barbara *News-Press*, August 3, 1886.

27. *Bad Company*, by Joseph Henry Jackson.

28. Reward Circular—1870s, Wells Fargo.

29. John J. Valentine Letter, April 10, 1894.

CHAPTER 9

1. *California: For Health, Pleasure & Residence*, by Charles Nordhoff.

2. *Ibid.*

3. *California of the South*, by Walter and J. P. Lindley, M.D.

4. *The Boom of the Eighties*, by Glen S. Dumke.

5. Pasadena *Daily Union*, September 5, 1887.

6. *Millionaires of a Day, etc.*, by Theodore Strong Van Dyke.

7. *Ibid.*

8. Los Angeles *Times*, June 15, 1887.

9. *The Story of San Diego*, by Walter Gifford Smith.

10. *The Boom of the Eighties, op. cit.*

11. *A Truthful Woman in Southern California*, by Kate Sanborn.

12. *To and Fro in Southern California*, by Emma H. Adams.

13. Santa Barbara *News-Press*, April 7, 1893.

14. San Francisco *Examiner*, as quoted in *U.S. West: the Saga of Wells Fargo*, by Beebe and Clegg.

15. *The Big Four*, by Oscar Lewis.

16. *The California Illustrated Magazine*, October 1892.

17. *The Overland Monthly*, August 1887.

18. Santa Barbara *News-Press*, May 12, 1885.

19. *A Truthful Woman in Southern California,* by Kate Sanborn.

20. *Country in the Sun,* by Scott O'Dell.

21. *Highways and Byways of California,* by Clifton Johnson.

22. *Beyond the Rockies,* by Charles August Stoddard.

23. *Southern California,* by Charles A. Keeler.

24. "The Heathen Chinee," first stanza of the poem by Bret Harte.

25. *Highways and Byways,* by Clifton Johnson.

26. *History of California,* vol. V, by H. H. Bancroft.

27. *Beyond the Rockies,* by Charles August Stoddard.

28. *Ten Years in Paradise,* by Mary Bowden Carroll.

29. *California and the Californians,* by David Starr Jordan.

30. *Tourists' Guide Book to Southern California,* by G. Wharton James, 1895.

31. *The Road is Yours,* by Reginald M. Cleveland and Samuel T. Williamson.

32. *California Highways,* by Ben Blow.

33. Los Angeles *Times,* January 18, 1896.

34. San Francisco *Chronicle,* February 24, 1896.

35. San Francisco *Call,* February 4, 1896.

36. Letter from Conrad Tieck to Peter R. Barrett, November 28, 1897.

CHAPTER 10

1. Santa Barbara *News-Press,* quoted in *Santa Barbara County History,* by Owen O'Neill.

2. *Motorland,* May–June 1959.

3. *Ibid.*

4. *The Wheel and the Bell,* by Mark Townsend Hanna, quoting a manuscript by Glen S. Dumke.

5. Santa Barbara *News-Press,* July 6, 1902.

6. *Get A Horse!* by M. M. Musselman.

7. *Outing,* October, 1904.

8. *The Wheel and the Bell,* by Mark Townsend Hanna.

9. *The Automobile Handbook,* by L. Elliot Brookes.

10. *The California Earthquake of April 18, 1906, etc.,* by Andrew C. Lawson.

11. Los Angeles *Times,* April 21, 1906.

12. *Motorland,* May–June, 1959.

13. *Santa Barbara County History,* by Owen O'Neill.

14. Quoted in *Oxcart to Airplane,* by Hunt and Ament.

15. Santa Barbara *News-Press,* June 13, 1910.

16. Los Angeles *Times,* May 24, 1914.

17. *Oxcart to Airplane*, by R. D. Hunt and W. S. Ament.
18. *Tin Lizzie*, by Philip Van Doren Stern.
19. Walker A. Tompkins in Santa Barbara *News-Press*—July 24, 1960.
20. *California Coast Trails*, by J. Smeaton Chase.
21. *On Sunset Highways*, by Thomas D. Murphy.
22. *Fortune Favors The Brave, etc.*, by Benjamin S. Harrison.

CHAPTER 11

1. *Motorland*, July–August, 1959.
2. *California Highways & Public Works*, September 9, 1950.
3. *California Highways*, by Ben Blow.
4. *California Highways & Public Works*, September 9, 1950.
5. *The Road is Yours*, by Cleveland and Williamson.
6. Los Angeles *Times*, May 24, 1924.
7. *California Highways*, by Ben Blow.
8. *Lawyers of Los Angeles*, by W. W. Robinson.
9. *The Wheel and the Bell*, by Hanna.
10. *East Cabrillo Boulevard, etc.*, (brochure), by Pearl Chase.
11. *California Historical Society Quarterly*, March 1953.
12. *California*, by John Walton Caughey.
13. *San Luis Obispo County History*.
14. *Oxcart to Airplane*, by Hunt and Ament.
15. *Linehaul*, by Samuel W. Taylor.
16. *Oxcart to Airplane*, by Hunt and Ament.
17. Quotations from recording of interview with Vincent Lucich, July 17, 1960 at Frank Carter's Lounge, Post Street, San Francisco.

CHAPTER 12

1. *California in Our Time—1900–1940*, by Robert Glass Cleland.
2. *Touring Topics*, January, 1931.
3. "The Lancer" by Harry Carr, Los Angeles *Times*, Jan. 2, 1935.
4. *Boy and Girl Tramps of America*, by Thomas Minehan.
5. *Back to Work: The Story of PWA*, by Harold L. Ickes.
6. Santa Barbara *News-Press*, July 31, 1935.
7. *Boy Transiency in America*, by George E. Outland.
8. *California in Our Time*, by Cleland.
9. *Fortune*, April, 1939.

10. *Fortune,* April, 1939.

11. *Associated Press,* May 15, 1960.

12. *San Francisco Bay,* by Harold Gilliam.

13. *Hollywood: the Movie Colony, the Movie Makers,* by Leo C. Rosten.

14. Radio Broadcasts at Los Angeles, July 1, 1939.

CHAPTER 13

1. *A Brief History of the California Division of Highways, etc.,* 1960.

2. *The Los Angeles Story: The Dream Department,* by Samuel W. Taylor, Ford Motor Co. Project, 1958.

3. Division of Highways brochure, July 1958.

4. Correspondence, Frederic Lane to author, Nov. 30, 1959.

5. *The Economist,* July, 1960.

6. *McCall's Magazine,* "Florida or California, Which?" by Samuel Grafton, May 1959.

7. *Reader's Digest,* ". . . And Sudden Death," by J. C. Furnas, July, 1934.

8. San Francisco *Chronicle,* July 31, 1959.

9. Los Angeles *Examiner,* Vincent X. Flaherty column, June 1, 1960.

10. Correspondence, Lewis A. Lapham to author, October 26, 1959.

11. Jim Bishop column, King Feature Syndicate, June 19, 1960.

12. Santa Barbara *News-Press,* "Notebook" (column) by Thor M. Smith, June 26, 1960.

CHAPTER 14

1. *The Life of Serra,* by Maynard Geiger, O.F.M., Washington, D.C., 1959.

2. *The Road,* by Hilaire Belloc.

3. Sarasota *Herald-Tribune,* Stan Windhorn column, May 5, 1960.

4. *Delaplane in Mexico,* by Stanton Delaplane and Robert de Roos, New York, 1960.

5. Los Angeles *Times,* series by Charles Hillinger, June 17, 1960.

BIBLIOGRAPHY

GENERAL

Books

Bancroft, Hubert Howe: *History of California*, 7 vols., San Francisco, 1884–90.
————: *History of North Mexican States and Texas*, 2 vols., San Francisco, 1884–89.
Cowan, Robert E., and Robert Granniss Cowan: *A Bibliography of The History of California*, 3 vols., San Francisco, 1933.
Drury, Aubrey: *California, An Intimate Guide*, New York, 1935.
Eldredge, Zoeth Skinner: *History of California*, 5 vols., New York, 1915.
Hanna, Phil Townsend: *California Through Four Centuries: A Handbook of Memorable Historical Dates*, New York, 1935.
Hittle, Theodore H.: *History of California*, 4 vols., San Francisco, 1897.
Hunt, Rockwell D.: *California Firsts*, San Francisco, 1957.
Hunt, R. D. and W. S. Ament: *Oxcart to Airplane*, Los Angeles, 1929.
James, George Wharton: *California, Romantic and Beautiful*, Boston, 1914.
Maas, Carl (ed.): *The Penguin Guide to California*, New York, 1947.
O'Dell, Scott: *Country of The Sun: Southern California—An Informal History and Guide Key*, New York, 1957.
Rydell, Raymond A.: *Cape Horn to The Pacific*, Berkeley, California, 1952.
Stone, Irving: *Men to Match My Mountains—The Opening of the Far West, 1840–1900*, Mainstream of America Series, New York, 1956.
Works Progress Administration, Federal Writers' Project: *California*, New York, 1939.
————, Federal Writers' Project: *Los Angeles*, New York, 1939.
————, Federal Writers' Project: *San Diego*, San Diego 1937.
————, Federal Writers' Project: *San Francisco and the Bay Area*, 1939.
————, Federal Writers' Project: *Santa Barbara*, New York, 1941.

CHAPTER 1

Books

Andrews, Roy Chapman: *Meet Your Ancestors, A Biography of Primitive Man*, New York, 1945.
Boscaña, Father Geronimo: *Chinigchinich*, Biobooks, Oakland, 1947.
Brebner, J. Bartlet: *The Explorers of North America, 1492–1806.* London, 1933.
Brennen, Louis: *No Stone Unturned*, New York, 1959.
Cervé, Wishar Spenle: *Lemuria, The Lost Continent of the Pacific*, San Jose, California, 1931.
De Camp, L. Sprague: *Lost Continents*, New York, 1954.
Drake, Francis, compiler: *The World Encompassed by Sir Francis Drake.* London, 1854.

Gifford, Edward Window and Gwendoline Harris Block: *California Indian Nights Entertainment*, Glendale, California, 1930.

Heiter, R. F. and M. A. Whipple: *The California Indians—A Source Book*, Berkeley, California, 1957.

Jackson, W. R., Jr.: *Early Florida Through Spanish Eyes*, Hispanic-American Studies, ed. R. S. Boggs, Coral Gables, Florida, 1959.

Keiser, A.: *The Indians in American Literature*, Washington, D.C., 1933.

Kroeber, Alfred L.: *Handbook of Indians of California*, Smithsonian Institute, Washington, D.C., 1932.

Reed, Ralph Daniel: *Geology of California*, Tulsa, Oklahoma, 1933.

Schurz, William Lytle: *The Manila Galleon*, New York, 1939.

Wagner, Henry R.: *Cryptography of the Northwest Coast of America to the Year 1800*, Berkeley, California, 1937.

————: *Juan Rodríguez Cabrillo, Discoverer of the Coast of California*, San Francisco, 1941.

Wissler, Clark: *Indians of The United States: Four Centuries of Their History and Culture*, The American Museum of Natural History Science Series. New York, 1948.

Wright, Ione Stuessy: *Voyages of Alvaro de Saavedra Cerón 1527–29*, Coral Gables, Florida, 1951.

Periodicals

Geiger, Maynard: "Dates of Palou's Death and Lasuén's Birth Determined," *California Historical Society Quarterly*, March, 1949.

Indians of California, Past and Present: American Friends Service Committee.

Sokol, A. E.: "California: A Possible Derivation of the Name," *California Historical Society Quarterly*, March, 1949.

Wright, Irene A. (trans.): "Voyage of Pedro de Unamuno to California in 1587," *California Historical Society Quarterly*, July, 1923.

CHAPTER 2

Books

Bolton, Herbert Eugene: *Fray Juan Crespí, Missionary Explorer on the Pacific Coast, 1769–1774*, Berkeley, California, 1927.

————: *Outpost of Empire—The Story of the Founding of San Francisco*, New York, 1931.

Browne, J. Ross: *Resources of The Pacific Slope—With a Sketch of the Exploration and Settlement of Lower California*, San Francisco, 1869.

Bustamente, C. M.: *Los Tres Siglos de Mexico*, Jalapa, 1870.

Cady, Theron G.: *Tales of the San Francisco Peninsula*, San Carlos, California, 1948.

Chapman, Charles E.: *Founding of Spanish California: The Northwestward Expansion of New Spain, 1687–1773*, New York, 1916.

Cleland, Robert Glass: *From Wilderness to Empire*.

Crow, John A.: *The Epic of Latin America*, New York, 1946.

Eldredge, Zoeth S.: *The March of Portolá and The Discovery of The Bay of San Francisco—The Log of The San Carlos and Original Documents*, Trans. E. J. Molera, San Francisco, 1909.
Fages, Pedro: *A Historical, Political and Natural Description of California*, Trans. Herbert Ingram Priestley, Berkeley, California, 1937.
Font, Pedro: *Font's Complete Diary: A Chronicle of The Founding of San Francisco*, Trans. and ed. Herbert Eugene Bolton, Berkeley, California, 1931.
Ford, Richard: *Gatherings From Spain*, New York, 1906.
Herring, Hubert: *A History of Latin America From the Beginnings to the Present*, New York, 1957.
Mackey, Margaret G., and Louise P. Sooy: *Early California Costumes 1769–1850*, Stanford, California, 1949.
Miller, Max: *Land Where Time Stands Still*, New York, 1952.
Priestley, Herbert Ingram: *José de Gálvez*, Berkeley, 1916.
Venegas, Miguel: *Juan María de Salvatierra, Apostolic Conqueror of the Californias.* Trans., ed., and annotated Marguerite Eyer Wilbur, Cleveland, 1929.

Periodicals

Raup, H. F. and William B. Pounds, Jr.: "Northernmost Spanish Frontier in California—As Shown By The Distribution of Geographic Names." *California Historical Society Quarterly*, March, 1953.

CHAPTER 3

Books

Bauer, Helen: *California Mission Days*, 1951.
Beechey, Frederick W.: *Narrative of a Voyage to The Pacific and Bearing's Strait, in the Years 1825–1828*, 2 vols., London, 1831.
De la Pérouse, Jean François Galaup: *A Voyage Round the World*, London, 1799.
DuHaut-Cilly, Capt. August Bernard: *Account of California in the Years 1827–1828*, Trans. Charles Franklin Carter.
Egenhoff, Elisabeth L.: *Fabricas*, San Francisco, 1952.
Engelhardt, Fray Zephyrin: *The Franciscans in California.* Harbor Springs, Michigan, 1897.
———: *The Missions and Missionaries of California*, 4 vols., San Francisco, 1908–1915.
James, George Wharton: *In and Out of the Old Missions of California*, Boston, 1927.
Repplier, Agnes: *Junípero Serra, Pioneer Colonist of California*, New York, 1933.
Rezánov, Nikolai P.: *The Rezánov Voyage to Nueva California in 1806*, San Francisco, 1926.
Richards, Jarrett T., LL.B.: *Romance on El Camino Real*, St. Louis, 1914.
Stoddard, Charles Warren: *In the Footprints of the Padres:* San Francisco, 1912.
Vancouver, George: *A Voyage of Discovery to the North Pacific and Round the World*, London, 1798.
Von Langsdorff, G. H.: *Voyages and Travels in Various Parts of the World*, London, 1813.
Webb, Edith Buckland: *Indian Life at the Old Mission*, Los Angeles, 1952.

Periodicals

Powers, Laura Bride: "The Missions of California," *The Californian*, July, 1893.
Smith, Frances Rand: "The Mission of Nuestra Senora de la Soledad," *California Historical Society Quarterly*, March, 1944.
Stanger, Frank M.: "The Hospice or Mission San Mateo," *California Historical Society Quarterly*, September, 1944.
Stephens, W. Barclay: "Time and the Old California Missions," *California Historical Society Quarterly*, December, 1958.

CHAPTER 4

Books

Atherton, Gertrude: *California, An Intimate History*, New York, 1927.
Bryant, Edwin: *What I Saw in California in the Years 1846–1847*, New York, 1848.
Cleland, Robert Glass: *California Pageant*.
Dana, Richard Henry: *Two Years Before the Mast*, New York.
Davis, William Heath: *Sixty Years in California, 1831–1846*, San Francisco, 1889.
Fisher, Anne B.: *The Salinas—Upside Down River*, The Rivers of America, New York, 1945.
Fricot, Desiré (trans.): *California Unveiled (La California Dévoilée)*, Paris, 1850.
O'Brien, Robert: *This is San Francisco*, New York, 1948.
Richman, Irving Berdine: *California Under Spain and Mexico 1535–1847*, Boston, 1911.
Robinson, Alfred: *Life in California*, San Francisco, 1891.
Robinson, W. W.: *Land in California*, Berkeley, California, 1948.
————: *Los Angeles From the Days of the Pueblo*, San Francisco, 1959.
Sanchez, Nellie van de Grift: *Spanish and Indian Place Names of California, Their Meaning and Their Romance*. San Francisco, 1914.
Thomas, William H.: *On Land and Sea; or, California in the Years 1843, '44, and '45*, Chicago, 1892.
Von Kotzebue, Otto: *Voyage of Discovery in the South Sea*, London, 1821.
Works Progress Administration: Federal Writers Project; *Almanac For Thirty-Niners*, Palo Alto, California, 1938.

Periodicals

Ballard, Helen M.: "San Luis Obispo County in Spanish and Mexican Times," *California Historical Society Quarterly*.
Bowman, J. N.: "The Peraltas and Their Houses," *California Historical Society Quarterly*, September, 1951.
Camp, Charles L. (ed.): "The Journal of a 'Crazy Man'—The Narrative of Albert Ferdinand Morris," *California Historical Society Quarterly*, June and September, 1936.
Harrington, Johns: "After Father Serra on California's Royal Road," *Westways*, March and April, 1938.
Ogden, Adele: "Boston Hide Droughers Along California Shores," *California Historical Society Quarterly*, December, 1929.

Williams, Mary Floyd: "Mission, Presidio and Pueblo," *California Historical Society Quarterly*, July, 1922.

CHAPTER 5

Books

Abbot, Willis J.: *The Naval History of The United States*, vol. II, New York, 1886.
Carson, Kit: *Autobiography*, ed. M. M. Quarte, Chicago, 1935.
Caughey, John W.: *Gold is the Cornerstone*, Berkeley, California, 1948.
Colton, Walter: *Three Years in California, 1846–1849*, New York, 1850.
Downey, Joseph T., *The Cruise of The Portsmouth, 1845–1847; A Sailor's View of The Naval Conquest of California*, ed. Howard Lamar, New Haven.
Frémont, J. C.: *Memoirs of My Life*, vol. I, Chicago and New York, 1881.
————: *Narratives of Exploration and Adventure*, ed. Allan Nevins, New York, 1956.
Guinn, J. M.: *History of the State of California and Biographical Record of Santa Cruz, San Benito, Monterey, and San Luis Obispo*. Chicago, 1903.
Meyers, William H.: *Naval Sketches of The War in California: Reproducing Twenty-eight Drawings Made in 1846–47 by Meyers*, descriptive text by Captain Dudley W. Knox, Introduction by Franklin Delano Roosevelt, New York, 1939.
Quigley, Hugh: *The Irish Race in California and On the Pacific Coast*, San Francisco, 1878.
Royce, Josiah: *California From The Conquest in 1848 To The Second Vigilante Committee*, New York, 1948.
Ryan, William R.: *Personal Adventures in Upper and Lower California, 1848–49*, 2 vols., London, 1850.
Taylor, Bayard: *Eldorado, or Adventures in The Path of Empire*, New York, 1860.
Vestal, Stanley: *Kit Carson*, Boston, 1928.
Wilkes, Charles: *Western America Including California and Oregon*, Philadelphia, 1849.

Periodicals

Ames, George Walcott, Jr.: "Horse Marines: California, 1846." *California Historical Society Quarterly*, March, 1939.
(California Admission): Appendix to the *Congressional Globe*, Washington, 1850.
Californian, November 21, 1846.
Chinard, Gilbert: "When The French Came to California," *San Francisco Historical Society*, 1944.
Haines, Francis: "Tom Hill—Delaware Scout," *California Historical Society Quarterly*, June, 1946.
"How The West Was Won," *Life*, seven issues commencing with April 6, 1959.
Kemble, John Haskell, ed.: "Journal of Lt. T. A. M. Craven, USN," *California Historical Society Quarterly*, September, 1941.
Spier, Robert F. G.: "Food Habits of the 19th Century California Chinese," *California Historical Society Quarterly*, March, 1958.

CHAPTER 6

Books

Banning, Captain William and George H. Banning: *Six Horses*, New York, 1930.
Bates, D. B.: *Incidents on Land and Water or Four Years on The Pacific Coast*, Boston, 1858.
Brewer, William H.: *Up and Down California, 1860–1864*, ed. Francis P. Farquhar, New Haven, 1930.
California Register: *The State Register and Year Book of Facts: For the Year, 1857*, San Francisco, 1857.
Gilliam, Harold: *San Francisco Bay*, New York, 1957.
Hall, Frederic: *History of San Jose*, San Francisco, 1871.
Harris, Charles A.: *Old Time Fairhaven*, New Bedford, Mass., 1947.
Hungerford, Edward: *Wells Fargo—Advancing the American Frontier*, New York, 1949.
Johnson, C. W.: *Along the Pacific by Land and Sea—Through the Golden Gate*, Chicago, 1916.
Lang, Walter B., ed.: *The First Overland Mail: Butterfield Trail*, 1940.
Ornsby, Waterman L.: *The Butterfield Overland Mail*, San Marino, 1942.
Soares, Celestino: *California and The Portuguese (How the Portuguese Helped Build up California)* Drawings by Jorge Barradas, San Francisco, 1939.
Stinson, A. L.: *History of The Express Business*, New York, 1881.
Winther, Oscar Osburn: *Via Western Express and Stagecoach*, Palo Alto, California, 1945.
————: *Express and Stagecoach Days in California*, Palo Alto, California, 1935.

Periodicals

Butterfield, D. A.: *Prospectus of Butterfield's Overland Dispatch*, New York, 1865.
Mitchell, Annie R.: "Major James D. Savage and the Tulareños." *California Historical Society Quarterly*, December, 1949.
Rensch, Hero Eugene: "Wood's Shorter Mountain Trail to San Diego," *California Historical Society Quarterly*, June, 1957.
Stuart, Reginald R., trans.: "The Burrell Letters," *California Historical Society Quarterly*, December, 1949.
Truman, Major Ben C.: "Nights of the Lash: Old Time Stage Drivers of the West Coast," *The Overland Monthly*, St. Louis, 1860.
Warren, Viola Lockhart: "Dr. John S. Griffin's Main, 1846–53," *California Historical Society Quarterly*, November and December, 1954.
Wilber, Marguerite Eyer, trans.: "A Frenchman in the Gold Rush," *California Historical Society Quarterly*, September, 1926.

CHAPTER 7

Books

Bell, Major Horace: *Reminiscences of a Ranger or Early Times in California*, Los Angeles, 1881.

Hittle, Theodore H.: *History of California*, vol. III, San Francisco, 1898.
Jackson, Joseph Henry: *Bad Company*, New York, 1939.
McGowan, Edward: *McGowan vs California Vigilantes*, an annotated edition of Edward McGowan's *Narrative of Edward McGowan*, Foreword by Joseph A. Sullivan, Biobooks, Oakland, Cal., 1946.
Morse, Harry N.: *Memoirs*.
Phillips, Michael James: *History of Santa Barbara County*, vol. I, The S. J. Clarke Publishing Co., Los Angeles, San Francisco, Chicago 1927.
Ridge, John Rollin: *The Life and Adventures of Joaquin Murieta*, San Francisco, 1854.
Streeter, William A.: *Recollections of Historical Events*, 1843–78.

Periodicals

Alta California, July 2, 1851.
Sacramento *Union*, June 2, 1857.
San Francisco *Alta*, August 23, 1853.
Santa Barbara *Gazette*, 1855.
Westways, September, 1952.

CHAPTER 8

Books

Bancroft, Herbert Howe: *History of California*, vol. VI.
Banning, Capt. William G. and George Hugh Banning: *Six Horses*, The Century Co., New York, 1930.
Beebe, Lucius and Charles Clegg: *U.S. West: The Saga of Wells Fargo*, New York, 1949.
Black, Samuel F.: *San Diego County California*, 2 vols., Chicago, Ill., 1913.
Boggs, Mae Helene Bacon (compiler), *My Playhouse was a Concord Coach*, Howell and North, Oakland, California, 1942.
Carlson, Vada F. and Ethel-May Dorsey: *This is Our Valley*, (Santa Clara Valley Historical Society), Westernlore Press, 1959.
Cleland, Robert Glass: *Transportation in California Before the Railroads*, Annual Publication, Historical Society of Southern California, vol. II, Part I, 1918.
Conkling, Roscoe P. and Margaret B.: *The Butterfield Overland Mail*, 1857–1869, Arthur H. Clark Co., Glendale, Cal., 1947.
Dana, Richard Henry: *Two Years Before The Mast*.
Eldredge, Zoeth Skinner: *History of California*, vol. IV.
Frederick, J. V.: *Ben Holliday*, (*The Stage Coach King*.) Glendale, Cal., 1940.
Guillermo, Prieto: *San Francisco in the Seventies*, San Francisco, Cal., 1938.
Hafen, Leroy R.: *The Overland Mail* (1849–69), Cleveland, O., 1926.
Hall, Frederick: *The History of San Jose & Surroundings*, San Francisco, 1871.
———: *History of Monterey County*, San Francisco, 1881.
Hittell, John S.: *The Commerce & Industries of the Pacific Coast*, A. L. Bancroft Co., San Francisco, 1882,
Jackson, Joseph Henry: *Bad Company*.

Jesperson, Senator Chris N.: *History of San Luis Obispo County*, San Luis Obispo, Cal., 1939.

Krythe, Maymie: *Port Admiral (Phineas Banning 1830–85)*, California Historical Society, San Francisco, 1959.

Los Angeles County, (Historical Sketch), L. Lewin & Co., Los Angeles, 1876.

MacMullen, Jerry: *Paddle-Wheel Days in California*, Stanford University Press, Stanford, 1944.

Marin County History, Alley-Bowen Co., San Francisco, 1880.

Menefee, C. A.: *Historical & Descriptive Sketch Book, Sonoma, etc.*, Napa, 1873.

Mills, James: *Historic Landmarks of San Diego County*, San Diego, 1959.

Newmark, Harriss: *Sixty-four Years in California*.

Quinn, J. M.: *Historical and Bibliographical Record of Monterey and San Benito Counties* (State History), Los Angeles, 1910.

Robinson, W. W.: *The Story of Ventura County*.

Rogers, Cameron: *A County Judge in Arcady*.

Rusling, General James F.: *Across America or The Great West and Pacific Coast*, New York, 1875.

Sala, George A.: *America Revisited*, 2 vols., London, 1882.

Thompson and West: *History of San Luis Obispo*, 1883.

Truman, Major Benjamin C.: *Occidental Sketches*.

Turrill, Charles B.: *California Notes*, San Francisco, 1876.

Valentine, John J.: *Letter*, April 10, 1894.

Wiltsee, Ernest A.: *The Pioneer Miner & The Pack Mule Express*, California Historical Society, San Francisco, 1931.

Periodicals and *Newspapers*

Alta California, Feb. 24, 1866.

The Butterfield Overland Mail, (frontispiece).

California Chronicle, May 4, 1854.

Los Angeles *Semi-Weekly News*. April, 1864.

New York *Herald*, Sept. 26—Nov. 19, 1858.

Sacramento *Union*, Sept. 3, 1857.

Reward Circular, 1870's, Wells Fargo.

San Francisco *Argonaut*, Sept. 29, 1890.

San Francisco *Bulletin*, Oct. 16, 17, 1858, May 12, 1859.

San Jose *Telegraph*, Oct. 16, 1858.

San Juan Bautista Historical Monument, No. 180.

Santa Barbara *News-Press*, Aug. 3, 1886.

This Is Monterey, May, 1960.

Truman, Major Ben. C.: "The Knights of the Lash," *Overland Monthly*, March–April, 1898.

CHAPTER 9

Books

Adams, Emma Hildreth: *To and Fro in Southern California*, Cincinnati, 1887.

Alverson, M. B.: *Sixty Years of California Song*, San Francisco, 1913.

Bancroft, Herbert Howe: *History of California*, vol. V.

Blow, Ben: *California Highways*.

Brooks, Benjamin: *What The Finger Wrote*, (Historical Sketch of the County of San Luis Obispo), 1917.

Carroll, Mary Bowen: *Ten Years in Paraise*, San Jose, Cal., 1903.

Cleveland, Reginald M. and S. T. Williamson: *The Road is Yours*, New York, 1951.

Disturnell's Business Directory & Gazetteer of the West Coast of North America, 1882–83.

Dumke, Glenn S.: *The Boom of the Eighties in Southern California*, San Marino, Cal., 1944.

Fifty Years of Schwinn-Built Bicycles, The Story of the Bicycle & Its Contributions to Our Way of Life, 1893–1945, Arnold Schwinn & Co., Chicago, Ill.

Greenwood, Grace: *New Life in New Lands* (Notes on Travel), Lippincott, Philadelphia, 1873.

Guinn, J. M.: *A History of California and an Extended History of Its Southern Coast Counties*, 2 vols., Los Angeles, 1907.

Harte, Bret: *Poems*.

Holden, Charles Frederick: *Life in the Open in Southern California*, G. P. Putnam's Sons, New York, 1906.

Johnson, Clifton: *Highways and Byways of California*, American Highways & Byways Series, The Macmillan Co., New York, 1908.

Jordan, David Starr: "California and The Californians," reprint of an essay that appeared in *Atlantic Monthly*, November, 1898, A. M. Robertson, San Francisco, Calif., 1907.

Keeler, Charles A.: *Southern California*.

Lee, S. M.: *Glimpses of Mexico & California*, Boston, Mass., 1887.

Lewis, Oscar: *The Big Four*.

Lindley, Walter & J. P. Widney: *California of the South*, Complete Guide Book to Southern California, D. Appleton & Co., New York, 1888.

Newmark, Harris: *Sixty Years in Southern California*, 1853–1913 (Revised Edition), Knickerbocker Press, New York, 1926.

Nordhoff, Charles: *California: For Health, Pleasure and Residence*, A Book for Travelers and Settlers, Harper and Bros., New York, 1873.

Nordhoff, Charles: *Peninsular California*, New York, 1888.

O'Dell, Scott: *Country In The Sun*.

Robinson, Marshall: *A Trip To Southern California*, Carson, 1879.

Rogers, Cameron: *A County Judge In Arcady, Charles Fernald, The Selected Private Papers of a Pioneer Jurist*, Arthur H. Clark Co., Glendale, Cal., 1954.

Sanborn, Kate: *A Truthful Woman In Southern California*.

Sayward, W. T.: *All About Southern California*, San Francisco, 1875.

Smith, Walter Gifford: *The Story of San Diego*.

Southworth, John Robert: *Santa Barbara & Montecito, Past and Present*. Santa Barbara, Cal., 1920.

Stoddard, Charles Augustus: *Beyond The Rockies, A Spring Journey in California*, Charles Scribner's Sons, New York, 1894.

Truman, Ben. C.: *Homes and Happiness in The Golden State of California*, San Francisco, 1883.

Van Dyke, Theodore Strong: *Millionaires Of A Day*.

Wharton, James G.: *Tourist's Guide Book To Southern California*.

————: *Travelers Handbook To Southern California*. Los Angeles, 1895.
Wilson, Neill C. and Frank J. Taylor: *Southern Pacific, The Roaring Story of a Fighting Railroad*, McGraw-Hill Book Co., New York, 1952.
Wood, Stanley: *Over The Range To The Golden Gate*, Chicago, 1903.

Periodicals and Newspapers

The California Illustrated Magazine, October, 1892.
Los Angeles *Times*, June 15, 1887.
————, Jan. 18, 1896.
The Overland Monthly, August 1887.
Pasadena *Daily Union*, Sept. 5, 1887.
San Francisco *Call*, Feb. 4, 1896.
San Francisco *Chronicle*, Feb. 24, 1896.
San Francisco *Examiner*, (As quoted in *U.S. West: The Saga of Wells Fargo* by Beebe & Clegg).
Santa Barbara *News-Press*, May 12, 1885.
————, April 7, 1893.
Letter from Conrad Tieck to Peter R. Barrett, Nov. 28, 1897.

CHAPTER 10

Books

Brewer, William H.: *Up and Down California* (1860–64), New Haven, Conn., 1926.
Brookes, L. Elliot: *The Automobile Handbook*.
Chase, J. Smeaton: *California Coast Trails*.
Cleveland, Reginald M. and S. T. Williamson: *The Road Is Yours*, New York, 1951.
Gregory, J. M.: *The Story of The Road*, new edition, 1939.
Hanna, Mark Townsend: *The Wheel and The Bell* (containing a manuscript by Glen S. Dumke).
Harrison, Benjamin S.: *Fortune Favors The Brave: The Life and Times of Horace Bell, Pioneer Californian*, Ward Richie Press, Los Angeles, 1953.
Hart, Val: *The Story of American Roads*, William Sloane Associates, New York, 1950.
Hunt, Rockwell D. and William S. Ament: *Oxcart To Airplane*, Los Angeles, 1929.
Lawson, Andrew C.: *The California Earthquake of April 18, 1906*, Report of the Earthquake Investigating Committee in 2 vols. with atlas, Washington, D.C., 1908.
Murphy, Thomas D.: *On Sunset Highways, A Book of Motor Rambles in California*, The L. C. Page Co., Boston, 1915.
Musselman, M. M.: *Get a Horse, The Story of the Automobile in America*, Lippincott, Philadelphia, 1950.
O'Neill, Owen H.: *History of Santa Barbara County*, Santa Barbara, Cal., 1920.
Stern, Philip Van Doren: *Tin Lizzie*.

Periodicals and *Newspapers*

California Addresses by President Roosevelt, California Promotion Committee, San Francisco, 1903.
The Los Angeles *Times*, April 21, 1906.
————, May 24, 1914.
Motorland, May, June 1959.
Outing, October, 1904.
Santa Barbara *News-Press*, July 6, 1902.
————, June 13, 1910.
Santa Barbara *News-Press*, Stories by Walker A. Tompkins, July 24, 1960.

CHAPTER 11

Books

Blow, Ben: *California Highways*, San Francisco, 1920.
Caughey, John Walton: *California*, New York, 1940.
Cleveland, Reginald M., and S. T. Williamson: *The Road Is Yours*, New York, 1951.
Hanna, Mark Townsend: *The Wheel and The Bell*, Los Angeles, 1950.
Hart, Val: *The Story of the American Road*, William Sloane Associates, New York, 1950.
Hunt, Rockwell D. and William S. Ament: *Oxcart to Airplane*, Los Angeles, 1929.
Robinson, W. W.: *The Story of Ventura County*, Los Angeles, 1956.
————: *Lawyers of Los Angeles*, Los Angeles, 1959.
San Luis Obispo County History, San Luis Obispo, 1898.
Santa Barbara: A Guide to the Channel City & its Environs, WPA Southern California Writers Project, Hastings House, New York, 1941.
Spaulding, William A.: *History and Reminiscences of Los Angeles, City and County*, vol. I, Los Angeles, 1930.
Storke, Thomas M., with Walker A. Tompkins: *California Editor*, Los Angeles, 1958.
Taylor, Samuel W.: *Linehaul*, San Francisco, 1959.

Periodicals and Newspapers

A Million Miles a Day, The Story of Greyhound, Chicago, 1906.
California Highways and Public Works, Centennial Edition, September 1950.
California Historical Society Quarterly, March, 1953.
East Cabrillo Boulevard, Etc., Brochure by Pearl Chase.
Jack O'Grady Guide to 101, Ventura, Cal., 1959.
Los Angeles *Times*, May 24, 1924.
Motorland, July and August, 1959.
Pioneers of the Highway. Bay Area Business, San Francisco, 1949.
Sunset (magazine), October, 1930.
The Santa Barbara Earthquake, Bulletin of the Seismological Society of America, December, 1925.

Touring Topics, Files 1925, 1926, 1927, Los Angeles.
Quotations from recording of interview with Vincent Lucich, July 17, 1959, at Frank Carter's Lounge, Post St., San Francisco.

CHAPTER 12

Books

Cleland, Robert Glass: *California in Our Time, 1900–1940*, New York, 1947.
Collins, Henry Hill, Jr.: *America's Own Refugees*, Princeton University Press, Princeton, N.J., 1941.
Gilliam, Harold: *San Francisco Bay*, Doubleday & Co., New York, 1959.
Hays, Arthur Garfield: *Democracy Works*, Random House, New York, 1939.
Hunt, Rockwell D., ed.: *California and The Californians*, vol. II New York, 1930.
Ickes, Harold L.: *Back To Work, Story of PWA*, The Macmillan Co., New York, 1935.
Japanese Evacuation from The West Coast, 1942. Washington, D.C. 1943.
Minehan, Thomas: *Boy and Girl Tramps of America*, Farrar and Rinehart, New York, 1934.
Outland, George E.: *Boy Transiency In America*, Santa Barbara State College Press, Santa Barbara, Cal. 1939.
Rosten, Leo C.: *Hollywood: The Movie Colony, The Movie Makers*, Harcourt Brace, New York 1941.
Sinclair, Upton: *The Epic Plan for California*, N.Y. 1934.
Wardlow, Chester: *U.S. Army in World War II, The Transportation Corps: Movements, Training, and Supply*, Washington, D.C., 1956.

Periodicals and Newspapers

Associated Press, May 15, 1960.
Carr, Harry: "The Lancer," Los Angeles *Times*, Jan. 2, 1935.
Fortune April, 1939.
Motorland, March–April 1959.
Radio Broadcasts at Los Angeles, July 1, 1939.
Santa Barbara *News-Press*, July 31, 1935.
Touring Topics, January, 1931.

CHAPTER 13

Books

Geddes, Norman Bel: *Magic Motorways*. Random House, New York, 1940.
Taylor, Samuel Woolley: *Linehaul—The Story of Pacific Intermountain Express*, Library of Western Industry, Filmer Publishing Co., San Francisco, 1959.
———: *The Los Angeles Story, The Dream Department*, 1959, Ford Motor Project.

Periodicals

A Brief History of the California Division of Highways and the California State Highway System, (Compiled by Right of Way Department, Standing Committee on Education) Educational Training Program Text, Sacramento, Calif. 1960.

Bishop, Jim, Column, June 19, 1960, King Features Syndicate.

Division of Highway Brochure, July, 1958.

Economist Magazine, London, July, 1960.

Flaherty, Vincent X., Column, June 1, 1960, Los Angeles *Examiner*.

Furnas, J. C.: "And Sudden Death," *Reader's Digest*, July 1934.

Grafton, Samuel: "Florida or California, Which?" *McCall's*, May, 1959.

More Than Fourteen Million People Want My Property. Sacramento, Calif. 1958, Division of Highways.

San Francisco *Chronicle*, July 31, 1959.

Smith, Thor M., "Notebook," Column in Santa Barbara *News-Press*, June 26, 1960.

Trade Area Directory of Santa Barbara and County, 1960–61, Santa Barbara *News-Press*.

Correspondence: Fredric Lane to author Nov. 30, 1959.

Lewis A. Lapham to the author Oct. 26, 1959.

CHAPTER 14

Books

Belloc, Hilaire: *The Road*, Harper and Brothers, New York.

Delaplane, Stanton and Robert de Roos: *Delaplane in Mexico, A Short Happy Guide*, Coward-McCann, Inc., New York 1960.

Geiger, Fr. Maynard: *Life of Junípero Serra*, vol. I, Washington, D.C., 1959.

Woodward, Arthur, trans.: *The Sea Diary of Fr. Juan Vizcaíno to Alta California in 1769*, Glen Dawson, Los Angeles, 1959.

Scott, Carroll Dewilton: Best Four Hundred Poems, vol. 2. (Manuscript.)

Periodicals

Hillinger, Charles, Series in Los Angeles *Times*, June 17, 1960.

Windhorn, Stan, Column, Sarasota *Herald-Tribune*, May 5, 1960.

INDEX

About the author

Like his father and grandfather before him, the late Felix Riesenberg, Jr., was a prolific writer. Newspaper editor, traveler, reviewer, and historian, he had done extensive research on the Spanish Mission Trail long before he wrote *The Golden Road* for The American Trails Series. An earlier book, *The Golden Gate*, which was a best seller, and a later work, *Balboa*, were indicative of his early and lasting interest in California. There, during the years he worked as reporter, shipping editor, and daily columnist for the *San Francisco News*, he owned a 22-foot sloop. His cruises in the San Francisco Bay led him to writing not only his first book and his first best seller, but lay behind the inspiration for many of subsequent tales of explorers, pirates, captains, and naval heroes he was to write for teen-age readers. In addition to some twenty books for adults and young people alike, Mr. Riesenberg wrote short stories, magazine articles, and television plays. Having spent several years at sea, he wrote many adventure stories about ships, fishermen, and merchant seamen, for youngsters. One of these, *The Crimson Anchor*, written in 1948, won the *New York Herald Tribune* award as the best book for older children published that year. Other works about the sea included such adult nonfiction as *Sea War: The Story of the U.S. Merchant Marine in World War II*, which grew out of his experiences in the merchant marine as a lieutenant, senior grade, during World War II. He later served as a technical advisor for two motion picture companies making merchant marine training films. At the time of his death, Mr. Riesenberg and his wife were living in Sarasota, Florida, where they had made their home for several years.